WHAT PHILOSOPHERS KNOW

D1400186

Philosophy has never delivered on its promise to settle the great moral and religious questions of human existence, and even most philosophers conclude that it does not offer an established body of disciplinary knowledge. Gary Gutting challenges this latter view by examining detailed case studies of recent achievements by analytic philosophers such as Quine, Kripke, Gettier, Lewis, Chalmers, Plantinga, Kuhn, Rawls, and Rorty. He shows that these philosophers have indeed produced a substantial body of disciplinary knowledge, but he challenges many common views about what philosophers have achieved. Topics discussed include the role of argument in philosophy, naturalist and experimentalist challenges to the status of philosophical intuitions, the importance of pre-philosophical convictions, Rawls' method of reflective equilibrium, and Rorty's challenge to the idea of objective philosophical truth. The book offers a lucid survey of recent analytic work and presents a new understanding of philosophy as an important source of knowledge.

GARY GUTTING holds the Notre Dame Chair in Philosophy at the University of Notre Dame. His most recent publications include *The Cambridge Companion to Foucault*, 2nd edition (2005), *Foucault: A Very Short Introduction* (2005), and *French Philosophy in the Twentieth Century* (2001).

WHAT PHILOSOPHERS KNOW

Case Studies in Recent Analytic Philosophy

GARY GUTTING

University of Notre Dame

CAMBRIDGE UNIVERSITY PRESS
Cambridge, New York, Melbourne, Madrid, Cape Town, Singapore,
São Paulo, Delhi, Dubai, Tokyo, Mexico City

Cambridge University Press
The Edinburgh Building, Cambridge CB2 8RU, UK

Published in the United States of America by Cambridge University Press, New York

www.cambridge.org
Information on this title: www.cambridge.org/9780521672221

First published 2009
Third printing with corrections 2010

Printed in the United Kingdom at the University Press, Cambridge

A catalogue record for this publication is available from the British Library

Library of Congress Cataloguing in Publication data
Gutting, Gary.
What philosophers know : case studies in recent analytic philosophy / Gary Gutting.
p.   cm.
Includes bibliographical references and index.
ISBN 978-0-521-85621-8 (hardback) – ISBN 978-0-521-67222-1 (pbk.)
1. Analysis (Philosophy)–Case studies.   I. Title.
B808.5.G88 2009
146′.4–dc22
2009000059

ISBN 978-0-521-85621-8 Hardback
ISBN 978-0-521-67222-1 Paperback

To Anastasia
always my first and best reader

Contents

Acknowledgments   *page* IX

Introduction   I

PART I: HOW DOES THAT GO? THE LIMITS
OF PHILOSOPHICAL ARGUMENT

1 Quine's "Two Dogmas": argument or imagination?   II

2 Argument and intuition in Kripke's *Naming
   and Necessity*   31

3 The rise and fall of counterexamples: Gettier,
   Goldman, and Lewis   51

4 Reflection: pictures, intuitions, and philosophical
   knowledge   73

PART II: ARGUMENTS AND CONVICTIONS

5 Turning the tables: Plantinga and the rise
   of philosophy of religion   105

6 Materialism and compatibilism: two dogmas
   of analytic philosophy?   122

7 Was there a Kuhnian revolution? Convictions
   in the philosophy of science   151

8 Conviction and argument in Rawls' *A Theory
   of Justice*   173

PART III: PHILOSOPHICAL TRUTH AND KNOWLEDGE

9   Rorty against the world: philosophy, truth, and objectivity   197

10   Philosophical knowledge: conclusions
     and an application   224

References   243
Index   248

Acknowledgments

While I was writing this book there were two philosophers whom I was most anxious to have read it: Phil Quinn and Dick Rorty, both of whom died before it was finished. I profited greatly from their reactions to an earlier volume (*Pragmatic Liberalism and the Critique of Modernity*), and know that this book is much the worse without the benefit of their wisdom. I can, at any rate, take this occasion to acknowledge their personal inspiration to me and their remarkable contributions to the American philosophical enterprise.

I thank the students who took part in the seminars in which I developed initial versions of much of the material in this book: Brian Boeninger, Claire Brown, Karen Chan, Daniel Colon, Kevin Connolly, Scott Hagaman, Ryan Greenberg, John Infranca, Nathan King, Buket Korkut-Raptis, Kevin Leary, James McGhee, Abigail Palko, Brad Thammes, Chris Tucker, Charles Tyler, and Gloria Wasserman. Thanks also to the audiences at Emory, Tulane, and Wheaton College, where I presented parts of this book.

I am particularly grateful to those who read and commented on drafts of various chapters: Paddy Blanchette, David Chalmers, Mike DePaul, Ernan McMullin, Al Plantinga, Jeff Speaks, Leopold Stubenberg, Fritz Warfield, and Paul Weithman. Thanks also to Hilary Gaskin for her continuing support of my work and for her superb editorial sense, and to her assistant editor, Gillian Dadd. As so often, I owe a special debt to Karl Ameriks, not only for his careful reading but also for many hours of extraordinarily helpful conversation.

My children, Edward, Tom, and Tasha, continue to inspire and delight; and my wife, Anastasia, makes every day bright with love.

Introduction

I knew from the beginning that the title of this book would set me up as a straight man for witty colleagues: "*What Philosophers Know* – that'll be a short book, won't it?" Or, a bit more subtly, "Shouldn't that title be a question?"

It's not that philosophers lack disciplinary pride. They are quite impressed with how smart they are – in contrast, say, to historians, who, as a member of their clan once pointed out to me, are impressed by how much they know. Of course, the history of philosophy has at regular intervals thrown up imposing monuments of cognitive pretension. Almost every great philosopher claims to have put us on a path to sure knowledge. But the claim is always to have been the first to do this, so that each successive monument is built on the ruins of all the others. As a result, perceptive outsiders (and most insiders, for that matter) have made the disagreement of philosophers a byword.

The failure to reach agreement suggests a failure of argument. Philosophy, especially analytic philosophy, sees itself as distinctively committed to rigorous argumentation. We teach our students how to argue, claim to establish our views by argument, and criticize opponents for offering arguments that are invalid or based on dubious premises. The days are long gone when adequate philosophical argument had to be valid deduction from self-evident premises. We allow that a good philosophical argument may be inductive or based on premises expressing widely shared common-sense judgments. There has, in particular, been a strong recent trend to support a philosophical theory as the best explanation of various data, corresponding to the "obvious facts" about, say, knowledge, reference, or morality. But even with the most generous plausible sense of proof, philosophical arguments are not adequate to settle the great disputes about, say, the existence of God, the nature of the mind, the reality of freedom, or the basic principles of morality.

Of course, some philosophers (sometimes even enough to constitute a school or movement) find some arguments convincing and, if they are right, they may well in some sense know the truth about the disputed issues. But, throughout the philosophical community as a whole, it seems that there is almost always fundamental disagreement about even the strongest arguments, so that we can never say that *philosophy as a discipline* knows the answer to any central philosophical question. In contrast to disciplines in the formal, physical, biological, and even (sometimes) social sciences, there seems to be no body of philosophical truth that our discipline can authoritatively assert to the wider intellectual world. The physicists can rightly tell their students, "This is what we know," whereas philosophers can only say "Some of us think this, others that." It seems that, as critics of philosophy (and many philosophers themselves) have said through the ages, there is no established body of philosophical knowledge because there is no end to philosophical disagreement.

I maintain, nevertheless, that there is a body of disciplinary philosophical knowledge achieved by (at least) analytic philosophers of the last fifty years. I agree that this knowledge does not encompass answers to the standard "big questions" about God, freedom, mind, and morality. But I do claim that it is a substantive body of knowledge and one of great cultural significance. Those without access to this knowledge will be severely limited in the essential reflective dimension of human existence.

My discussion belongs to the disdained and marginalized domain of *metaphilosophy*, and I hasten to assure the reader that "I, too, dislike it."[1] But I've tried to avoid the two features that have typically made metaphilosophy so unsatisfying: a dogmatic attitude that derives the nature of philosophy from controversial philosophical doctrines (e.g., idealist metaphysics or empiricist epistemology) and an abstract, overly generalized approach that pays no attention to the details of philosophical practice. As the reader will see, I am much more positively disposed to Richard Rorty's effort to characterize philosophy in its historical and cultural context, but in the end I conclude that he paints with too broad a brush and with a palette limited by his assumptions of what successful philosophy would have to do.

My approach, by contrast, derives from that of historians and philosophers of science, who focus on case studies of exemplary instances of the disciplines they are trying to understand, thereby avoiding the perils of both a priorism and abstraction. Just as philosophers reflecting on science start from close studies of exactly what Galileo, Newton, and

---

[1] Marianne Moore, "Poetry," *The Complete Poems of Marianne Moore*, New York: Macmillan, 1967, 36.

Darwin achieved and how they did it, so I propose to develop an understanding of what Quine, Kripke, Rawls, *et al.* have achieved in philosophy.

I take my exemplars from recent analytic philosophy first because, despite a good deal of work on the continental side of the street, I think of myself as an analytic philosopher. More important, analytic philosophy works from a self-understanding that seems to commit it to claims of knowledge. Unlike those in other humanistic disciplines – and even some who claim the name of philosopher – we disdain what Wallace Stevens called "the tired romanticism of imprecision."[2] We undertake to state exactly what we mean and prove with step-by-step lucidity that it is true. If philosophical knowledge exists anywhere, we should expect it to exist in the analytic realm.

I've further restricted myself to more recent analytic philosophy (the last fifty years), both for the sake of a coherent focus and to minimize the hermeneutic difficulties of dealing with work removed from our own milieu. Beyond that, I've tried to choose cases that cover an important range of topics without exceeding by too much my own limited set of competences. I realize that I've omitted many obviously excellent examples and included some that others may find inappropriate. Nonetheless, I'm content that my case studies at least provide a helpful starting point for my topic.

In searching for philosophical knowledge, I begin with three achievements for which some of the strongest cognitive claims have been made by many philosophers: W. V. O. Quine's "refutation" of the analytic-synthetic distinction, Saul Kripke's rehabilitation of necessity in metaphysics and the philosophy of language, and Edmund Gettier's counterexamples against the standard definition of knowledge. How often have we heard (or told others) that Quine refuted the analytic-synthetic distinction, that Kripke proved that there are necessary a posteriori truths, and that Gettier showed that knowledge cannot be defined as justified true belief? But, although I entirely agree that Quine, Kripke, and Gettier have achieved something of philosophical importance, a careful reading of their exemplary texts does not reveal any decisive arguments for the conclusions they are said to have established. Chapters 1–3 make this point through a detailed analysis of these texts.

Nonetheless, I maintain that these exemplary pieces of philosophy have generated important philosophical knowledge. In chapter 4 I argue first

[2] Wallace Stevens, "Adult Epigram," *Collected Poetry and Prose*, The Library of America, 1997, 308.

that they contribute to a body of "second-order" knowledge about the prospects of general philosophical pictures. The notion of a *picture*, which I take from Kripke, applies to broad views such as empiricism, material-ism, and theism, which have been understood and defended in various ways over the philosophical centuries.[3] Philosophers of great imaginative power, such as Quine and Kripke, can, without establishing its truth, make a strong case for a picture's potential for fruitful development. Even though they provide no sound argument for finally accepting the picture as correct, they develop very good reasons for taking it seriously and working to develop it. This is what Quine did for his holistic picture of knowledge in "Two Dogmas" and what Kripke did for his metaphysical picture of necessity in *Naming and Necessity*. Reflection on our first three case studies will give some detail regarding the process – which I call *persuasive elaboration* – that supports a picture's viability and fruitfulness. Whereas Quine and Kripke support their pictures without formulating them theoretically, other cases (e.g., that of Goldman's reliabilism) sup-port a picture by demonstrating its ability to generate a series of increasingly more detailed and adequate theories.

But chapter 4 also argues that there is a substantial body of first-order philosophical knowledge – knowledge not about philosophical pictures but about the subject-matter (language, necessity, knowledge, etc.) treated by those pictures. Such knowledge is typically about the nature of fundamental *distinctions* and the limits of their application. It is often ignored because it is not ordinarily the goal of philosophical reflection but a by-product of (generally unsuccessful) efforts to answer standard "big questions." So, for example, even those who do not accept Kripke's overall account of reference and necessity can appreciate and appropriate his use of rigid designation to distinguish naming from description. Knowledge of important distinctions is often not the result of any one individual's work but rather accumulates over time, one philosopher following another in refining and deepening our understanding of a distinction, and the philosophical community as a whole implicitly incorporates the results into its future thinking. Our case studies will reveal many instances of this process.

---

[3] Corresponding to a given picture are, again following Kripke, a variety of *theories* that provide detailed formulations of the picture. Theories range from a given philosopher's highly similar, successive efforts to express a picture – e.g., Plato's dualism in *Phaedo* and *Republic* – to vastly different formulations from different philosophers at widely separated times – e.g., Plato's, Descartes', and David Chalmers' formulations of dualism. We will later discuss the role of theories in developing and defending pictures.

We will also see some striking cases in which what presents itself as a challenge to a distinction turns out to be a positive contribution to our understanding it. I will argue, for example, that Quine should be ultimately seen as contributing to our understanding of the analytic-synthetic distinction, not refuting it. Similarly, the upshot of many years of Gettier epistemology has been to establish the fundamental soundness of the characterization of knowledge (in distinction from mere true opinion) as justified true belief – a result refined, however, by an understanding of the limits of the (extensive) domain in which the characterization is valid.

The claim that there is a substantive body of philosophical knowledge will lead many critics to ask for an account of the nature and justification of such knowledge. I argue, however, that although this question is interesting in itself as a further philosophical or psychological topic, answering it is not a necessary condition for showing that philosophy has produced authoritative knowledge. Our case studies show that the knowledge exists, quite apart from any account of how this is possible. The last part of chapter 4 develops this point in the context of recent debates about intuition in philosophy. I distinguish three main sorts of intuitions, discuss their role in philosophical knowledge, and reflect on recent critiques of intuitions by naturalist and "experimentalist" philosophers. I conclude that, whether or not there is a special faculty of philosophical (e.g., modal) intuition, establishing the nature and reliability of any such faculty is not required to show that there is a body of authoritative philosophical knowledge.

Our next four case studies (chapters 5–8) continue the case for philosophical knowledge but also focus on the central role played by pre-philosophical *convictions* in the development of this knowledge. What I will call the "foundationalist" conception of philosophy, which demands argument from uncontroversial premises, rejects the introduction of such convictions as intellectually irresponsible. But one of the most important results of recent philosophy has been the inadequacy of this foundationalist conception, a result that opens the door to a positive role for pre-philosophical convictions. Chapter 5 introduces this role by discussing Alvin Plantinga's transformation of the philosophy of religion from the criticism to the defense and development of religious convictions. It might seem that only religiously committed philosophers will deploy pre-philosophical convictions. But chapter 6 shows, through discussions of David Chalmers' zombie argument and Peter van Inwagen's consequence argument, how materialist or naturalist convictions play an essential role in debates about consciousness and freedom. Similarly, chapter 7 argues that one major effect of Thomas Kuhn's historicist challenge to the positivist account of science was to reveal that philosophers of science accepted the rationality of science as a pre-philosophical conviction. Kuhn's work also highlighted the irreducible role of judgment in the knowledge of scientific disciplines, a result that also applies to philosophy.

Chapter 8 presents John Rawls' *A Theory of Justice* as a detailed example of the philosophical development and defense of pre-philosophical convictions, in this case liberal democratic convictions about a just society. Rawls' case for his two principles of justice is a useful model of how non-foundationalist argumentation can lead to philosophical knowledge. His work is also a good example of how convictions arise not from disengaged intellectual intuitions but from practices that are central to our identities.

Convictions typically express major philosophical pictures and so can be judged viable or not depending on the success of the persuasive elaboration of these pictures. Also, established philosophical distinctions are essential means for clarifying and evaluating convictional claims. Accordingly, although convictions are initially held independent of philosophical arguments, their intellectual viability requires that they pass the test of philosophical scrutiny. Because convictions provide answers to the traditional big questions, their essential tie to philosophy maintains the discipline's connection to its founding questions, even though they have no decisive philosophical answers.

Our final case study, in chapter 9, looks at the work of Richard Rorty as an example of philosophizing that itself concerns the metaphilosophical topics we have been exploring. Here I both examine Rorty's modes of argumentation (which turn out to fit the modes at work in our other case studies) and respond to Rorty's rejection of philosophy as a body of disciplinary knowledge. I argue that, ironically, Rorty's rejection follows only if we assume that philosophical knowledge has to meet the foundationalist ideal of proof from indisputable premises. I also examine Rorty's debate with McDowell on truth to reject the suggestion that my claims to philosophical knowledge depend on an incoherent notion of objectivity.

My concluding chapter 10 summarizes the case for philosophical knowledge and illustrates the importance of such knowledge outside the discipline of philosophy by showing the relevance of philosophical results to the evaluation of religious convictions.

Like many, I became a philosopher because I wanted to know the truth about the great questions of human life; and, like even more, I learned soon enough that there was little likelihood of finding decisive philosophical answers to these questions. This utterly common experience led me to expect that this book would be an essentially skeptical exercise. I have been delighted to find that I was wrong. Skepticism about philosophy derives from the assumption of philosophical foundationalism, itself refuted by philosophical reflection. Once we give up this assumption, we are able to see philosophy for what it is: a major source of humanistic knowledge, fully entitled to the respect and deference accorded other successful cognitive enterprises.

PART I

How does that go? The limits of philosophical argument

CHAPTER I

Quine's "Two Dogmas": argument or imagination?

TWO SORTS OF KNOWLEDGE?

A lot of our knowledge derives from sense experience: from what we see, hear, touch, etc. Other things we know – about mathematics and logic, for example – seem quite independent of sense experience; we know them simply by thinking – about, for example, the definition of a triangle or the meaning of the term "implies." Philosophers have long recognized this fact by a distinction between knowledge that is *a posteriori* (derived from sense experience) and knowledge that is *a priori* (derived from mere thinking, independent of sense experience). This distinction concerns the ways in which we know. Two further distinctions suggest themselves, one concerning what our knowledge is about (its content) and the other concerning its stability (or, to use the standard logical term, its modality). First, there is a distinction between knowledge about the world we encounter through our experience and knowledge derived from the meanings of the concepts (or words) we use to think. Philosophers, at least since Kant, have called knowledge about the world *synthetic*, and knowledge about meanings *analytic*. Second, there is a distinction between knowledge that is *contingent* (about what can change, such as the color of a leaf) and knowledge that is *necessary* (about what cannot change, such as the fact that blue is a color).

Philosophers have focused intensely on these distinctions, not only because they seem important for understanding knowledge in general but also because they seem crucial for understanding the nature of philosophical knowledge itself. It has been generally agreed that a posteriori knowledge is the domain of the empirical sciences (including the everyday perceptions from which they originate); so if philosophy is to be an autonomous discipline, it must have access to a distinctive domain of a priori truths. Beginning with Plato, many philosophers (those often called rationalists) have maintained that such knowledge derives from

II

intellectual, as opposed to sensory, intuitions of necessary truths about fundamental realities. Other philosophers, often called empiricists, reject intellectual intuitions, maintaining that only sense experience (hence science) yields knowledge of reality. Accordingly, philosophical knowledge, if there is any, must be both a priori and analytic. Kant, rejecting both intellectual intuition and empiricism, made a profound effort to show that philosophical (like, he thought, mathematical) knowledge is a priori *and* synthetic. Philosophy in the first half of the twentieth century was split among those who reasserted the rights of intellectual intuition (idealists), those who continued Kant's philosophy of the synthetic a priori (neo-Kantians), and those who revived empiricism (logical positivists). In the English-speaking world, from the 1920s through the 1950s, empiricism in the form of logical positivism defined much of the philosophical agenda. As a result, the analytic-synthetic distinction was at the heart of epistemological discussions and underlay the conception of philosophy as an autonomous body of knowledge. The leading logical positivist, Rudolf Carnap, was particularly prominent in explicating and defending the distinction.

Willard van Orman Quine, who had worked with Carnap in Vienna during a post-doctoral year (1932), early on developed qualms about the distinction, which he began to articulate in discussions with Carnap. These discussions continued intermittently, both in person and by letter, through the 1930s and into the 1940s. Quine comments that he had not thought of his "strictures over analyticity as the stuff of revolution. It was mere criticism, a negative point with no suggestion of a bright replacement."[1] But eventually Quine came to see his criticisms in a broader and deeper context. He says that "in June and July of 1947 a triangular correspondence on the issue developed among [Nelson] Goodman, Morton White, and me."[2] Others in the philosophical community got wind of an important development, and Quine was invited to present a paper on the topic at the 1950 meeting, in Toronto, of the APA Eastern Division.

In December 1950, Quine read "Two Dogmas of Empiricism" to the APA, and a printed version appeared in *The Philosophical Review* the following year. In the words of Richard Rorty, the paper "rocked the audience back on its heels" and, after its publication, "went on to become the most discussed and influential article in the history of 20th-century

---

[1] W. V. Quine, "Two Dogmas in Retrospect," *Canadian Journal of Philosophy* 21 (1991), 265–74; citation 267.
[2] Ibid., 268.

Anglophone philosophy."[3] Although Quine had advanced similar ideas as early as 1936, "Two Dogmas" gave canonical form to his attack on the positivists' analytic-synthetic distinction and the related doctrine of reductionism. It became common wisdom that Quine had, in this article, refuted positivism by undermining two of its main doctrines. As the editors of a recent collection of essays on Quine's article put it: "In the wake of 'Two Dogmas', and of related early articles by Quine . . . most contemporary analytic philosophers assumed that it is impossible to draw a clear and sharp distinction between empirical propositions and propositions that are true solely because of their meaning."[4] Similarly, William Lycan, writing in 1991, said: "It has now been nearly forty years since the publication of 'Two Dogmas of Empiricism'. Despite some vigorous rebuttals during that period, Quine's rejection of analyticity still prevails – in that philosophers en masse have either joined Quine in repudiating the analytic-synthetic distinction or remained (however mutinously) silent and made no claims of analyticity."[5] The result, Tyler Burge tells us, was that "Quine's frontal attack on both primary principles of logical positivism in the early 1950s marked the true end of the movement."[6]

The usual assumption is that Quine prevailed by the rational force of his arguments. Even Richard Rorty, no friend of claims to decisive philosophical argument, describes Quine's case in "Two Dogmas" as "a model of succinct and convincing argumentation."[7] I do not think that a close reading of Quine's paper sustains this view. There is no doubt that he undermined the distinction in the minds of most philosophers. But this was not a matter of cogent argumentation.

THE FIRST DOGMA AND QUINE'S CRITIQUE OF ANALYTICITY

Quine states the positivist doctrines he is attacking (the "two dogmas" of empiricism) as follows:

1. "a belief in some fundamental cleavage between truths which are *analytic*, or grounded in meanings independently of matters of fact, and truths which are *synthetic*, or grounded in fact."

---

[3] "An Imaginative Philosopher: the Legacy of W. V. Quine" (obituary notice), *Chronicle of Higher Education*, February 2, 2001.
[4] H.-J. Glock, K. Glürt, and G. Keil (eds.), *Fifty Years of Quine's "Two Dogmas"* (*Grazer Philosophische Studien* 66 (2003)), 1. Also published as a book by Rodopi, 2003.
[5] William Lycan, "Definition in a Quinean World," in J. Fetzer, D. Shatz, and G. Schlesinger (eds.), *Definitions and Definability: Philosophical Perspectives*, Dordrecht: Kluwer, 1991, 111–31.
[6] "Philosophy of Language and Mind: 1950–1990," *Philosophical Review* 101 (1992), 6.
[7] "An Imaginative Philosopher."

2. "Reductionism: the belief that each meaningful statement is equivalent to some logical construct upon terms which refer to immediate experience."[8]

The focus of his discussion, however, is the analytic-synthetic distinction, with the second dogma discussed, as we shall see, mainly because it supports an argument for the distinction.

Quine's attack on the distinction turns on his insistence that there is no satisfactory characterization of the term "analytic." Leibniz, for example, spoke of analytic truths (or "truths of reason") as "true in all possible worlds," language Quine dismisses as merely "picturesque" (20). Similarly, Kant defined "an analytic statement as one that attributes to its subject no more than is already conceptually contained in the subject," but this, Quine says, "appeals to a notion of containment which is left at a metaphorical level" (21). We could, he allows, depoeticize Leibniz's possible-worlds characterization of analytic statements by replacing it with the paraphrase "could not possibly be false," an expression he takes as equivalent to "having a denial that is self-contradictory." But Quine is unimpressed with this line of explanation because "the notion of self-contradictoriness, in the quite broad sense needed for this definition of analyticity, stands in exactly the same need of clarification as does the notion of analyticity itself. The two notions are the sides of a single dubious coin" (20).

We may wonder why there is supposed to be a problem here, since Quine's own statement of the first dogma seems to have defined "analytic" as "grounded in meanings independent of matters of fact," a definition that corresponds, he tells us, to Kant's use of the term. Quine, however, does not think that we can take "meanings" as an unproblematic starting point. One problem for Quine arises if we think of meanings as having a special ontological status, like, for example, Platonic Forms or Aristotelian essences, which exist either separate from ordinary material things or as irreducible elements of them. Quine has no stomach for such "obscure intermediate entities" (22), although here, at least, he offers no argument to support his revulsion. He does suggest that we can avoid positing reified meanings by making a clear distinction between meaning and reference (naming). Presumably, his target here is the classic Platonic argument from the essential role of idealized concepts in knowing to the existence of Forms that exemplify these concepts. This argument, he implies, fails when we realize that we need not understand a term's having meaning as a matter of its referring to a non-linguistic reality that also has

---

[8] W. V. O. Quine, "Two Dogmas of Empiricism," in his *From a Logical Point of View*, Cambridge, MA: Harvard University Press, 1953, 20. Further references will be given in the text.

that meaning. "Once [following Frege and Russell] the theory of meaning is sharply separated from the theory of reference, it is a short step to recognizing as the primary business of the theory of meaning simply the synonymy of linguistic forms and the analyticity of statements" (22).

But even if Quine is right that the distinction of meaning and reference undermines one classic argument for an ontology of meanings (essences), it does not follow that we should reject any such ontology as the basis for an account of meaning. Indeed, someone who sees some sort of analytic-synthetic distinction as prima facie plausible – given, for example, our ready ability to see the difference between statements such as "All bachelors are unmarried" and "All bachelors are neurotic" – can very effectively invoke an ontology of essences to explicate the distinction. If there are essences corresponding to different kinds of things, then analytic statements can be defined as just those that are true in virtue of what we know about essences.

Quine does offer what might seem to be an argument against the existence of essences when he says: "it makes no sense to say of the actual individual, which is at once a man and a biped, that his rationality is essential and his two-leggedness accidental or vice versa" (22). But this, as Quine himself points out, is a claim that follows only if we adopt "the point of view of the doctrine of meaning" (22); that is, if we choose to take linguistic descriptions rather than essences as ultimate. It's clear that Quine himself endorses this choice, but he offers no reasons for doing so.[9] His discussion simply assumes a nominalistic standpoint that disallows from the start any defense of the analytic-synthetic distinction on ontological grounds.

Elsewhere, Quine suggests that ontological commitments can be justified by quasi-scientific arguments from explanatory simplicity. "Our acceptance of an ontology is, I think, similar in principle to our acceptance of a scientific theory . . . : we adopt, at least insofar as we are reasonable, the simplest conceptual scheme into which the disordered fragments of raw experience can be fitted and arranged" ("On What There Is," 16). However, "simplicity, as a guiding principle in constructing conceptual schemes, is not a clear and unambiguous idea," and Quine, like Carnap, sees ontological issues as ultimately settled by pragmatic considerations, which depend on "our various interests and purposes" (19). It is far from clear, however, that there are

---

[9] Quine does offer an argument (the "mathematical cyclist" argument) against essentialism in *Word and Object*, but, as Plantinga has shown, this argument is not effective. See Quine, *Word and Object*, Cambridge, MA: MIT Press, 1960, 199; and Alvin Plantinga, *The Nature of Necessity*, Oxford: Oxford University Press, 1974, 23–5.

any generally shared interests and purposes that require a minimalist ontology. Quine himself concludes that "the question what ontology actually to adopt still stands open, and the obvious counsel is tolerance and an experimental attitude." Here he explicitly includes the necessities his case against analyticity rejects: "Let us also pursue mathematics and delve into its platonistic foundations" (19). It seems that, even from Quine's own stand-point, his exclusion of meanings as a basis for analyticity is a personal pref-erence, not a justified philosophical position. Quine, as he himself puts it, prefers a "desert landscape" that excludes the aesthetically offensive "rank luxuriance" of modal ontologies.[10]

But, we recall, Quine is making a case against the claims of *empiricists*, who are not likely to object to his ontological picture or to his call for a strictly linguistic understanding of meaning. So even if he is begging some ontological questions, his argument may have significant force. But Quine's ontological assumptions alone are not sufficient to make his case. He recognizes that even his strictly linguistic understanding of meaning might still allow for an analytic-synthetic distinction.

A first point is that there seems to be no problem at all with one class of "narrowly" analytic statements: those (e.g., "All unmarried men are unmarried") that are logically true, that is, true solely in virtue of their logical form. Problems arise only with "broadly" analytic statements (e.g., "All bachelors are unmarried"), which become logically true statements only if we substitute an appropriate term with the "same meaning" – e.g., "unmarried man" for "bachelor." (Quine notes on pp. 23–4 that Carnap's explanation of analyticity in terms of state-descriptions applies only to the narrow sense.)

Given this, why not just say that a broadly analytic truth is one that reduces to a logical truth upon substitution of appropriate synonyms for its non-logical terms? Because, says Quine, "the notion of synonymy . . . is no less in need of clarification than analyticity" (23). Like self-contradic-tion, synonymy, on Quine's account, is just as dubious a notion as the "meaning" assumed by analyticity. The question we need to return to, of course, is why Quine thinks all these concepts are insufficiently clear.

In any case, Quine is open to the thought that synonymy (and hence meaning and analyticity) can be adequately explicated. One obvious sug-gestion is that two expressions are synonymous when one is the *definition* of the other. Given this, why not say that "broadly" analytic truths are those that reduce to "narrowly" analytic truths (logical truths) by *definition*? Although, Quine says, some find this "soothing," it is an unhelpful

---

[10] "On What There Is," *From a Logical Point of View*, 4.

explication, since definition always presupposes synonymy (except for the trivial case of stipulative definition: "the explicitly conventional introduction of novel notations for purposes of sheer abbreviation," 24). He supports his claim by canvassing the main types of definition: lexicographical (an empirical report on accepted synonymies), philosophical explication (which presupposes and tries to improve on accepted synonymies), and formal definitions (which are various ways of correlating an "inclusive language" with that part of it consisting of "primitive notation" – all falling under one of the previously noted types of definition).

Quine finds more promising (section 3, 27ff.) the idea that two terms are synonymous when they can be *interchanged* in any statement without affecting the statement's truth value. Suppose, for example, that "bachelor" and "unmarried man" are interchangeable *salva veritate*. Then, substituting one for the other into the narrowly logical truth, "Necessarily all and only bachelors are bachelors," we conclude that, necessarily, all and only bachelors are unmarried men. Assuming that any necessary truth is analytic,[11] it follows that "All and only bachelors are unmarried men" is analytic. From this we can conclude that "bachelor" and "unmarried man" are cognitively synonymous (since an analytic truth depends on sameness of meaning).

But, Quine says, this argument has "an air of hocus-pocus" (29) that is connected with its reliance on the notion of necessity. All it shows is that, *if* we have a language that includes the adverb "necessarily," then we can show that interchangeability entails cognitive synonymy. "But can we condone a language which contains such an adverb? Does the adverb really make sense? To suppose that it does is to suppose that we already have made satisfactory sense of 'analytic'" (30).

To drive home his point about necessity, Quine notes that we can construct a language in which any predicates that are true of exactly the same objects are interchangeable (this is what is meant by an "extensional language"). In such a language, not only "bachelor" and "unmarried man" are interchangeable but also "creature with a heart" and "creature with kidneys." Here, obviously, interchangeability ensures truth but not synonymy, since the latter requires necessity (i.e., not just "All bachelors are unmarried," which may just contingently happen to be true, but "Necessarily, all bachelors are unmarried"). When we enrich our language

---

[11] At the time of "Two Dogmas," this was an unproblematic assumption. Later, of course, Kripke convinced many that there are necessary truths that are a posteriori and so not analytic. In any case, there is no reason to think that "All bachelors are unmarried" is necessary a posteriori.

with modal notions such as necessity, we can readily define analyticity, and, given that, define synonymy (in terms of what Quine archly calls "interchangeability *salva analyticitate*") for all syntactical categories (31–2). But the root notion of necessity remains in need of clarification. Once again, Quine's argument turns on a declaration about what is and what is not sufficiently "clear."

It might seem that Quine's problems with "analytic" stem from the vagueness of ordinary language and can be overcome by defining the term in an artificial language à la Carnap. Within such a language, analytic statements could be specified in various ways by the semantical rules of a language L. We might, for example, have a semantical rule that simply specified that certain statements were analytic or analytic-in-L. Quine maintains, however, that such a rule would itself involve "analytic" in its formulation and so would provide only a circular definition. There is also the alternative of simply saying that analytic statements are just those specified as true by semantical rules. But then the question arises of what is meant by a semantical rule. Surely not just any statement in L specifying that a certain class of statements is true is a semantical rule; if that were so, then all true statements of L would be analytic. The only option is to say that semantical rules are those that specify statements as true in virtue of their meaning, which puts us back into the circle. Accordingly, "semantical rules determining the analytic statements of an artificial language are of interest only in so far as we already understand the notion of analyticity; they are of no help in gaining this understanding" (36).

Quine concludes that "for all its a priori reasonableness, a boundary between analytic and synthetic statements simply has not been drawn." The claim that there is such a distinction "is an unempirical dogma of empiricists, a metaphysical article of faith" (37).

But has Quine successfully argued, even in the context of empiricism, for this conclusion? What exactly has he established? He has surveyed a number of ways of defining analyticity and, apart from those he dismisses as merely metaphorical or picturesque, found all of them wanting on grounds of circularity. In two cases – that of explaining synonymy in terms of definition and that of formally distinguishing the set of analytic sentences via semantical rules – the circularity is strict: the process of specifying the analytic presupposes that we already understand analyticity. But in the other cases, most notably the definitions of synonymy via self-contradiction and via interchangeability, the notion of "circularity" is much broader. To use Quine's own metaphor, it is not a matter of being "flatly circular" but of having "the form, figuratively speaking, of a closed curve in space" (30). What Quine means here is that, as he so often reiterates, even if analyticity is not defined strictly in its own terms, it is defined in terms that are equally in need of clarification. His argument turns on his claim that necessity, self-contradiction, and sameness of meaning are not sufficiently intelligible in their own terms.

This claim is, on the face of it, odd, since "self-contradictory" (even in the "broad" sense in which not only "bachelors are not bachelors" but also "bachelors are married" are unacceptable) is an ordinary-language expression that many people use with apparent understanding. The same is even more obviously true of "necessary" and "have the same meaning." At a minimum, such terms have some intuitive content, based on common linguistic use. This point was very effectively developed by Grice and Strawson in their famous response to Quine. They note that there are "plenty of distinctions, drawn in philosophy and outside it, which still await philosophical elucidation, but which few would want on this account to declare illusory."[12] (The distinction between *moral* and *immoral* would seem an obvious example.) In such cases, Grice and Strawson plausibly suggest, the existence of an "established use" of the distinction is sufficient evidence for its existence. So, for example, the expressions "analytic" and "synthetic" have an established use in the sense that "those who use the terms...do to a very considerable extent agree in the applications they make of them." Moreover, "this agreement extends not only to cases which they have been *taught* to so characterize, but to new cases." When such an established use is in place, we are justified in "saying that there are kinds of cases to which the expressions apply; and nothing more is needed for them to mark a distinction."[13] Further reflection may suggest challenges to this view,[14] but Quine simply assumes that the established use of the analytic-synthetic distinction is not sufficient evidence for its existence.

There may, of course, still be reasons why our understanding of the complex of terms that are inter-definable with "analytic" requires further philosophical clarification, but Quine's arguments provide no reasons for thinking this might be so, nor, if it is, why the needed clarification must take the form of an account that replaces these terms with others of an entirely different character. Fundamental terms in a given domain (e.g., mathematics) are often found to be interconnected and, given that each

---

[12] H. P. Grice and P. F. Strawson, "In Defense of a Dogma," *The Philosophical Review* 55 (1956), 141–58; citation, 142.
[13] Ibid., 143.
[14] See, for example, Scott Soames, *Philosophical Analysis in the Twentieth Century, Volume I: The Dawn of Analysis*, Princeton, NJ: Princeton University Press, 2003, 371–3.

has its own intuitive content, we often find that a "wide enough" circle of inter-definition is sufficient to count as understanding. Of course, we can always hope to improve our understanding of the analytic-synthetic distinction by further philosophical reflection, but this is certainly not Quine's project, since he proposes simply to eliminate the distinction.

In this regard, it is worth reflecting a bit further on Quine's critique of Carnap's effort to understand analyticity in terms of semantical rules. The critique seems to ignore the fact that there are degrees of understanding a concept, not a simple stark gap between understanding and not understanding. The fact that we all agree on a large number of obvious cases of analytic statements suggests that we do have a significant preliminary understanding of the notion. Why couldn't the semantical rules of an artificial language be a plausible means for developing and clarifying this understanding (as, for example, Peano's axioms help clarify our intuitive notion of number)? Carnap himself described his own formal work on analyticity in such terms: "Our [semantical] rules are meant . . . neither as assertion nor as mere nominal definition . . . Their purpose is, rather, the explication of an inexact concept already in current use . . . we advance the claim that the defined concept embraces what philosophers have meant, intuitively but not exactly, when they speak of 'analytic sentences.'" [15] When Quine ignores the significance of our competence in using the analytic-synthetic distinction, he is begging the question against not only ordinary-language philosophers such as Grice and Strawson but also against fellow formal-language philosophers such as Carnap.

The general structure of Quine's argument against the "first dogma" is this:

(1) The analytic-synthetic distinction is viable only if "analytic" can be adequately clarified.
(2) "Analytic" can be adequately clarified only by giving an account of it in terms of concepts clearer than that of *true in virtue of meaning*.
(3) All accounts of "analytic" are in terms of concepts no clearer than *true in virtue of meaning*.
(4) Therefore, "analytic" cannot be adequately clarified.
(5) Therefore, the analytic-synthetic distinction is not viable.

---

[15] Richard Creath (ed.), *Dear Carnap, Dear Van: The Quine–Carnap Correspondence and Related Work*, Berkeley: University of California Press, 1990, 430. Grice and Strawson, "In Defense of a Dogma," make a similar point.

(1) is acceptable in the trivial sense that "analytic" is a technical philosophical term that requires some sort of definition. In support of (3), Quine discusses a number of ways of clarifying "analytic," showing that they are either strictly circular or at best define "analytic" via terms such as "self-contradictory" or "necessary," which we understand no better than we do "true in virtue of meaning." This doesn't strictly prove (3), but it does effectively present a challenge for those who would reject (3) to provide the required definition of "analytic." For premise (2), however, "Two Dogmas" offers no defense at all, simply assuming that there is no way of making sense of the distinction short of a definition of "analytic" outside the circle of its kindred terms. The need to justify this assumption is apparent both from Carnap's prior approach to analyticity and from Grice and Strawson's subsequent approach.

Quine does, as several commentators have pointed out, have a reason for (2): his commitment to a thoroughly behaviorist account of language. Although his behaviorism is muted in "Two Dogmas," Quine connects it to the question of analyticity in both earlier and later writings.[16] The point is most evident in *Word and Object*, where, in response to the criticism that "the standard of clarity that I demand for synonymy and analyticity is unreasonably high," he says: "yet I ask no more, after all, than a rough characterization in terms of dispositions to verbal behavior."[17] But, despite Quine's suggestion that this is an entirely reasonable demand, behaviorist accounts of thought and language are highly questionable, a point that became widely accepted at least in the wake of Chomsky's famous 1959 critique of B. F. Skinner's *Verbal Behavior*.[18] As John Burgess recently remarked, Quine's insistence that "a distinction between analytic and synthetic" must be "directly manifested in observable behaviour . . . dates his classic paper more than any other feature."[19] Here, Burgess suggests, Quine has not learned "to think outside the Skinner box."[20] In any case, Quine's argument in "Two Dogmas" against analyticity either offers no reason for its demand that the "circle" of

---

[16] For details, see Richard Creath, "Quine on the Intelligibility and Relevance of Analyticity," in Roger F. Gibson, Jr. (ed.), *The Cambridge Companion to Quine*, Cambridge: Cambridge University Press, 2004, 47–64.

[17] *Word and Object*, 207. Fifty years after "Two Dogmas," in a contribution to an anniversary retrospective on that article, Quine made the same point: "Repudiation of the first dogma, analyticity, is insistence on empirical criteria for semantic concepts" ("Two Dogmas in Retrospect," 272).

[18] Noam Chomsky, Review of *Verbal Behavior*, *Language* 35 (1959), 26–58.

[19] John Burgess, "Quine, Analyticity and Philosophy of Mathematics," *Philosophical Quarterly* 54 (2004), 38–55; citation, 52.

[20] Ibid., 51.

terms surrounding "true in virtue of meaning" ("necessity," "synonymy," "self-contradictory," etc.) be defined in other terms; or it (implicitly) offers a highly controversial behaviorist reason.

We see, then, that Quine's critique of the analytic-synthetic distinction is based on unjustified controversial assumptions. Given the strongly empiricist context of his discussion, it is not surprising that he begins by assuming that there is no basis for the distinction in an ontology of essences. But his assumption that the distinction must be explained in terms outside the circle of meaning/synonymy/necessity excludes solidly empiricist moves such as basing the distinction on our established use of "analytic" (Grice and Strawson) or at least on a formal explication of that use (Carnap). Nor is Quine's highly debatable behaviorism an adequate justification for this assumption.

Despite the frequent claims that Quine refuted the analytic-synthetic distinction, some commentators have noted the conspicuous weakness of his arguments in "Two Dogmas," but they typically discount the problem. Scott Soames, for example, reads Quine as arguing against opponents who think of analyticity in terms of two key claims: "T1. All necessary (and all apriori) truths are analytic" and "T2. Analyticity is needed to explain and legitimate necessity." Given T1 and T2, necessity makes sense only in terms of analyticity; that is, we must understand a necessary truth as one that is true in virtue of its meaning. "Two Dogmas," however, showed that efforts to explicate analyticity wind up appealing to necessity (or equivalent notions), so that we have no non-circular understanding of analyticity. Soames thinks that nowadays "very few philosophers would accept T1 or T2, since Kripke has shown that there are necessary truths that are a posteriori and so not analytic and that necessity is a metaphysical notion that can stand on its own without explication in terms of analyticity." But, Soames maintains, in the mid-twentieth century, T1 and T2 were generally accepted, by both logical positivists and ordinary-language philosophers, so "Quine's circularity argument . . . was, and was seen to be . . . a powerful objection to the then dominant conception of analyticity."[21]

But Soames, like Quine, simply assumes that analyticity itself requires definition outside of its circle of kindred terms. Only given this, can we argue from the fact that we have no explicit non-circular understanding of analyticity, but only an implicit understanding in use, to the conclusion that we have no right to make the analytic-synthetic distinction. Without

---

[21] Soames, *Philosophical Analysis, Volume I*, 361.

this assumption, which Carnap as well as Grice and Strawson rejected, the argument loses its force.

Here, as we have seen, the case of Carnap is particularly instructive. Quine ignores the fact that Carnap is not trying to introduce the notion of an analytic truth *ab novo*, but is rather explicating an already intuitively understood concept. Given the preliminary, informal understanding we have of the distinction between what is true in virtue of meaning and what is not, Carnap's explication is neither circular nor arbitrary. Here we should also note that Carnap's positivism was entirely consistent with Quine's holistic picture of epistemology, which we will be discussing below. Carnap had himself earlier endorsed a holistic picture (as we shall see, Quine cites him in support of holism), agreeing that any individual claim (logical or empirical) can be rejected for the sake of a more adequate overall account. The only difference is that for Carnap revising logical claims is a matter of making a pragmatic judgment that a new conceptual framework would be a more effective means to scientific goals, not a matter of adjusting to falsifying empirical data. Analytic statements arise from metascientific (philosophical) judgments, not from the ordinary scientific process of empirically testing hypotheses. Quine, by contrast, sees no room for judgments that look at science from a meta-standpoint and so finds no sense in distinguishing analytic statements from the ordinary empirical judgments of scientists.[22] But Quine's disagreement with Carnap derives from an empiricism so radical that it excludes even pragmatic judgments about science that are not themselves the results of empirical tests. This radical empiricism is a pre-philosophical conviction, not something Quine is able to support by philosophical argument.

There is, therefore, no basis for claiming that "Two Dogmas" refuted logical positivism. Moreover, since Quine's radical empiricism amounts to an insistence that positivism put no limits on its empiricism, there is an important sense in which he is more positivist than Carnap. Putnam, indeed, said that Quine was "the last and greatest of the logical positivists, in spite of his criticism of the movement."[23] More accurate, however, is Isaacson's formulation, according to which Quine is definitely a positivist but, precisely because of his rejection of analytic truths, not a *logical* positivist.[24]

[22] On the differences between Quine and Carnap on the analytic-synthetic distinction, see Daniel Isaacson's thorough and perceptive "Quine and Logical Positivism," in Gibson (ed.), *Cambridge Companion to Quine*, 214–69. On the point I am making here, see especially 246–7.

[23] Hilary Putnam, "The Greatest Logical Positivist," in his *Realism with a Human Face*, ed. James Conant, Cambridge, MA: Harvard University Press, 1990, 269.

[24] Isaacson, "Quine and Logical Positivism," 217.

Another suggestion made by some commentators is that, although the case against analyticity is weak in "Two Dogmas," Quine offered much better arguments in other places. Burge, for example, thinks that "Truth by Convention" (1936), as well as "Carnap and Logical Truth" (1960) and *The Philosophy of Logic* (1970) provide Quine's "strongest arguments" (206) against analyticity.[25] But even if Burge is right about Quine's arguments elsewhere, this provides no explanation of why "Two Dogmas" played such a central role in generating a consensus against the analytic-synthetic distinction. It is highly implausible that it was only after its publication in 1951 that philosophers came to appreciate the force of arguments Quine had offered fifteen years earlier in "Truth by Convention" or that readers of "Two Dogmas" somehow anticipated arguments that Quine would formulate only ten to twenty years later. In any case, Burge himself sees these arguments as effective against only one of the three concepts of analyticity implicit in Quine's discussions.

In a similar vein, some maintain that the full force of Quine's case against analyticity is developed only in *Word and Object* (1960). Donald Davidson notes that "Quine has often replied to criticisms of 'Two Dogmas' by pointing out that in *Word and Object* he had replaced what was left implicit or nebulous in 'Two Dogmas' with an explicit statement of his views, and he wished his views to be discussed on the basis of the book."[26] But even if *Word and Object* is the preferred statement of Quine's position, it was not this reformulation nine years later that made the analytic-synthetic distinction an object of doubt throughout the 1950s. In any case, *Word and Object* offered no improvement in the argument against analyticity, apart from making explicit Quine's questionable behaviorist assumptions. The real advance was to provide a much fuller and non-metaphorical account of Quine's holism. But this account, with its introduction of the indeterminacy of translation and of the inscrutability of reference, proved highly controversial from the outset, with debates continuing today not only about whether Quine was right but even about what he meant. It is, therefore, implausible to think that *Word and Object*, rather than "Two Dogmas," generated consensus about the inadequacy of the analytic-synthetic distinction.

A final suggestion is that the decisive case against the distinction emerged only from the many years of discussion that followed Quine's

---

[25] Tyler Burge, "Logic and Analyticity," *Grazer Philosophische Studien* 66 (2003), 199–249; citation, 204, 205.

[26] Donald Davidson, "Quine's Externalism," *Grazer Philosophische Studien* 66 (2003), 281–97; citation, 282.

paper. Gilbert Harman, for example, says that "few philosophers were converted to Quinean skepticism about the distinction at first, but there followed an intense exploration, in which numerous attempts to defend the distinction proved ineffective." This discussion, which Harman says lasted until "the late 60s," was as important as Quine's initial work "in showing that a certain philosophical line was not sustainable."[27] But what was "not sustainable" was the project of defining "analytic" without using kindred terms such as "necessary" or "self-contradictory." No one was able to meet that challenge, but this did not, as we have seen, show that there was no viable analytic-synthetic distinction. In the discussions that followed Quine's article, not only critics such as Grice and Strawson but also (as we will see below) some very sympathetic to Quine's approach, such as Hilary Putnam, asserted a genuine distinction between analytic and synthetic truths. Putnam, in fact, faults most of the replies to Quine for merely "refuting" him by citing clear cases of the distinction and ignoring the "important question" of "how is he wrong?"[28]

THE SECOND DOGMA AND QUINE'S HOLISTIC VISION

As we noted, Quine discusses the second dogma of empiricism, reductionism, not for its own sake but only for its connection with the analytic-synthetic distinction. He points out that if, for example, we could define two statements as synonymous (having the same meaning) if and only if "they are alike in point of method of empirical confirmation or infirmation" (37) we could, as we have seen, define analyticity in terms of synonymy and logical truth: a sentence is analytic if and only if it is synonymous with a logically true statement. "So, if the verification theory can be accepted as an adequate account of statement synonymy, the notion of analyticity is saved after all" (38).[29]

---

[27] Gilbert Harman, "Analyticity Regained?," *Noûs* 30 (1996), 392–400; 396.

[28] Hilary Putnam, "The Analytic and the Synthetic," in his *Mind, Language and Reality: Philosophical Papers*, Volume II, Cambridge: Cambridge University Press, 1975 (originally published 1962), 33–69; 34.

[29] As I read him, Quine agrees that if the verification account of statement-meaning is true, then the analytic-synthetic distinction is viable, but denies that the verification account is true, thereby rejecting this case for the analytic-synthetic distinction. Burge ("Logic and Analyticity," 203) maintains that Quine here puts forward a much stronger argument: "Meaning is if anything confirmation or infirmation. Confirmation and infirmation are holistic; they apply to whole theories, not to statements taken individually. So meaning is if anything something that attaches to whole theories, not statements, much less words, taken individually." From this it would follow directly that both the first and the second dogmas are false, since both imply that individual statements have meaning, which is denied by his argument's conclusion. But Quine never says in "Two Dogmas" that the only possible understanding of meaning is confirmation or infirmation.

As Quine was well aware, however, the stronger forms of verificationism had been thoroughly discredited by the time he was writing. So, for example, he only briefly evokes and quickly dismisses Carnap's version of "radical reductionism," which maintained that any meaningful statement can be translated into a statement about sense experiences (40). Quine further notes that it might be that two statements are confirmed by the same empirical methods even if they are not entirely translatable into statements about sense experience. Indeed, as long as it makes sense to speak of individual statements being confirmed or disconfirmed, it would seem to make sense to speak of an analytic statement as a limiting case that is confirmed by every experience. In fact, it is just this minimal "reductionist" claim that concerns Quine, since a common line of thought supporting it also supports the analytic-synthetic distinction. The line of thought is this: the truth of any statement "does obviously depend both upon language and upon extralinguistic fact" (41). For example, "Brutus killed Caesar" would be false if Brutus had not been involved in Caesar's death or if "killed" meant "begat" (36). Given this, there is a natural, but, Quine claims, ill-founded, inclination to conclude that "the truth of a statement is somehow analyzable into a linguistic component and a factual component" (41). The factual component must, for an empiricist, be the experiences that confirm the statement – which amounts to the dogma of reductionism (in its weakest form). The notion of an analytic as opposed to a synthetic statement is simply the notion of a statement whose truth depends only on its linguistic component.

The idea Quine sees as his main threat is not that the meaning of a statement depends somehow on its relation to experience but merely that *a statement is a unit of meaning*, and hence capable of confirmation by experience (regardless of whether that experience constitutes its meaning). This apparently innocuous claim is the famous second dogma of empiricism. Specifically, Quine's concern is that if individual statements can be confirmed by experience, then we must allow that each such statement has an "empirical component" in addition to its merely "linguistic component" (as illustrated above by "Brutus killed Caesar"). Once this is admitted, Quine thinks, analytic statements can be defined as those that have a null empirical component (are confirmed by all experiences) and synthetic statements as those that have a non-null

---

He merely says that, if individual statements had meaning in the verificationist sense, then the two dogmas would be true, but that individual statements do not have meaning in the verificationist sense.

empirical component (and so are confirmed by some experiences but not others). The issue for Quine, then, is not really reductionism but holism: not the semantic question of whether meaning is determined by empirical content but the epistemological question of whether individual statements can be confirmed by empirical evidence. Quine presents such holism as a "countersuggestion" to the "reductionist" belief that "each statement, taken in isolation from its fellows, can admit of confirmation or infirmation." To the contrary, Quine suggests, "our statements about the external world face the tribunal of sense experience not only individually but only as a corporate body" (41). Quine offers no defense of this claim apart from an appeal to the authority of Carnap, who had endorsed Duhem's famous claim that deriving an empirically testable consequence from a scientific hypothesis requires auxiliary hypotheses about the circumstances of the test and the reliability of our instruments.[30]

It's hard, however, to see how Duhem's thesis is supposed to support Quine's conclusion. Duhem was making the logical point that what is entailed by a negative experimental result is a denial not of the hypothesis itself but of the conjunction of the hypothesis and further, auxiliary, hypotheses that are needed to deduce the false experimental claim. So, for example, Newton's laws of motion, of themselves, predict nothing about the motions of the planets around the sun, since deriving such motions requires further assumptions about the masses of the sun and the planets, their relative positions to one another, the presence or absence of forces other than the sun's gravitational attraction – not to mention assumptions about the reliability of the telescopes we are using to make astronomical observations.

The upshot is that, in any realistic scientific case, we can never argue logically: $H \rightarrow O$; $\sim O$; therefore, $\sim H$. Logic gives us only: $H \mathbin{\&} A \rightarrow O$; $\sim O$; therefore, $\sim H \vee \sim A$. But, as many, beginning with Duhem himself, have noted, this logical point is entirely consistent with the epistemological claim that there might be good reason to deny H. There might, all things considered, be evidence for thinking that all the auxiliary assumptions (A) are true, from which it follows that there is good reason to think that H is false. Accordingly, Duhem's logical point does not support the epistemic conclusion that a particular scientific hypothesis cannot be disconfirmed (or confirmed) by empirical test. The fact that an empirically refuted hypothesis can still be asserted without *logical* contradiction does

---

[30] Only in a footnote added in the reprint of "Two Dogmas" in *From a Logical Point of View*, did Quine cite Duhem (41, n. 17).

not mean that such an assertion is *rationally* justified. There is even less basis for moving, as Quine does, from Duhem's logical point about a hypothesis and the auxiliary assumptions needed to test it, to a general holism for which the ultimate "unit of empirical significance" is neither the word nor the statement but "the whole of science" (42).

In the final section (6) of "Two Dogmas," Quine complements his rejection of the dogmas with an alternative to the conception of knowledge based on them. The discussion here is notably free of argument and mainly relies on a set of striking metaphors. He begins with a metaphor of the totality of our beliefs ("so-called knowledge") as a "man-made fabric" that has contact with experience only on its periphery. (Alternatively, he speaks of a force field with experience as its boundary conditions.) Pressure from experience can require, on pain of contradiction, revision of the statements making up the fabric, but the entire system "is so underdetermined by its boundary condition, experience, that there is much latitude of choice as to what statements to reevaluate in the light of any single contrary experience" (42–3).

Different statements are thought of as at different "distances" from the periphery, but, regardless of how near or far it is from the boundary, any given statement can be maintained in the face of apparently refuting experience or revised to save other statements. There is no distinction of statements to which we are committed no matter what (analytic statements) and those whose acceptability depends on the contingencies of what is experienced (synthetic statements). Similarly, "it is misleading to speak of the empirical content of an individual statement" (43).

In an effort to go beyond a metaphorical formulation, Quine introduces the notion of germaneness: certain statements are more or less germane to certain sense experiences; that is, we are more or less likely to revise them in the event of "recalcitrant" experiences. If I walk down a street and see only frame houses, I will be more inclined to revise my previous belief that there were brick houses on the street and less inclined to decide that I was having a hallucination. The belief that the street has brick houses is more germane to experience than is the belief that I am not hallucinating. This terminology allows Quine to introduce a more flexible parallel to the rigid distinction of analytic from synthetic statements. But it is hard to see how talk of "germaneness" is any less metaphorical than, say, conceptual containment.

Although many have found this holistic picture of knowing attractive, Quine provides no serious line of argument to support it. Tyler Burge, who says he thinks "Quine's holism about confirmation is insightful and his rejection of the second dogma correct," nonetheless (but understandably) also concludes that Quine's arguments "against the second dogma are unsound." He allows that "Quine had a gift for making these arguments exciting" but agrees that "the metaphors, slogans, and observations invoked to recommend them do not . . . make them cogent." Rather, Quine's holism "is not argued anywhere in depth"; "the view rides the waves of assertion and metaphor." Further, Quine's later ideas (indeterminacy of translation, inscrutability of reference, ontological relativity, etc.), which are based on "extensions of his argument against the second dogma," are "no better grounded than the grandiose metaphysics of Whitehead or Bradley."[31]

One final aspect of Quine's vision is his naturalism, which appears only at the end of the essay. His epistemological picture is of a system of beliefs, all in principle revisable, with the revisions made to adjust most appropriately to new experiences. But what, then, are the standards of appropriateness; that is, the goals that guide the effort of revision? There would seem to be a number of possibilities: to maximize human happiness, to conform with a religious vision of reality, etc. Quine, however, without justification or comment, begins speaking of the system of our beliefs as that of science, directed exclusively to the goal of "predicting future experiences in the light of past experiences" (44), implicitly committing himself to the naturalist assumption that there is nothing to know except the truths of empirical science.

Quine concludes with brief comments on the implications of his epistemological view for the ontology of science. Since all statements are revisable, all scientific entities must be regarded as posits, acceptable just to the extent that they assist in our effort to predict the future. There is no difference in principle between macroscopic physical objects and sub-atomic particles – or, for that matter, the Greek gods. There are just different degrees to which such posits are helpful for achieving our scientific goal. Quine even treats mathematical entities – e.g., classes – as posits in this sense. The result is that ontological questions are entirely reduced to scientific questions. But scientific questions are now resolved in the way that Carnap, for example, had proposed to resolve ontological questions, understood as questions about the choice of a "convenient conceptual scheme or framework for science" (45). Carnap maintained a distinction between ontological questions, to be decided by pragmatic considerations of which conceptual framework was most convenient for

---

[31] Burge, "Logic and Analyticity," 204, 205.

science, and scientific hypotheses, to be evaluated by their adequacy to experience. But such a distinction depends on the analytic-synthetic distinction that Quine rejects. So, in the Carnapian sense, what Quine proposes is a reduction of scientific questions to ontological questions. Quine's epistemic naturalism is complemented by a thoroughgoing ontological pragmatism.

Even more than the critique of the second dogma, this final statement of Quine's holistic vision of knowledge and reality is strikingly unargued. As Richard Creath notes, "there is no explicit argument . . . We are left to conclude that the elegance and coherence of his positive views were intended by Quine to *be* the argument."[32] Quine's holism, along with his related naturalism and pragmatism, seems supported by nothing more than persuasive rhetoric. His presentation is impressive as a philosophical manifesto or program, but not as a cogent argument for a conclusion.

[32] Creath, "Quine on the Intelligibility and Relevance of Analyticity," 56.

CHAPTER 2

Argument and intuition in
Kripke's Naming and Necessity

In January 1970, just about twenty years after Quine's revolutionary APA paper, Saul Kripke gave a series of lectures at Princeton that launched a counter-revolution. "The impact of the lectures," Scott Soames tells us, "was profound and immediate, and over the years their influence has grown." In drastic contrast to Quine's paper, Kripke's lectures provided, among other things, "a compelling defense of the metaphysical concepts of necessity and possibility . . . forceful arguments that there are necessary truths that are knowable only aposteriori, and apriori truths that are contingent . . . and a persuasive defense of the intelligibility of essentialism – i.e., the claim that it makes sense to characterize objects as having some of their properties essentially."[1] Soames' view of Kripke's effectiveness is widely shared. As Christopher Hughes puts it, "Certain Kripkean views [the metaphysical views mentioned by Soames as well as many of Kripke's key claims in the philosophy of language] . . . are, if not uncontroversial, as close to uncontroversial as any interesting views in analytic philosophy."[2] This consensus is all the more remarkable because, especially regarding necessity, Kripke rehabilitated positions that seemed to have been definitively buried by analytic philosophers from Frege, through the logical positivists, to Quine. Given analytic philosophers' commitment to rigorous argument as the hallmark of their discipline, we might expect that Kripke's lectures will be models of compelling argument. I will examine the case Kripke makes for three of the main theses that are widely held to be decisively established in *Naming and Necessity*: (1) there are essential as well as contingent properties that characterize things (essentialism); (2) proper names are not descriptions but rigid designators; (3) there are necessary truths that are knowable

---

[1] Scott Soames, *Philosophical Analysis in the Twentieth Century, Volume II: The Age of Meaning*, Princeton, NJ: Princeton University Press, 2003, 336.
[2] Christopher Hughes, *Kripke: Names, Necessity, and Identity*, Oxford: Oxford University Press, vii.

a posteriori. In every case, we shall see that the discussion is primarily driven not by argument but by intuition.

Given Quine's influential strictures against necessity we might expect Kripke – who was Quine's student at Harvard – to offer a thorough defense of this controversial notion. He, however, insouciantly forges right ahead without, as they say, a by-your-leave:

> We ask whether something might have been true, or might have been false. Well, if something is false, it's obviously not necessarily true. If it is true, might it have been otherwise? Is it possible that, in this respect, the world should have been different from the way it is? If the answer is "no", then this fact about the world is a necessary one.[3]

He goes on to "stipulate" that "an analytic statement is, in some sense, true by virtue of its meaning and true in all possible worlds" (39). It's almost as if "Two Dogmas" had never been written. A little later, however, Kripke averts in a footnote (without mentioning names) to Quinean qualms about necessity:

> By the way, it's a common attitude in philosophy to think that one shouldn't introduce a notion until it's been rigorously defined (according to some popular notion of rigor). Here I am just dealing with an intuitive notion and will keep on the level of an intuitive notion. (39, n.11)

In the face of Quine's strictures against necessity, Kripke simply asserts the rights of his contrary intuitions as a starting point.

A bit later, Kripke makes it clear that his commitment to necessity goes beyond accepting necessarily true *statements*. He notes that philosophers (more tolerant than Quine) often are willing to allow necessity of statements (de dicto necessity) but balk at necessity of *properties* (de re necessity, or *essentialism*). Kripke, however, thinks there are essential properties.

He briefly mentions Quine's influential objection to essentialism: that whether a property is necessary to an object depends on how the object is described. If the number 9 is referred to as *the successor of 8*, it is necessarily odd, but if it's referred to as *the number of planets*, it is not. From this Quine concludes that there is no objective fact of the matter as to whether a given number is essentially odd or not; any apparent necessity

---

[3] Saul Kripke, *Naming and Necessity*, Cambridge, MA: Harvard University Press, 1980, 36. Further references will be given in the text.

is merely relative to the way we have chosen to refer to it. Kripke does not reply directly to this argument, but notes how Quine's line of thought would extend to an everyday, non-technical case.[4] If we ask whether winning the 1968 election is a necessary or a contingent property of Nixon, the answer, according to Quine, depends on whether we refer to him under the description "the man who won the election in 1968." If we do so describe him, then *winning the 1968 election* is necessary; if we refer to him simply as "Nixon," then it is not. Kripke, however, demurs. An ordinary person, he says, would have no disagreement with someone who pointed to Nixon and said, "That's the guy who might have lost in '68," and certainly would not be hospitable to the response that this is so only if we describe the guy as "Nixon" and not as "the winner of the 1968 election." The ordinary person, according to Kripke,

> would say, and with great conviction, "Well, of course, the winner of the election might have been *someone else*. The actual winner, had the course of the campaign been different, might have been the loser . . . So, such terms as 'the winner' and 'the loser' don't designate the same object in all possible worlds. On the other hand, the term 'Nixon' is just a *name* of *this man*." (41)

Accordingly, Kripke concludes, it's not, as is sometimes maintained, that essentialism is "just a doctrine made up by some bad philosopher," that the "notion has no intuitive content" and "means nothing to the ordinary man" (41). On the contrary, it takes someone with a philosophical theory (Quine, for example) to call essential properties into question. There's significant intuitive support for at least the meaningfulness of necessary properties. Of course, "some philosophers think that something's having intuitive content is very inconclusive evidence in favor of it." But, Kripke tells us, "I think it is very heavy evidence in favor of anything, myself" (42).

Of course, many philosophers think that essential properties are, on the contrary, highly unintuitive. Why is that? One important reason, Kripke suggests, is that the question of essential properties is equivalent to the question of identity across possible worlds; both ask about what it takes to be a particular individual in any particular possible world. But answering such a question would seem to require our having necessary and sufficient conditions for being Nixon. And, Kripke admits, outside of mathematics,

---

[4] Soames points out (*Philosophical Analysis, Volume II*, 347–50) that Kripke can directly challenge Quine's argument by denying its implicit assumption that we refer to objects only through descriptions. If, as Kripke holds, names are not descriptions but rather rigid designators, then Quine's argument fails. Kripke does not seem to make this point explicitly, and, in any case, as we shall see, his defense of the rigid-designator thesis, like the rest of his "response" to Quine, is based on appeals to intuition.

we simply can't formulate necessary and sufficient conditions for being anything. If we can't formulate the (necessary and sufficient) conditions for being Nixon, how can we talk about properties that he has in all possible worlds (his essential properties)?

Kripke's answer is that the question is based on "the wrong way of looking at what a possible world is" (43). The question assumes that, when we inquire about Nixon's properties in possible worlds, we first need to formulate criteria for being Nixon, use these criteria to find Nixon in a given world, and then see if he has the relevant properties in that world. (For example, we look into possible worlds to see if there are any in which Nixon is non-human.) But this, Kripke says, "intuitively speaking . . . seems to me not to be the right way of thinking about the possible worlds" (43–4). As he sees it, "a possible world is given by the descriptive conditions we associate with it" (44). Here Kripke once again invokes ordinary language. He acknowledges that it might seem that we have to specify possible worlds through purely qualitative descriptions (that is, without referring to an individual who *has* the relevant qualitative properties). But, he responds, "that is not the way we ordinarily think of counterfactual situations" (45). Rather, we just point to (or name) someone and ask ourselves what might have happened to him. The idea that we have to look into worlds (with a special modal telescope?) is a misleading result of the technical apparatus of possible-world semantics – for which Kripke admits his work in modal logic may bear some responsibility.

It is at this point that Kripke's defense of essentialism connects with his views on naming. If we can refer to Nixon in various possible worlds without first describing him, then the name "Nixon" must be capable of picking out Nixon quite apart from any purely qualitative description of him. In other words, the name "Nixon" must be able to designate Nixon in any possible world in which he might exist. To say this is, in Kripke's terminology, to say that "Nixon" is a *rigid designator*. More generally, for Kripke a name (a proper name, that is) is a rigid designator: it refers to its referent in any possible world in which that referent exists. It is precisely because we can rigidly designate Nixon (by calling him "Nixon") that we can stipulate truths about him in various possible worlds. Once again, Kripke puts forward his view that names are rigid designators as an "intuitive thesis" (48). We will see much more of Kripke's development of this thesis in the next section.

Like Kripke's general defense of essentialism, his claims about which properties are in fact essential are based on intuitions. "For example, supposing Nixon is in fact a human being, it would seem that we cannot think of a possible counterfactual situation in which he was, say, an inanimate object; perhaps it is not even possible for him not to have been a human being" (46). This is the sort of evidence that shows that being human (or, at least, not being inanimate) is an essential property of Nixon. Or, to take another example, think about a table, which, in accord with current scientific theory, we regard as composed of molecules. Suppose that this is in fact true: the table is made up of a collection of molecules. Kripke agrees that, epistemically, we could have learned (and still could learn in the future) that the table is not composed of molecules. But suppose that in metaphysical fact the table is so composed. Then, Kripke asks, "could anything be this very object and not be composed of molecules?" His response: "Certainly there is some feeling that the answer to that must be 'no'. At any rate, it's hard to imagine under what circumstances you would have this very object and find that it is not composed of molecules" (47). Here Kripke's essentialism connects with his thesis that there are necessary a posteriori truths. That Nixon is human and that this table is composed of molecules are, if true, necessary truths. But knowing these metaphysical necessities depends on our empirical evidence that, for example, Nixon is not a robot but an organism or that the molecular hypothesis is true.

It is apparent that Kripke's "rehabilitation" of necessity in general and essentialism in particular is mainly based on the fact that the notion makes intuitive sense (has "intuitive content"). Sometimes he talks as if the intuition just corresponds to the way he sees things; other times, he appeals to an intuition that he claims is implicit in the language and thought of ordinary people. For example, he appeals to ordinary-language intuitions in response to Quine's objection that so-called essential properties are relative to our mode of reference. On the other hand, he rejects the objection tied to the problem of transworld identity because it is based on a way of thinking about possible worlds that he himself finds intuitively wrong. Then, when his intuition is challenged by philosophers who insist (presumably based on their own intuitions) that possible worlds have to be described entirely qualitatively, Kripke once again invokes ordinary ways of thinking and talking about counterfactual situations. Finally, regarding specific judgments about which properties are in fact essential, he states his own intuitions and invites us to see if we share them. We will return to this central role of intuitions in the final section of this chapter.

NAMES: DESCRIPTIONS OR RIGID DESIGNATORS?

Kripke defends his thesis that names are rigid designators as an alternative to the view – pretty much standard at the time of his lectures – that names are, or must be understood in terms of, definite descriptions. He begins by distinguishing, in the standard way, names (proper names) from (definite) descriptions: for example, "Walter Scott" vs. "the author of *Ivanhoe*." How are descriptions and names related? Mill thought that names have no connotation (meaning), only denotation (reference), whereas descriptions have both. Frege and Russell, however, thought that a name is really just a disguised or abbreviated description. Kripke admits (27–9) that there are strong arguments favoring the Frege–Russell view: (1) Except for special cases in which we can point to an object named, it seems we need to use a description of the object to refer to it. So, unless a name is a description, it's hard to see how, in general, we're able to use names to refer. (2) We sometimes discover that two names have the same referent and so can say, for example, "Hesperus is Phosphorus." Such an identity statement seems to be contingent, not necessary, but in Mill's view it would have to be necessary, since it would merely express Hesperus' identity with itself. But on the Frege–Russell view, we can more plausibly say that the identity is a contingent one between the Evening Star and the Morning Star. (3) It makes sense to ask whether a given name has any referent, whether, for example, the Loch Ness monster exists. But it's hard to see what sense there is to such a question unless it's asking whether there's anything that corresponds to a given description. On Mill's view, it would seem, we'd have to ask, "Does this thing (referred to by its name) exist?," thereby assuming a positive answer to the question.

Kripke says he's not prepared to respond to all these arguments for the Frege–Russell view, but he is nonetheless "pretty certain" that the view is false (29). He notes that many philosophers (e.g., Searle) have rejected this view but have substituted one that retains its spirit. Their move has been to deny that the referent of a name is determined by a single definite description but to maintain that it is determined by a "cluster" or "family" of definite descriptions. This "cluster-concept" view of names seems to maintain the virtues of the Frege–Russell view while avoiding some obvious problems (e.g., if "Aristotle" means "the teacher of Alexander," then "Aristotle taught Alexander" becomes a necessary truth). Accordingly, Kripke focuses his discussion on this version of descriptivism.

The idea of the cluster theory is, first of all, that, when I use a name (say, "Aristotle") to refer, then there is a description given by a cluster of properties (say, *being the teacher of Alexander, being the inventor of logic,* etc.) all of which I think belong to Aristotle. I also think that these properties pick out Aristotle uniquely (that is, as a group, they apply to Aristotle and to no one else). Of course, either there is or there is not a unique thing that in fact has all (or most) of the properties I think belong to Aristotle. If there is such a thing, then, according to the theory, "Aristotle" refers to it; if there is no such thing, then there is nothing referred to by "Aristotle"; that is, Aristotle does not exist. Finally, the description theory holds that, when I use "Aristotle" as a name, I know a priori that, if Aristotle exists, Aristotle has all or most of the properties in the cluster associated with him.

Kripke expresses the above account of naming in the following six general theses (71):

(1) For every name (X) there is a cluster of properties (ϕ) such that A (the person using X) believes ϕX.
(2) Some of these properties (ϕ) are believed by A to pick out some individual uniquely.
(3) If most of the ϕs are satisfied by a unique object, y, then X refers to y.
(4) If there is no unique object that satisfies most of the ϕs, then X does not exist.
(5) The statement "If X exists, then X has most of the ϕs" is known a priori by A.
(6) The statement "If X exists, then X has most of the ϕs" expresses a necessary truth (in A's idiolect).[5]

Kripke notes that including (6) yields a strong form of the cluster theory (held, he says, by John Searle), according to which a description not only fixes the reference of a name but also gives its meaning (necessary and sufficient conditions for its application). He rejects this strong version on intuitive grounds: "It is just not, in any intuitive sense of necessity, a necessary truth that Aristotle had [any of] the properties commonly attributed to him" (74). On the contrary, it's intuitively obvious that Aristotle might not have had any of these properties. The remaining five theses constitute a weaker version of the cluster theory, on which Kripke concentrates most of his attention.

Kripke allows that (1) can be stipulated as true by definition, but he thinks (2)–(5) are false, refutable by counterexample. So, regarding (2), he points out that many people who use the name "Cicero" may know nothing more of Cicero than that he was a famous Roman orator and even be aware that this description does not pick out a unique individual. A similar situation holds for "Richard Feynman," which for the less informed is simply the name of a famous physicist, not distinguishable by

---

[5] I omit a further, "non-circularity" condition that Kripke also discusses.

those who use the term from, say, Gell-Mann. With this, descriptivism must give up its fundamental claim that referring requires a uniquely specifying description of what is referred to.

Against (3), Kripke asks us to consider a case in which I think of Gödel as the man who proved the incompleteness of arithmetic, although in fact someone else (let's say Schmidt) gave the proof. In such a case, it would not follow, as (3) requires, that I am using "Gödel" to refer to Schmidt. Schmidt satisfies the relevant φs, but I still refer to Gödel. Accordingly, even if there is someone other than Gödel who has the cluster of properties that I think describe Gödel, I will still be referring to Gödel rather than to that person. Reference does not go to whoever happens to satisfy the associated description.

Thesis (4) is refuted by the same counterexample that refuted (2). If all I believe of Cicero is that he was a famous Roman orator, there is no unique individual picked out by the description associated with my use of "Cicero." But it does not follow that "Cicero" has no referent (that there is no Cicero, given the way I use the term "Cicero"). Kripke further notes that I can use a name (e.g., "Jonah") to refer even if there is no one at all (not just no unique individual) who satisfies the associated description. There may, as biblical scholars claim, have been someone the book of Jonah was about, even though no one did any of the things that, on the basis of the biblical story, I believe Jonah did.

Finally, thesis (5) fails because, for example, my knowledge that Gödel discovered the incompleteness of arithmetic is obviously not a priori. Accordingly, it is not true that I know a priori that, if Gödel exists, then Gödel discovered the incompleteness of arithmetic.

Here, if anywhere, Kripke's case seems based on solid argumentation: a modus-tollens refutation of descriptivism via uncontroversial counterexamples. Who could sincerely deny that Aristotle might not have been chosen to tutor Alexander, or that there are people who know nothing of Cicero except that he was a Roman orator? Here Kripke's intuitions merely express what is utterly obvious to anyone.

But do the counterexamples settle the issue? Do they refute the descriptivist theory? For one thing, descriptivists may argue that Kripke's theses (1)–(6) don't accurately characterize their theory. But even if they accept Kripke's characterization, descriptivists may argue that Kripke has not looked at the right set of descriptions. Regarding his counterexample to (3), for example, they might deny that, when we use the name "Gödel" to refer, we associate it with the description "the person who proved the incompleteness of arithmetic." Perhaps it makes more sense to say that the associated description is "the person most people think proved the incompleteness of arithmetic." If so, the Gödel–Schmidt counterexample becomes irrelevant. For, then, (3) takes the form: "If y is the person most people think proved the incompleteness of arithmetic, then 'Gödel' refers to y"; and y is Gödel, not Schmidt.

To this, Kripke's response is two-fold: first, he thinks there are new counterexamples to the revised description (for example, if most people came to believe that Schmidt proved the incompleteness of arithmetic, there could still be someone who thought Gödel did, and that person's use of "Gödel" would not refer to Schmidt). The description would have to be further revised to avoid such examples. Second, Kripke claims that the revised description leads to an unacceptable circularity. The revision requires that, when most people say "Gödel proved the incompleteness of arithmetic," they are referring to Gödel and not Schmidt. But the revision also requires that, when most people refer to Gödel, they are thinking of him as "the person most people think proved the incompleteness of arithmetic," since this is the new associated description. So, when I try to refer to Gödel, I do it by referring to whoever it is that most people refer to as the person who proved the incompleteness of arithmetic. Well, who is that? Who do most people refer to as the person who proved the incompleteness of arithmetic? According to the revised description they merely refer to whoever most people refer to when they refer to whoever proved the incompleteness of arithmetic. In other words, "we attribute this achievement to the man to whom we attribute it," a circular attribution from which we cannot escape by providing an independent criterion of reference (89).

Kripke allows, though, that the descriptivist has a response to the circularity charge. As Strawson has pointed out, although there is a vicious circularity in giving a description in terms of one's own reference, there is no circularity in a description in terms of someone else's reference. So, for example, I may refer to Gödel via the description, "The person Joe thinks proved the incompleteness of arithmetic." Joe may, in turn, refer to Gödel via the description, "The person Harry thinks proved the incompleteness of arithmetic," and so on for everyone who uses "Gödel" to refer, until, presumably, we reach someone who has actually seen Gödel and referred to him via a description such as "The man I saw at Princeton ten years ago." Kripke doesn't deny that this might work to fix the reference of "Gödel," but he notes that the chain of references might turn out to be circular (maybe Harry's description is in terms of the person Joe thinks proved the incompleteness of arithmetic) or there might not be any chain that leads back to Gödel. In any case, we have no way of knowing whether such things might be the case. Accordingly, "you cannot use this as your identifying description with any confidence" (90).

There is, of course, no reason to think that ingenious descriptivists could not find ways of evading even this assault. The key question would seem to be whether there is any limit to the thrust-and-parry of counter-example debate, any point at which we can reasonably conclude that a certain set of counterexamples does refute a philosophical theory. For Kripke, however, even this question is ultimately irrelevant, since, according to him, *any* philosophical theory is wrong:

> The cluster concept theory of names is . . . really a nice theory. The only defect it has is probably common to all philosophical theories. It's wrong. You may suspect me of proposing another theory in its place, but I hope not, because I'm sure it's wrong if it's a theory. (64)

Kripke does not, however, see this as a skeptical conclusion because he does not think that philosophical disputes are ultimately about what is the *true theory* but about what is the *correct picture*. I will discuss in some detail later this distinction of picture and theory, which I believe is central for our questions about philosophical knowledge. For the present, we can simply think of a *picture* as a highly general approach to a philosophical issue (for example: materialism or dualism regarding the relation of mind and body), with a *theory* being one of many possible precise formulations of a picture. Kripke, in any case, acknowledges the possibility that, if he developed his alternative view of names (the rigid-designator theory) "with sufficient precision in the form of six or seven or eight theses, it would also turn out that when you examine these theses one by one, they will all be false" (93). But that, he thinks, need not matter. The question is rather whether a theory is refutable simply because "there's some technical error here or some mistake there" or because "the whole picture given by this theory . . . [is] wrong from the fundamentals" (93). He believes that his theory will turn out to be false only in the first, innocuous sense, whereas the descriptivist theory is based on a picture that is fundamentally wrong. "What I am trying to present is a better picture" (94).

Kripke, then, is trying to show both that the descriptivist picture is fundamentally wrong and that his own picture is better than the descriptivist picture. His claim is that the first point emerges from the counterexamples he puts forward to theses (2)–(6). "What I think the examples I've given show is . . . that the whole picture given by this theory of how reference is deter-mined seems to be wrong from the fundamentals" (93). But just how is this supposed to happen? We have seen, in Kripke's discussion, the back-and-forth process of counterexample, response by defusing the example or modifying the theory, counterresponse by defusing the response or by further counterexample . . . What basis does Kripke have for claiming that, although he has clearly not brought this process to an end, he has shown that the picture on which descriptivism is based is fundamentally wrong?

There is one point at which he explicitly discusses the descriptivist picture as opposed to the specific theoretical version of it he has formulated. "The picture which leads to the cluster-of-descriptions theory is something like this," he says (91) and proceeds to describe a situation in which "one is isolated in a room," with no other speakers, and "determines the reference for himself by saying – 'By "Gödel" I shall mean the man, whoever he is, who proved the incompleteness of arithmetic'." Kripke says he doesn't deny that someone might do this: "There's nothing really preventing it. You can just stick to that determination," and, for example, wind up using "Gödel" to refer to Schmidt, if that's who meets the description. But, Kripke goes on, "that's not what most of us do" – and proceeds to sketch his own account of an initial rigid designation ("baptism") that is transmitted by a chain of uses of a name, each intending to have the same referent as the preceding speaker (91).

Admittedly, the locked-in-a-room procedure Kripke describes is "not what we do," but neither is it what any plausible version of the description theory says that we do.[6] The situation Kripke has described does not even express the cluster version of descriptivism, since it defines a name via a single description. Nor does the situation allow fixing reference, as Strawson suggests, by invoking another speaker's reference; nor does it take account of the possibility that Kripke's six theses may not be the necessary or best expression of the descriptivist picture. Indeed, it seems that he has done nothing more than present one particularly simple-minded theoretical version of descriptivism. Why characterize this as the descriptivist picture?

As to Kripke's effort to show that his rigid-designation picture is "better" than the descriptivist picture, this is merely a matter of stating, in a very preliminary and incomplete way, the main ideas of the picture. His most extended presentation begins:

Someone, let's say, a baby, is born; his parents call him by a certain name. They talk about him to their friends . . . Through various sorts of talk the name is spread from link to link as if by a chain. A speaker who is on the far end of this chain,

---

[6] John Searle says in his response to Kripke, "that is not the view any descriptivist known to me ever espoused and it is not surprising that Kripke gives no source for this strange view" ("Proper Names and Intentionalitiy," in his *Intentionality: An Essay in the Philosophy of Mind*, Cambridge: Cambridge University Press, 1983, 233).

who has heard about, say, Richard Feynman...may be referring to Richard Feynman even though he can't remember from whom he...ever heard of Feynman. He knows that Feynman is a famous physicist. A certain passage of communication reaching ultimately to the man himself does reach the speaker. He then is referring to Feynman even though he can't identify him uniquely. (91)

Kripke follows this exposition with some comments designed to show that the view he presents here is not the same as Strawson's descriptivist use of a similar chain of references, the main difference being that for Strawson successful reference depends on "how the speaker thinks he got the reference," whereas for Kripke all that matters is "the actual chain of communication" (93).

Kripke then remarks that in presenting his picture, he "has been far less specific than a real set of necessary and sufficient conditions for reference would be." He mentions, for example, that not all causal chains of communication lead to reference: there may well be such a chain going from today's children, speaking of Santa Claus, back to "a certain historical saint," but it's not likely that their "Santa Claus" refers to this person. Another difficult case for his account: a teacher (very confused, apparently) wants to tell his class that someone has squared the circle and does so by saying, "George Smith squared the circle," where George Smith is a neighbor of his, although he doesn't tell his students that. In such a case, Kripke says, there is a chain of communication from George Smith to the students, but it doesn't seem that, when they say (falsely) "George Smith squared the circle," they are referring to the teacher's neighbor. Such examples show that "more refinements need to be added to make this even begin to be a set of necessary and sufficient conditions. In that sense it's not a theory" (96). In fact, Kripke allows that adequate necessary and sufficient conditions of reference in terms of causal chains would be "very complicated" and "one might never reach a set" of them (94).

Finally, Kripke offers what he says might be "a rough statement of a theory": "An initial 'baptism' takes place. Here the object may be named by ostension, or the reference of the name may be fixed by a description. When the name is 'passed from link to link', the receiver of the name must, I think, intend when he learns it to use it with the same reference as the man from whom he heard it" (96). He remarks that it might be failure to keep the same intention that accounts for the Santa Claus case. On the other hand, he still thinks that the George Smith case "casts some doubt on the sufficiency of the conditions" (97).[7]

---

[7] There is also the important challenge of Gareth Evans' Madagascar counterexample to Kripke's view: the term "Madagascar" had been long used to refer to part of the African continent. Marco Polo,

What, then, warrants Kripke's immediately following conclusion that "I have presented a better picture than that given by description theorists" (97)? What he has presented seems no more plausible than did the descriptivist picture when he first explained it in contrast to Mill's view. He, by his own admission, has not formulated it in anything like the detail he formulated the description theory, and, nonetheless, there already seem to be troublesome counterexamples. There does not, then, seem to be any effective argument for Kripke's claim that names are rigid designators. This conclusion fits, moreover, with Kripke's own suggestion that his claim is an "intuitive thesis" (48). (See also his Preface to *Naming and Necessity*, where he refers to the claim as a "natural intuition" [5] and a "direct intuition" [14].)

This dominance of intuition – which, we have seen, Kripke himself emphasizes – may seem odd given that commentators on Kripke typically talk about the "arguments" whereby he has refuted the description theory. In particular, it is claimed that Kripke deploys three powerful kinds of arguments: "modal arguments," "epistemic arguments," and "semantic arguments."[8] But in fact these "arguments" amount to nothing more than the various counterexamples that Kripke offers to the descriptivist theory. In the expositions of Hughes and of Fitch, for example, modal arguments correspond to the Aristotle counterexample against descriptivist thesis (6), epistemic arguments to the Feynman counterexample against thesis (2), and semantic arguments to the Gödel counterexample against thesis (3). As we have seen, Kripke himself does not regard these counterexamples in themselves as decisive against the descriptivist picture.

The "modal argument" is sometimes formulated in a somewhat different way. Soames, for example, at one point puts it like this:

P1. Names are rigid designators.
P2. Standardly, the descriptions associated by speakers with names are not rigid designators.[9]

---

misunderstanding his informants, used it to refer to the island off the east coast of Africa. Kripke's causal account would seem to require that "Madagascar" still refers to the mainland, which it obviously does not. (See Gareth Evans, "The Causal Theory of Names," in his *Collected Papers*, Oxford: Oxford University Press, 1985.) Kripke briefly discusses this and similar counterexamples in his "Addenda" to *Naming and Necessity*, concluding "I leave the problem for further work" (163).

[8] See, for example, Nathan Salmon, *Reference and Essence*, Oxford: Basil Blackwell, 1982, 23–31; Hughes, *Kripke*, 7–15; G. W. Fitch, *Saul Kripke*, Montreal: McGill Queen's University Press, 2004, 34–9.

[9] The qualification "standardly" is required because there are some cases of definite descriptions that do rigidly designate their referents; for example, "the successor of 22" refers to 23 in all possible worlds.

C. So, names are standardly not synonymous with descriptions associated with them by speakers.[10]

According to Soames, "this argument was immediately recognized to be a powerful challenge to descriptivism about the meanings of proper names and it continues to be accepted by a great many philosophers to this day."[11]

But P1 simply assumes what is at stake in the debate between Kripke and descriptivists: that names are not descriptions but rather rigid designators. Kripke's entire discussion is intended to show the superiority of his rigid-designation picture, so how can an argument that simply assumed this superiority have been decisive? Soames is right to present Kripke's rigid-designation thesis as an ultimate premise, not a conclusion. But since this is a premise Kripke can justify only as part of his alternative to the descriptivist picture of naming, it is misleading to claim that this "modal argument" is a decisive refutation of descriptivism.[12]

THE NECESSARY A POSTERIORI

So far, we have discussed Kripke's anti-Quinean view of necessity and his rejection of the descriptivist view of names in favor of his own rigid-designator view. We look, finally, at how Kripke weaves these two threads together in his account of identity statements involving proper names (e.g., "Hesperus is Phosphorus"). As Kripke sees it, such statements are another example of necessary a posteriori truths. We must discover their truth by experience, not, for example, by reflection on the meaning of their terms. But, given their truth, they are necessarily true. We have already seen that attributions of essential properties ("Nixon is human," "This table is made of molecules") can be necessary a posteriori. Given the existence of essential properties, which an object has in every possible world in which it exists, and given that an object's name is a rigid designator, which refers to the object in every world in which it exists, it

---

[10] Soames, *Philosophical Analysis, Volume II*, 343.   [11] Ibid.

[12] Here "descriptivism" refers to the view that a name is simply a description, which, apart from some exceptional cases, does not rigidly designate. "Descriptivism" can also be applied to views that agree with Kripke that all names are rigid designators but replace his causal account of how reference is achieved with an account in which description plays a central role. As we will see in chapter 4, almost all philosophers did eventually come to agree with Kripke that names are rigid designators, at which point Soames' modal argument would be unproblematic. But the key to Kripke's success was getting philosophers to accept his view that names are rigid designators, not constructing the obvious argument from this premise to the conclusion that names are not descriptions.

follows that such an attribution is a necessary truth, since it is true of the object in all possible worlds.[13] Many philosophers, of course, have thought that a necessary truth must be a priori. Kripke, however, notes that the *a priori* is an epistemological notion, about how we know something, whereas the *necessary* is a metaphysical notion, about how something is in reality. Short of an independent philosophical argument connecting the two, there is no reason the two notions must go together. (We will discuss this issue further below.)

Kripke extends his idea of necessary a posteriori truths to statements of identity that involve proper names, for example, "Cicero is Tully" or, most famously, "Hesperus is Phosphorus." Such identities are, he says, all both metaphysically necessary and known from experience.

He develops this claim through a detailed discussion of the Hesperus–Phosphorus example. There are those who say "Hesperus is Phosphorus" is a contingent truth. It is, they say, easy to describe a possible situation in which Hesperus is not Phosphorus: suppose people saw a bright heavenly body in the eastern morning sky and called it "Hesperus," then saw an exactly similar body in the western evening sky and called it "Phosphorus"; later astronomical investigation showed that these are two distinct bodies. Kripke agrees that this could happen, but he denies that, in the case described, Hesperus would not be identical with Phosphorus. What, he asks, would the people assigning the names "Hesperus" and "Phosphorus" have done in the possible but counterfactual case described? They wouldn't have assigned both names to the same heavenly body (say what we now call Venus), since then Hesperus would be Phosphorus. So they would have either assigned the names to two bodies, each different from Venus; or, at best, assigned one of the names to Venus (suppose that was "Hesperus") and the other to another body (suppose that was "Phosphorus"). Kripke, however, wants to say that this would be just a case of the names "Hesperus" and "Phosphorus" being assigned to objects other than the ones to which we assign them.

But why should we believe this, rather than that it would be a case of Hesperus and Phosphorus not being the same heavenly body? Kripke offers two related distinctions to support his view. First, there is a distinction between epistemic possibility and metaphysical possibility, between what

---

[13] Soames makes this point: once we "sharply distinguish" epistemic and metaphysical possibility, "and both rigid designation and the existence of nontrivial essential properties of objects are accepted, the necessary a posteriori follows unproblematically" (*Philosophical Analysis*, Volume II, 377).

might be true "for all we know" and what is really possible. So, for example, before Andrew Wile's 1994 proof, we didn't know for sure whether Fermat's Last Theorem was true; in this sense it might have turned out to be false. But the possibility merely corresponded to our ignorance: it wasn't really (metaphysically) possible that Fermat's Last Theorem not be true; the possibility was merely epistemic (relative to our lack of knowledge). Kripke's suggestion is that the same is true of "Hesperus is Phosphorus." "For all we knew," the referents of "Hesperus" and "Phosphorus" might have turned out to be different, but in reality they couldn't have, since the identity, if true, is necessarily true. The difference between this case and that of Fermat's Last Theorem is that it required empirical observation to learn that Hesperus is Phosphorus. But this, Kripke maintains, simply shows that a necessary truth can be known a posteriori.

There is, nonetheless, a difference between the Hesperus–Phosphorus case and the case of Fermat's Last Theorem. In the mathematical example, it is not true that the theorem might have turned out to be false. Any apparent disproof of it would have turned out to be mistaken. In the Hesperus–Phosphorus case, this is not so. Here "it might have turned out either way" (104); in particular, Hesperus might have *turned out* not to be Phosphorus. From this it seems to follow that Hesperus might *not have been* Phosphorus, which is to say that it is not Phosphorus necessarily. Kripke, however, insists that the distinction between epistemic and metaphysical possibility applies even here. But it takes the form of a distinction between the qualitative epistemic situation – that is, the total evidence I have that a given state of affairs obtains – and the state of affairs that actually (metaphysically) obtains. I can be in the identical qualitative epistemic situation regarding Hesperus and Phosphorus (that is, have exactly the same experiences of seeing bright heavenly bodies in the relevant locations) but have it turn out in one case that there was only one body and in the other that there were two. The identical qualitative epistemic situation can exist with either Hesperus and Phosphorus being identical or their not being identical. In particular, we could have had compelling inductive evidence that Hesperus is Phosphorus, even though Hesperus and Phosphorus were different planets. This is what leads us to say that Hesperus might have turned out not to be Phosphorus. This is true, but only in the epistemic sense that our total evidence might be the same, whether Hesperus was or was not Phosphorus. It is not true in the sense that, in reality (metaphysically), Hesperus might or might not actually be Phosphorus.[14] In

---

[14] Later Kripke suggests that we might mark the relevant distinction by agreeing that (before investigation) *Hesperus might turn out not to be Phosphorus*, where the "might" has a merely

reality, since "Hesperus" and "Phosphorus" name the same entity in all possible worlds, the identity must hold.

It does seem that Kripke's deployment of the epistemic–metaphysical distinction enables him to interpret the counterfactual cases in a way consistent with claim that "Hesperus is Phosphorus" is necessary.[15] This, however, does not prove that the claim is correct. The fact remains that, if "Hesperus" means "the heavenly body we see at dusk in the west" and "Phosphorus" means "the heavenly body we see before sunrise in the east," then Hesperus need not be identical with Phosphorus: the identity is not a necessary truth. It seems, in other words, that to establish positively that "Hesperus is Phosphorus" is necessarily true, Kripke needs the assumption that proper names are rigid designators rather than descriptions. More fully, his claim about necessity of identities has no basis apart from his claim about naming, which, as we have seen, is grounded in intuition rather than argument.

KRIPKE AND INTUITIONS

It is, in any case, time to reflect in a more systematic way on the distinction, on which I have been insisting, between argument and intuition. In one sense, of course, there need be no deep contrast between the two. It is a truism, emphasized from Aristotle on, that arguments require premises and that, since there is no going to infinity with arguments for premises, arguments must rely on premises that are not themselves justified by argument. If we define "intuition" simply as "statement accepted without argument," then intuition becomes an essential part of argument. Then, however, everything will depend on the nature of the intuitions that provide the ultimate premises of an argument.

Ideally, these intuitions would express utterly obvious truths – e.g., of logic, mathematics, or sense perception; truths that simply need no support other than our immediate awareness that they are so. Of course, philosophers have been famous for taking seriously challenges to even such obvious truths, and there is, at least, much to be learned from efforts to refute radical skepticism. There is even more to be learned from suggestions – for example, by idealists or materialists – that what we take to be obvious truths in our ordinary frameworks of thought and

epistemic significance, but denying that (after investigation) *Hesperus might have turned out not to be Phosphorus*, where the "might have" has a metaphysical sense (143, n.72).

[15] Soames offers a thorough discussion of Kripke's case here (*Philosophical Analysis, Volume II*, 380–95).

experience might need to be rejected from the standpoint of some (philosophically or scientifically) superior framework. But neither of these points should keep us from recognizing that arguments from obvious truths to substantial conclusions about controversial philosophical topics would be major intellectual achievements and would constitute genuine philosophical knowledge. Skeptical concerns would not alter the fact that virtually all of us do firmly accept the claims skepticism questions, and, even if there are compelling cases for revising our ordinary frameworks, it remains absurd to deny "obvious truths" within the frameworks within which they are obvious.[16]

If, then, Kripke's arguments relied only on obvious truths in the above sense, there would be no point to insisting that his case is based on intuition rather than argument. But, apart from some of his counter-examples (which are, for other reasons, less than argumentatively decisive), Kripke's intuitions are far from obvious. At their strongest, they correspond to common-sense assumptions that are built into at least some of our ordinary-language usage. As Hughes says of Kripke's defense of essentialism: "The view that things have at least some of their proper-ties . . . essentially . . . is not just the view of Aristotle, or Aquinas, but also the view of the man on the Clapham omnibus – or so Kripke argued. And he persuaded, if not everyone, nearly everyone."[17] But why should analytic philosophers, who had a long history of distrusting essentialism, have suddenly changed their minds because Kripke – even if correctly – pointed out that de re necessity is part of common talk and thought? They surely already knew this, and, in any case, why should appeals to common sense suddenly be thought to overcome what so many had seen as Quine's decisive objections – e.g., by the mathematical cyclist argu-ment – to de re modality? Similar questions could be raised about the rapid acceptance of Kripke's other theses – similarly defended – about the nature of proper names and the existence of necessary a posteriori truths.

Kripke rightly points out that "ordinary people" have no problem referring to Nixon without specifying criteria for his existence or that we typically distinguish between epistemic possibility (what might be as far as we know) and metaphysical possibility (what must be no matter what we

---

[16] So, for example, it is one thing to claim that there are good scientific reasons for denying the existence of color, but quite another to claim that, from the standpoint of everyday perception, the sky is not blue. A proof for, say, God's existence, that used premises no more controversial than that the sky is blue (as asserted within the framework of ordinary experience) would be very impressive indeed.

[17] Hughes, *Kripke*, 84.

think). But such common-sense intuitions are too close to philosophically disputed claims to be more than starting points for discussion. They may be the modal parallels to "folk psychology" or "folk physics," if indeed they do express views that are deeply embedded into our everyday thought. Even so, as we know from the cases of other folk beliefs, they may not be entirely reliable and might be superseded by alternative views that have greater coherence or explanatory power. Kripke himself, as we saw above, cites various ways in which the descriptive theory of names seems clearly superior to the rigid-designator theory. In his Preface he makes a point of acknowledging the power of the descriptivist picture: "The natural and uniform manner by which these ideas appear to account for a variety of philosophical problems – their marvelous coherence – is adequate explanation for their long appeal" (5).

Moreover, we must keep in mind that descriptivists too can cite instances of ordinary usage that fit their picture better than Kripke's. Ordinary people, for example, would say that there are descriptive limits to what our term "Nixon" could turn out to refer to. It could not – to use Searle's example – refer to a bar stool in a 1950s New Jersey pizzaria, although Kripke's account allows for this.[18] In yet other cases, an intuition seems to have little or no claim to grounding in ordinary thought and speech but merely expresses the reflective judgment of Kripke and other like-minded philosophers; for example, that a table is necessarily composed of molecules, which even Kripke expresses with some hesitation ("there's some feeling that" this must be the case (47)).

But if Kripke's intuitions don't provide sufficient basis for his conclusions, why were philosophers so impressed with his achievement? It is sometimes suggested that the answer lies in Kripke's earlier work in modal logic. Hughes, for example, says that this work helped "demarginalize" modality "by providing a semantics for modal logic" and "by vigorously and effectively addressing Quinean worries about whether quantification into modal contexts made sense."[19] But these technical achievements had not removed philosophical doubts. In spite of the work of Kripke and others between 1955 and 1965 on modal logic, "before the appearance of *Naming and Necessity*, quite a few philosophers had doubts about the philosophical respectability of modal logic, and indeed about the philosophical

---

[18] Searle, *Intentionality*, 249–50. Kripkeans, of course, would try to formulate their causal-transmission account to exclude such cases, which they would argue are rather changes in the reference of a term.
[19] Ibid.

respectability of the concepts of possibility and necessity."[20] This is not surprising since, insofar as Kripke's semantics for modal logic provides an interpretation for quantification into modal contexts, it *presupposes*, as Quine had said it would have to, the truth of essentialism. Accordingly, as Plantinga pointed out, Quine was correct that "a natural or standard interpretation of quantified modal logic . . . will be no more intelligible than [the] ancient distinction between essential and accidental properties of objects."[21] In any case, it is hard to understand why *Naming and Necessity* made such a difference, since it scarcely refers to the new developments in modal logic, offers no response to Quine's specific objections, and relies far more on intuition than on argument to support its claims.

[20] Hughes, *Kripke*, 81.
[21] Alvin Plantinga, *The Nature of Necessity*, Oxford: Oxford University Press, 1974, 238.

CHAPTER 3

The rise and fall of counterexamples: Gettier, Goldman, and Lewis

For all their analytic acuity, Quine and Kripke were dealing with a sweeping range of issues that, we might think, make it hard to stay on the narrow path of rigorous argument and call for flights of philosophical imagination or depths of intuitive penetration. Perhaps we should look at a narrower issue that has allowed analytic philosophers to focus their argumentative resources on specific, well-defined points. Here an obvious choice is the search for a definition of knowledge that has occupied epistemologists since the early 1960s. The choice seems particularly appropriate, since epistemology has been driven by what may seem to be the purely argumentative power of counterexamples, which, we have seen, constituted Kripke's most effective use of argument in *Naming and Necessity*. We begin with Gettier's two famous counterexamples and the debate they spawned over the definition of knowledge, then move to Alvin Goldman's use of counterexamples in his seminal paper, "What Is Justified Belief?," and conclude with the more complex forms of argumentation deployed in David Lewis' recent but already classic "Elusive Knowledge."

TWO COUNTEREXAMPLES THAT SHOOK
THE EPISTEMOLOGICAL WORLD

Plato, in the *Theatetus* and the *Meno*, suggested defining knowledge as *justified true belief*. Although he himself does not unequivocally endorse the idea and although for centuries the topic was little discussed outside commentaries on Plato, the definition seems intuitively right and earlier analytic philosophers such as Ayer and Chisholm had put forward definitions along its lines. On reflection, almost everyone will agree that we believe what we know and that what we really know must be true. Further, true belief alone cannot be knowledge. It's not enough that I just

51

luckily happen to believe what's true; knowledge also requires some sort of basis (justification) for what I know, although it is not easy to say just what this involves. Hence: knowledge is justified true belief. But in a brief article, published in *Analysis* in June 1963, Edmund Gettier offered two counterexamples to this definition that were quickly accepted as decisive.[1]

The counterexamples are cases in which someone (Smith) has a belief that seems to be clearly true and justified, but seems, with equal clarity, not to have knowledge of what he believes.[2] For example, Smith might have good reason to believe that Jones owns a Ford (he's seen him driving one, has heard him repeatedly say that he owns one, etc.) and so believes and is justified in believing that Jones owns a Ford. Further, given that Smith is justified in believing that Jones owns a Ford, he is also justified in believing any claim that he believes because he has logically deduced it from "Jones owns a Ford"; for example, that *either* Jones owns a Ford *or* Brown (another acquaintance of Smith's) is in Barcelona. Suppose that Smith does deduce this disjunctive statement and, accordingly, believes it. His belief in this disjunction is justified, since his belief in the first disjunct is justified. Of course, supposing that the first disjunct is true, the entire disjunctive statement is also true, and we will have no hesitation in saying that Smith knows it. But, Gettier says, suppose that the first disjunct, although well justified, is in fact not true (perhaps Jones has been lying and only rents the car he drives) but that Brown, entirely unbeknown to Smith, is in Barcelona. Once again, the disjunction will be true (because the second disjunct is), and Smith will be justified in believing it (because his belief in the first disjunct is justified and he has inferred the disjunction from this justified belief). In such a case, there is a proposition ("Smith owns a Ford or Brown is in Barcelona") that: (a) Smith believes; (b) Smith is justified in believing; and (c) is true. By the definition of knowledge, it follows that Smith knows this proposition. But surely Smith does not know it. It is, as Gettier says, just the "sheerest coincidence, and entirely unknown to Smith" that Brown is in Barcelona, and this is the fact that makes what Smith believes true. To know that Jones owns a Ford or Brown

---

[1] Edmund Gettier, "Is Justified True Belief Knowledge?," *Analysis* 23 (1963), 121–3.

[2] There are simpler counterexamples, more intuitive and closer to real life, that would make Gettier's point. One example: I look at a clock I have good reason to think is reliable and see that it reads 12 p.m. and so come to have the belief that the time is 12 p.m. It is indeed 12 p.m., but what I don't know is that the clock is stopped at 12 p.m., so it was just sheer luck that I saw it at the one time when it happened to be right. In this case, I believe it's 12 p.m. and my belief is both justified and true. But surely I don't know that it's 12 p.m. I begin with Gettier's much more convoluted and unrealistic case both because of its seminal role and because its oddity and complexity are typical of the counterexamples needed to keep the Gettier debate going.

is in Barcelona, Smith would have to have some reason to believe that Brown is in Barcelona. Nonetheless, the disjunctive proposition Smith believes fits perfectly the definition of knowledge as justified true belief. There is, Gettier concludes, something wrong with the definition.

Accepting this case as a counterexample to the standard definition of knowledge depends on two presuppositions, both noted by Gettier. First, in the relevant sense of "justified," it is possible to be justified in believing a false proposition (in the example, Smith is justified in believing the false statement that Jones owns a Ford). Second, if p logically entails q, and I'm justified in believing p, and moreover I accept q because I have logically derived q from p, then I'm justified in believing q. Gettier presents both of these presuppositions as obvious, as they indeed seem to be.

There have been literally hundreds of papers written in response to the issues raised by Gettier's paper.[3] Almost everyone agrees that Gettier was correct: that his (or similar) counterexamples show that the standard analysis of knowing was incorrect and needed revision. Here, at least, we seem to have an example of a decisive philosophical argument. But is there any way to revise the definition of knowledge to avoid Gettier's counterexamples? At first it seemed to be a simple matter of adding a fourth condition in the definition of knowledge, one that would place further restrictions on the kind of justification required. One immediate suggestion, the "no-false-lemmas" revision,[4] was to require that the justification for what is known not be based on propositions that are false (recall that in Gettier's example, Smith derives his justified and true disjunctive proposition from the false claim that Smith owns a Ford).

But this revision falls to another sort of counterexample: suppose you are in a library and see your good friend Tom Grabit nervously take a book from the shelf, slip it into his backpack, and sneak out of the library when the guard is distracted. You are obviously justified in believing that Tom has stolen a book. But suppose that, quite unknown to you, Tom has a kleptomaniac identical twin who was in the library at exactly this time. Suppose also, though, that it was in fact Tom who stole the book. Then it would seem clear that, although your belief is justified, true, *and*

---

[3] For a careful, comprehensive – and, inevitably, mind-numbing – survey of the Gettier literature up to 1983, see Robert K. Shope, *The Analysis of Knowledge*, Princeton, NJ: Princeton University Press, 1983. For an excellent, much more accessible overview of the discussion (up to the end of the twentieth century), see Shope's article, "Conditions and Analyses of Knowing," in Paul Moser (ed.), *The Oxford Handbook of Epistemology*, Oxford: Oxford University Press, 2002.

[4] Michael Clark, "Knowledge and Grounds: A Comment on Mr. Gettier's Paper," *Analysis* 24(2) (1963), 46–8.

not based on any false beliefs, you do not *know* that Tom stole the book. The justification for your belief depends on the sheer chance of your not knowing evidence that would have undermined it.[5]

This counterexample, however, suggested another version of the fourth condition, one asserting that a justified belief is not a candidate for knowledge as long as there are truths (call them defeaters) that, if you did believe them, would undermine the justification of your belief. In short, the condition is that your belief be indefeasible (have no defeaters). So, in the case of Tom, if you knew about his identical twin, you would no longer be justified in believing that he had stolen the book. The problem is that your justification of your belief is defeasible (there is further information that, if you came to know it, would undermine your justification). Adding a fourth condition requiring that justification be indefeasible eliminates the library counterexample. This approach, introduced by Peter Klein, is an example of what has become known as the defeasibility analysis, which has been extensively developed.[6]

The need for further development is apparent from a variation on the library counterexample. Supposes you see Tom just as before and correctly conclude that he stole the book. But now further suppose that: (1) Tom's mother (a generally very honest woman) has testified to the police that Tom has an identical twin and that Tom was far away from the library at the time of the theft; (2) Tom's mother was, however, lying: Tom has no identical twin and was in the library. In this case, Klein's indefeasibility condition says you do not know that Tom stole the book, since if you had known (1), you would not have been justified in believing that he did. The fact that Tom's mother testified as she did defeats the justification of your belief that he stole the book. But surely you *do* know that Tom stole the book: the fact that you don't know about lying testimony to the contrary doesn't undermine your knowledge.

This last counterexample was based on the fact that what would by itself be a defeater of a claim to knowledge might itself have a defeater, which, so

---

[5] Another counterexample not based on false beliefs is the famous case of the barn, which I insert here for further reference: You are driving through a rural area and notice what surely seem to be barns in the fields you are passing. You quite justifiably form the belief that a particular one of the objects you are seeing is a barn – which in fact it is. What you don't know, however, is that the farmers in this area frequently put up (as a joke or to give an impression of prosperity) painted facades that merely seem to be barns. You were just lucky to have encountered one of the few real barns. In this case, we would not say that your belief that you are looking at a barn is a piece of knowledge, even though there are no false beliefs involved in your arriving at this belief.

[6] Peter Klein, "A Proposed Definition of Propositional Knowledge," *Journal of Philosophy* 68 (1971), 471–82.

to speak, overrides the initial defeater. In our case the defeater is "Tom's mother has testified that Tom was nowhere near the library but has an identical twin who was" and the defeater of this defeater is "Tom's mother is lying." This suggests that we revise our definition of indefeasible from "has no defeater" to "has no defeater that does not itself have a defeater." With this revision, we disarm the revised library counterexample.

Unfortunately, this revision is too strong, since it disarms all Gettier counterexamples. Take Gettier's original case, Smith's belief that Jones owns a Ford or Brown is in Barcelona. Applying our original defeasibility condition, we would conclude that this belief is not knowledge, because its justification depends on "Jones owns a Ford," which is defeated by "Jones does not own a Ford." But, once we take into account the new requirement (introduced to meet the revised library example), we see that this defeater is itself defeated by "Brown is in Barcelona": if I came to believe both "Jones does not own a Ford" and "Brown is in Barcelona," I would be justified in believing "Jones owns a Ford or Brown is in Barcelona." Similarly, in any other Gettier-type counterexample, the truth that I believe but do not know will defeat the defeater of my justification. There have, however, been many further wrinkles on the defeasibility approach (and many other approaches), and the discussion continues with ever increasing complexity.[7]

The increasing complexity of fourth-condition proposals and their apparently inevitable vulnerability to counterexamples have left little reason to think that trying to solve the Gettier problem by adding further conditions will ever move beyond the rococo futility in which it has been immersed for so long. But can't we at least conclude that the Gettier counterexamples refute the long-held view that justified true belief is knowledge? Can't we rightly claim, therefore, that philosophers now know that justified true belief is not the same as knowledge?

Of course, a modus tollens argument based on an utterly obvious counterexample is decisive. If I say that all women are under six feet tall, then the fact that a women is six-foot-four refutes my claim. But the force of the argument depends on the obviousness of the counterexample. In

---

[7] Robert Shope, for example, concludes his excellent briefer survey of the Gettier problem with a proposal that defines "S knows that h" in terms of a belief that is justified, true, and meets the further condition: "(iv) S's believing/accepting that h is justified in relation to epistemic goals either through S's grasping portions of a justification-explaining chain connected to the proposition that h or independently of anything making it justified." To this he must add a definition of the technical term "justification-explaining chain" (used in (iv)) in terms of four further conditions, one of which involves six sub-conditions (Shope, "Conditions and Analyses of Knowing," 56–7).

just what sense are the Gettier cases obvious? I suggest we can fruitfully judge the obviousness of a claim by the epistemic price of refusing to accept it. If I'm presented with a woman who certainly looks well over six feet and whose height has just been measured (by competent judges) as over six feet, denying her height requires me to deny the evidence of my own senses and the validity of a measurement I have every reason to think is reliable. To maintain my claim that there are no women over six feet will involve me in a cascade of epistemic absurdities that makes holding on to my claim a common-sense impossibility.

Gettier counterexamples do not have this sort of obviousness. It seems right – at least to most philosophers – that I wouldn't know that Jones owns a Ford or that there was a barn in the field (for this example, see note 5), but denying these claims does not contradict anything built into our everyday judgments. Whereas we frequently make judgments about whether *a* could or could not turn out to be P, we seldom if ever are called on to make judgments about whether someone in a Gettier-situation has knowledge. Similarly, it seems obvious to many of us that, in the barn case, I do not know that there is a barn in the field. But suppose I nonetheless maintain that I do know this: I saw what I had every reason to think was a barn, it turned out actually to be a barn, so I knew that it was a barn. Maintaining this is not a "common-sense impossibility," since, in everyday, common-sense life, the only ways of denying that a belief amounts to knowledge are to deny its truth or to deny that I am justified in holding it. Here what I believe is both true and justified. Intuitions about Gettier-cases, clear as they may be, are not part of our everyday, common-sense way of dealing with knowledge claims, so giving them up does not overwhelm us with epistemic absurdities.

In view of this, it is not surprising that some philosophers, notably Brian Weatherson and William Lycan, have recently been willing to swim against the tide of Gettier intuitions – and have done so with relative impunity. Weatherson, for example, suggests that the general plausibility and power of the standard justified-true-belief model could give us a reason for accepting it and overriding our intuitions in a few marginal cases.[8] William Lycan endorses a relatively slight revision of Clark's early no-false-lemmas definition of knowledge. He responds to counter-examples that involve no false assumptions, such as that of Tom Grabit in the library and that of the real barn amid the fakes, by maintaining that I *do* know that Grabit stole the book and that there is a barn in the field,

---

[8]   Brian Weatherson, "What Good Are Counterexamples?," *Philosophical Studies* 115 (2003), 1–31.

even if this might be a weaker sense of "know."[9] Such moves may also gain empirical support from studies suggesting that samples of non-philosophers are far from unanimous regarding Gettier intuitions.[10] It seems, then, that even Gettier's generally accepted negative conclusion has not been decisively established.

GOLDMAN ON JUSTIFIED BELIEF

But even if we accept this pessimistic conclusion, there is still more to the story. Even though the direct assaults of fourth-condition analysis have failed to solve the Gettier problem, they have helped produce new ways of thinking about knowledge that have revolutionized epistemology. Alvin Goldman, for example, suggested in 1967 that the Gettier problem could be handled by taking account of the causal connection between a belief and the reality it was about.[11] Why doesn't Smith know that Jones owns a Ford or Brown is in Barcelona? Because, Goldman says, what makes the proposition believed true is the fact that Brown is in Barcelona and there is no causal tie between Smith's belief in the proposition and this fact. By contrast, if Jones did in reality own a Ford, then this fact would be causally tied to Smith's belief – as e.g., part of the motive Jones had for saying he owned a Ford.

In typical fashion, this causal move required modification in the light of various counterexamples, one of the most important of which was the barn example: my true belief that there is a barn in the field is directly caused by the barn itself, despite the many fake barns that undermine my claim to know this truth. In response, Goldman modified his requirement to say that knowledge requires causal production by a generally reliable process (a process that, in the relevant situation, will typically produce true belief). Given the preponderance of fake barns in the field, ordinary perceptual processes are not very reliable. Further counter-examples led Goldman to give up the requirement that the fact known must be part of the reliable causal process – think of coming to believe that an object is in a room when what you actually see is a mirror image of the object which is, nonetheless, in the room out of your sight. But

---

[9] William Lycan, "On the Gettier Problem Problem," in Stephen Hetherington (ed.), *Epistemology Futures*, Oxford: Oxford University Press, 2006, 148–68.

[10] J. Weinberg, S. Nichols, and S. Stich, "Normativity and Epistemic Intuitions," *Philosophical Topics* 29 (2001), 429–60. In chapter 4, I will discuss the broader significance of this paper as an attack on philosophical intuitions.

[11] Alvin Goldman, "A Causal Theory of Knowing," *Journal of Philosophy* 64 (1967), 335–72.

Goldman was left with the powerful idea that knowledge (or at least justified belief) is in essence the result of a reliable causal process, an idea he developed into the original and powerful epistemological position known as reliabilism.

Goldman's development of this position in his seminal article, "What Is Justified Belief?,"[12] is an instructive example of epistemological work that arises out of the Gettier methodology of counterexamples but implicitly reveals the limits of that methodology and develops less argumentative means of philosophical understanding. A close reading of this article will provide a good basis for reflecting on the power and limitations of counterexamples.

Goldman first deploys counterexamples to refute the traditional view that a belief is justified if (though, of course, not only if) it is self-evident. (I omit a similar discussion in terms of incorrigibility.) A self-evident belief is plausibly construed as one that it is impossible to understand without believing. But Goldman points out that this formulation itself admits of two different readings, depending on whether we take "impossible" to mean merely "humanly impossible" or "logically impossible." He rejects the first reading on the grounds that "it seems unlikely that people's inability to refrain from believing a proposition [e.g., every event has a cause] makes every belief in it justified" (342).

As to the reading in terms of logical impossibility, Goldman thinks that it is logically possible to understand any belief (even a trivial logical truth) without believing it. Why does he think this? He notes that any proposition involves at least two components juxtaposed in a specific way (e.g., a subject and predicate connected by a copulative verb: grass is green). In the case of complex logical truths, we are able to grasp (understand) the proposition's components without being forced to believe the truth it expresses, although in simple cases, understanding does compel belief. For example, I can't understand "If p, then p" without believing it. But is it logically necessary that anyone – not just human knowers – who understands such a proposition will believe it? Or, on the contrary, "can't we conceive of psychological operations that would suffice to grasp the components and componential-juxtaposition of these simple propositions but do not suffice to produce *belief* in that proposition?" Goldman says, "I think we can conceive of such operations," from which it follows that

---

[12] Alvin Goldman, "What is Justified Belief?," in George Pappas (ed.), *Justification and Knowledge*, Dordrecht: Reidel, 1979, 1–23. Reprinted in E. Sosa and J. Kim (eds.), *Epistemology: An Anthology*, Malden, MA: Blackwell, 2000, 340–53. References will be to this reprint and will be given in the text.

any proposition can be understood without being believed (342). Accordingly, neither reading of "self-evident" provides a sufficient condition for justification.

How effective are Goldman's counterexamples against the characterization of justified belief in terms of self-evidence? A fully effective counterexample is one that provides an uncontroversial, paradigmatic case that contradicts a claim. Goldman's counterexamples do not, however, meet this standard. They are, rather, cases that may seem plausible given our rather confused understanding of the concepts in question but that also might be rejected in the light of fuller understanding. Consider Goldman's treatment of the thought that justification is self-evident in the sense of what it is "humanly impossible" not to believe. He allows that there may be propositions such as "Some events have causes" that we have "an innate and irrepressible disposition to believe." But he says it is "unlikely" that such a belief is in every case justified. Goldman's tentative language suggests something less than a compelling counterexample. The reason, I suggest, is that whether such beliefs are treated as justified will depend on the details of our full and final understanding of justification, not our a priori certainties about the limits of the concept. If, for example, we wind up regarding beliefs as justified as long as we cannot be faulted for holding them, then natural necessity may well be a grounds for justification. But short of a final definition of justification, we have no basis for making firm judgments about such a case.

There are similar problems with Goldman's critique of the claim that the logical possibility of not believing a proposition is sufficient for justification. He agrees that it may be logically impossible for us to understand but not believe elementary claims such as "if p, then p": any evidence that might seem to support my not believing this would be read instead as evidence that I didn't understand it. But, Goldman says, "I think we can conceive" of someone with a sufficiently different psychology who could understand elementary logical propositions and fail to believe them. This may be so in the sense that we don't know of anything preventing such a possibility, but then, by the same token, we don't know of anything preventing its denial. What we don't seem to have is sufficiently clear insight into what is essential to "understanding" a proposition to be sure how this understanding is related to believing what we understand.

In any case, reflecting on what he sees as various failed attempts to give conditions for justification, Goldman notices that they pay no attention to what caused a belief to be held and that the counterexamples were often based on oddities concerning the production of a belief. He further comments that a belief's cause is also relevant when we are deriving one belief from another. For example, my belief that p is not justified merely because it is entailed by a belief q that is justified. If my belief that p was caused in the wrong way, then it may still not be justified. For these reasons, Goldman suggests that we explore the possibility that justification is tied to the way in which I am caused to have a belief.

But what sort of cause ensures justification? Reviewing various examples of unjustified belief (based on only a quick glance, a hazy memory, or a biased sample) compared with justified belief (based on careful examination, a vivid memory, a random sample of sufficient size), Goldman notices that justification seems to be a matter of forming a belief through types of processes that are generally reliable (that is, usually produce true beliefs). After sensitizing us to various complexities and nuances of the idea of reliable processes (how reliable does a process have to be? how narrowly or broadly can we construe the type to which a process belongs? must reliable processes include only what goes on "in the mind"?), Goldman formulates his own reliabilist account of justification:

If S's believing p at t results from a reliable cognitive belief-forming process (or set of processes), then S's belief in p at t is justified. (347)

He notes, however, that, as it stands, the characterization is over-simplified. It works for belief-forming processes such as perception, which yield beliefs without deriving them from other beliefs. Such processes are "unconditionally reliable." But there are also processes that derive beliefs from other beliefs; for example, logical reasoning or memory. These are reliable processes, but only when the beliefs from which they start are true; they are, accordingly, "conditionally reliable." The above characterization works only for unconditionally reliable processes. For conditionally reliable beliefs, we need to add a proviso that the beliefs from which they begin (on which they operate) are themselves justified. We need, in other words, both a base-clause principle and a recursive principle:

(A) If S's belief results from an unconditionally reliable process, then it is justified.
(B) If S's belief results from a conditionally reliable process, and the beliefs on which this process has operated are themselves justified, then it is justified.

A belief that meets either or both of (A) and (B) is well-formed and so justified. Since it presents justification as a matter of how a belief has been generated, Goldman says that his theory is "Historical or Genetic." By contrast, traditional theories of justification, for which justification is a matter entirely of current mental states – for example, Cartesian foundationalism – he calls "Current Time-Slice" theories.

Interestingly, Goldman offers no positive case for his "Historical Reliabilism," but is content to defend it against counterexamples. A first objection is that some beliefs are justified by immediate introspection, not a temporally extended causal process. When, for example, I know that I am in pain or that $1 + 1 = 2$, my beliefs seem to be justified by my immediate apprehension, not the application of some process of inquiry. Goldman, however, says "I am not persuaded by either of these examples . . . a justified belief that I am 'now' in pain gets its justificational status from a relevant, though brief, causal history," and similarly for "the apprehension of logical or conceptual relationships" (348). Such a process is "very fast, and we cannot introspectively dissect it into constituent parts. Nonetheless, there are mental processes going on" (349).

Goldman is right that there is nothing compelling about the counterexample: how could I know that being justified in believing that I am in pain is definitely not the result of a temporally extended process? But, by the same token, how could I know, as Goldman claims, that there is a temporally extended process? He himself admits that there is no phenomenological description that can settle the issue, since we cannot "introspectively dissect" our experience "into its constituent parts." The only alternative would seem to be to cite neurological data supporting the claim that there are mental events occurring that take time to happen. But Goldman offers no such data and there would be major disputes as to whether the brain-processes that might be cited could be properly identified with the relevant mental processes. The counterexample is not compelling, but neither is Goldman's claim that it is wrong.

Another apparent counterexample is the existence of processes of belief formation such as wishful thinking that, even if they were reliable, would not confer justification. Goldman emphasizes that he is thinking of a case in which wishful thinking is not itself justified by some clearly reliable process, such as inductive argument. It is a question of having beliefs that are "formed purely by wishful thinking" (353, n.15) and turn out to be generally true. Here, Goldman says, his own intuitions ("and those of other people I have consulted") are "not entirely clear" (349), and his subsequent discussion does little to resolve the unclarities.

In any case, Goldman moves to a new counterexample that will require some revision of his reliabilist account of justification. The example is this: Suppose Jones' parents tell him (plausibly but falsely) that he had amnesia as a child and later fabricated an entire year's worth of false memories. He has every reason to believe his parents but in fact does not and continues to believe that the memories are correct (as indeed they are). Since Jones' memory-beliefs in fact result from a reliable process of recall, our theory says that they are justified. But, says Goldman, "intuitively, they are not justified" (350). How can we revise the theory to eliminate this flaw?

One suggestion is to add a condition requiring that S believe that his belief is caused by a reliable process. But Jones might believe that his memories are caused by a reliable process, even though his parents' testimony gives him good reason to believe the contrary. In that case, our new conditions would be met but "we wouldn't say that these beliefs are justified" (350).

To meet this difficulty, Goldman adds yet another clause to his conditions for justification: that S's (meta-)belief that his beliefs are caused by a reliable process is itself caused by a reliable process. One problem with this amendment is that it implies that non-reflective creatures (e.g., animals or young children, who do not have beliefs about their beliefs) cannot have justified beliefs. Another, deeper problem is that the solution is based on the idea that a belief is not justified simply because it was produced by a reliable process. In spite of this, the solution seems to assume that a meta-belief *is* justified simply because it is produced by a reliable process.

Goldman gives up on this sequence of revisions and instead proposes to rethink the Jones counterexample. Jones' problem is that he has ignored evidence (his parents' testimony) that he could and should have paid attention to. (Admittedly, doing so would have led him to be worse off epistemically, believing that true memories were false; but justification requires deciding according to the evidence we have, even if this turns out to be misleading.) This suggests a major revision in the reliabilist theory: justification is "not only a function of the cognitive process actually employed in producing it, it is also a function of processes that could and should be employed" (351). Accordingly, Goldman proposes one last revision of his theory:

If S's belief that p:

(i)   results from a reliable process; and
(ii) there is no (unconditionally or conditionally) reliable process available to S that, had he also used it, would have resulted in his not believing p; then, S's belief that p is justified.

There is still a problem about what exactly it means for a process to be "available" to a person at a given time: is a process available if it could have been, in principle, developed but only with massive amounts of time and effort? Even if we restrict ourselves to processes that are available in some entirely straightforward sense, do we mean that any such process must be maximally exploited (e.g., that a scientist must perform every experiment he can think of that might refute his hypothesis)? Since the answers to such questions are surely no, it remains vague as to just what "available" means here. Goldman, however, suggests that this may well correspond to the intrinsic vagueness of our ordinary notion of justification.

Although counterexamples are the driving argumentative force in Goldman's discussion, they are far from sufficient to make his case. As we have seen, many of his counterexamples against alternative characterizations of justified belief derive from intuitions that are far from compelling and could be readily ignored by those committed to a different view. Certainly, they are no more persuasive than are counterexamples Goldman rejects as having no force against his own account. On the other hand, Goldman does make good use of what he sees as effective counterexamples in diagnosing the essential flaws of views he rejects or of inaccurate formulations of his own approach. Analysis of counterexamples against the self-evidence and the incorrigibility approaches helps suggest Goldman's initial causal account, and reflection on counterexamples to this account lead to his introduction of his reliabilism. But it is striking that Goldman offers no arguments for his own accounts of justification but merely responds to various counterexamples that might be put forward. In the case of his final formulation, he does not even suggest any counterexamples. Overall, Goldman's case is grounded far more in his own intellectual imagination and intuitive sense of plausibility than in any argumentative techniques.

None of this is to say that Goldman's "What is Justified Belief?" is not a major contribution to our understanding of knowledge. The point is rather that this contribution cannot be plausibly viewed as deriving from the rigor of the arguments (mostly discussions of counterexamples) by which he supports his views. Goldman's epistemology is solidly rooted in the Gettier culture of counterexamples, but Goldman moves beyond this origin and "establishes" his conclusions, to the extent that he does, by means quite other than decisive modus tollens argument. Our next example, a more recent and much more free-wielding discussion by David Lewis, takes epistemology even further down this road.

DAVID LEWIS AND ELUSIVE KNOWLEDGE

David Lewis' "Elusive Knowledge" represents a rethinking of the issues about knowledge raised by the Gettier revolution in epistemology.[13] Whereas Gettier – and almost all the Gettierites – assumed that knowledge needs to be understood as a form of justified belief, for Lewis the essential feature of knowledge is its certainty.

Lewis begins with what he regards as the utterly obvious claim that "we know a lot." He gives no weight to skeptical arguments to the contrary: "it is one of those things that we know better than we know the premises of any philosophical argument to the contrary" (549). But this doesn't mean that he simply ignores skeptical arguments. Once we engage in epistemology ("the systematic philosophical examination of knowledge"), at least one skeptical argument seems compelling. It is based on the fact that knowledge must be infallible; that is, if S knows P, then S must be able to eliminate every possibility in which not-P. But how can S eliminate *every* possibility in which not-P? As Lewis says: "Let your paranoid fantasies rip – CIA plots, hallucinogens in the tap water, conspiracies to deceive, old Nick himself – and soon you find that uneliminated possibilities of error are everywhere" (549). Maybe there are a few limited domains of infallible knowledge (simple axioms, our present experience), but hardly any of the "lots" we know is infallible.

So the argument is straightforward: (1) To know is to know infallibly; (2) We have no (hardly any) infallible knowledge; (3) Therefore, we have no (hardly any) knowledge. Of course, any valid argument logically proves only that we must choose between the premises and the conclusion. Here, since premise (2) is undeniable, the choice is between giving up the claim that knowledge is infallible (fallibilism) and giving up the claim that we know a lot (skepticism). Given that choice, we will, Lewis says, all go with fallibilism. It is "the less intrusive madness," demanding "less frequent correction of what we want to say" (550). But unlike many of us, who are comfortable with fallibilism, Lewis does see it as "madness" – a claim that contradicts a strongly compelling intuition. Lewis pleads with his readers to feel the force of this intuition: "If you are a contented fallibilist, I implore you to be honest, be naïve, hear it afresh. 'He knows yet he has not eliminated all possibilities of error.' Even if you've numbed your ears, doesn't this overt, explicit fallibilism still sound wrong?" (530). As he puts

[13]   David Lewis, "Elusive Knowledge," *Australasian Journal of Philosophy* 74 (1996), 549–67. References will be given in the text.

it a bit later: "To speak of fallible knowledge, of knowledge despite uneliminated possibilities of error, just *sounds* contradictory" (549).

But Lewis' intuition is undermined if, as his argument suggests, it leads to skepticism. So the issue is, can he find a way to avoid the choice between fallibilism and skepticism: is there a way to be a non-skeptical infallibilist? Yes, Lewis suggests, provided we make knowledge *context-dependent*. Specifically, his idea is that it is only in the context of epistemology, where we're allowed and encouraged to "let [our] paranoid fantasies rip," that skepticism is unavoidable and we know (almost) nothing. In other, more mundane contexts, we know lots.

Many philosophers would develop the context-dependence idea in terms of justification, since, they think, "justification is the mark that distinguishes knowledge from mere opinion" (530). In particular, they would argue that in the context of epistemology, where standards of justification are so high that they cannot be met, we know nothing. In other contexts, however, with laxer standards, we know a lot. Lewis, however, rejects the claim that "justification is the mark of knowledge." First, there are cases of justified true belief that are not knowledge. We can imagine a lottery where the justification for believing that my ticket won't win is as strong as you like (just increase the total number of tickets). Nonetheless, even if it's true that my ticket won't win, I don't *know* that prior to the drawing. Second, there are cases of knowledge that are not *justified* true belief. There are, for example, no arguments for what we know by perception or memory. So Lewis concludes that we must break the link between knowledge and justification.

These two counterexamples against the justification view are hardly decisive. The logic of the lottery example is, as Lewis notes, exactly that of a certain class of Gettier examples (e.g., Tom in the library, the bogus barns) and may well be handled by maintaining the justification condition and adding others to defeat the example. Saying that perception and memory don't involve justification requires a quite narrow reading of justification (as argument as opposed, say, to experiential evidence) that many epistemologists would not accept. At best, Lewis has announced his rejection of justification in the analysis of knowledge and indicated the terrain on which he proposes to defend the claim.

In any case, Lewis proceeds to offer a definition of knowledge in terms of certainty rather than justification: "Subject S *knows* proposition P . . . iff S's evidence eliminates every possibility in which not-P" (531). But doesn't this definition lead right to skepticism? Well, says Lewis, it all depends on what we mean by "eliminate *every* possibility." Skepticism does follow immediately if "every" is taken to mean literally every possibility, with no restrictions. But quantifiers such as "every" are typically restricted to a limited domain of relevance (consider Lewis' example: "every glass is empty, so it's time for another round"). So, in the case of knowledge, S's evidence doesn't have to eliminate literally every possibility, just those that are relevant in the given context. In a given context, some possibilities may be properly ignored and others may not. Accordingly, Lewis adds what he calls a "*sotto voce* proviso" to his definition of knowledge: "S knows that P iff S's evidence eliminates every possibility in which not-P – Psst! – except for those possibilities that we are properly ignoring" (554).

The project of what Lewis calls his "modal epistemology" (554) consists in explaining the conditions that determine when a possibility is properly ignored (or, equivalently, what we properly presuppose) in a given context. He carries out this project by formulating seven rules:

1. Rule of Actuality: "The possibility that actually obtains is never properly ignored" (554).
2. Rule of Belief: "A possibility that the subject believes to obtain is not properly ignored" (555).
3. Rule of Resemblance: Given that two possibilities saliently resemble one another, if one of them may not be properly ignored, then neither may the other.

These first three rules are prohibitions. Lewis adds some permissive rules:

4. Rule of Reliability: Given reliable cognitive processes, we may (defeasibly) ignore the possibility that they may fail.
5. Rules of Method: We may (defeasibly) ignore the possibility that a sample is not representative and that the best explanation of the evidence is not true.
6. Rule of Conservatism: Possibilities that are generally ignored (and are generally known to be so ignored) may be properly ignored.

Finally, a rule that is "more a triviality than a rule" (although it turns out to be crucial):

7. Rule of Attention: A possibility not ignored is ipso facto not properly ignored.

Lewis' epistemological position combines his definition of knowledge with these seven rules.

Lewis' direct justification for this position is minimal. The definition of knowledge is presented as his firm intuition, although he's aware that others disagree with it. He has little to say on behalf of his seven rules apart from an implicit claim (more or less plausible from case to case) that they are intuitively obvious, although he does offer some elaborations of the rules and replies to a few objections.

Whatever the justification for Lewis' epistemological position, he maintains that, if we accept it, we can solve the lottery paradox and the Gettier problem, as well as reject fallibilism but still avoid skepticism.

The lottery paradox, as we saw, is that, no matter how low the odds of my winning are in a lottery that I in fact will not win, I cannot know ahead of time that I will lose. Lewis' definition provides a straightforward response. In concluding that I will lose the lottery, I am ignoring the possibility that I might win. But this possibility may not be properly ignored. Why not? Because it saliently resembles all the possibilities of other tickets winning, and one of these possibilities is actual (that of the ticket that will actually win). By the Principle of Actuality, I cannot ignore the possibility that the winning ticket will win. Therefore, by the Principle of Resemblance, I can't ignore the possibility that my ticket will win. It then follows by Lewis' definition of knowledge that I do not know that my ticket will not win, since this possibility excludes my not winning.

Some Gettier counterexamples fall readily to Lewis' definition of knowledge. I do not know, for example, that the real barn I see is in the field because I cannot properly ignore the possibility that it is bogus, given the prevalence of bogus barns in the area. On the other hand, a close relative of an original Gettier example seems less tractable: Nogot does not own a Ford and Havit does. However, I have good reason to think Nogot does own a Ford, since I frequently see him driving one; and I have good reason to believe Havit doesn't own a Ford, since I always see him taking the tram, not driving. Given my evidence, I conclude that either Nogot or Havit owns a Ford. This is justified true belief, but not knowledge.

Lewis first argues against my knowing that either Nogot or Havit owns a Ford on the grounds that I have not eliminated the following dual possibility: that (a) Nogot drives a Ford he doesn't own and (b) Havit neither drives nor owns a car. As in the lottery case, Lewis argues that this dual possibility saliently resembles actuality, which our first rule says may not be ignored: (a) the first disjunct, concerning Nogot, resembles actuality perfectly (i.e., the conjunct is true); (b) the disjunct concerning Havit, although it is not true, resembles actuality in two salient respects: the fact that Havit doesn't drive a car and the fact that people who don't drive a car usually don't own one. Since I cannot properly ignore this dual possibility and since, if it were true, my belief would be false, I do not know that either Nogot or Havit owns a car.

The dual possibility resembles another possibility that I may not properly ignore: that Nogot drives a Ford he owns and Havit neither drives nor owns a car. I may not properly ignore this possibility because I believe it (Rule of Belief). The dual possibility resembles this new possibility: it resembles the second conjunct, regarding Havit, exactly; and it resembles the first conjunct, regarding Nogot, rather well (according to the new possibility, Nogot drives a Ford but doesn't own it, whereas the dual possibility says Nogot both drives a Ford and owns it).

Whether this resolution works (assuming Lewis' epistemological position) depends on whether the possibilities in question "saliently resemble" one another. There is no problem in accepting salience when the resemblance is exact. But why should we accept Lewis' judgments of salience when resemblance is only partial? There seems to be no reason, given that Lewis has no discussion of what makes for a salient resemblance.

Lewis' responses to the lottery paradox and the Gettier counterexamples are by-the-way. His primary goal is to show how his infallibilist epistemology can avoid skepticism. At one level, the proviso that knowledge is not undermined by possibilities that are properly ignored seems to disarm skepticism. For any given context, there are some possible refuters of our beliefs that we can properly ignore. Epistemological standards vary increasingly from casual decisions to pick up a book, through reflection on whether to apply to law school, to jurors' votes in death-penalty cases. Surely, we might conclude, the possibilities that sustain radical skepticism (evil demons, brains in vats, etc.) are properly ignored in all contexts.

Of course, when we do epistemology, at least in its standard analytic mode, we do not ignore even the most extreme possibilities. Recall that, as an epistemologist, you are enjoined to "let your fantasies rip," to "find uneliminated possibilities of error everywhere" (559). So what, we might respond, since such possibilities are properly ignored in all contexts? But here Lewis stops us short by insisting on that apparent triviality, the Principle of Attention. If a principle *is not ignored*, then ipso facto it *is not properly ignored*. Since in epistemology we do attend to the most extreme possibilities, we are not, in the context of epistemological reflection, properly ignoring them. But there is no eliminating the extreme possibilities once they are admitted to consideration. "That," says Lewis, "is how epistemology destroys knowledge" (559).[14]

---

[14] Compare Bernard Williams' similar claim that, regarding ethical matters, reflection can destroy knowledge (*Ethics and the Limits of Philosophy*, Cambridge, MA: Harvard University Press, 1985).

It is also why, in Lewis' titular phrase, "knowledge is elusive. Examine it, and straightway it vanishes" (560).

Of course, the destruction occurs only in the rather outré context of epistemology. "The pastime of epistemology does not plunge us forever-more into its special context. We can still do a lot of proper knowing" (559). But should we allow the skeptic "even his very temporary victory" (560)? After all, the wedge for skepticism was Lewis' formulation of the Principle of Attention as "that which is not ignored at all *is not* properly ignored" (560), which in turn corresponds to Lewis' indicative-mood formulation of the *sotto voce* exception clause of his definition of knowledge: "except for those possibilities that we *are* properly ignoring" (554). Why not instead state the exception clause in the subjunctive: "except for those possibilities we *could* properly have ignored" (560)? Then, even in the context of epistemology, where we inevitably do not ignore (and so do not properly ignore) evil demons, etc., this attention will not destroy knowledge, since we could have properly ignored such possibilities.

Lewis's response to this objection is as follows:

> If you say this, we have reached a standoff. I started with a puzzle: how can it be, when his conclusion is so silly, that the sceptic's argument is so irresistible? My Rule of Attention, and the version of the proviso that made that Rule trivial, were built to explain how the sceptic manages to sway us . . . If you continue to find it eminently resistible in all contexts, you have no need of any such explanation. We just disagree about the explanandum phenomenon. (561)

Just how is Lewis arguing in this passage? He says that his definition of knowledge and Rule of Attention are designed to explain the fact that the skeptic's argument seems so convincing. The argument he has in mind moves from (i) the requirement that to know we must exclude every possibility that we are wrong and (ii) the fact that such an exclusion is almost never available, to the conclusion that we know almost nothing. Lewis agrees that there is no way around this argument unless we include a proviso in our definition of knowledge that allows for cases in which we properly ignore some possibilities that we are wrong. His critic ("you") endorses all of this. Where they differ is over the formulation of the exclusion clause. Lewis says it should exclude possibilities that we *do* properly ignore, his critic says it should exclude possibilities that we *could* properly ignore. According to Lewis, his version, but not his critic's, explains how the skeptic's argument seems convincing.

Why so? In the end, of course, both Lewis and his critic show why the skeptic's argument does not establish its conclusion that we know almost nothing. The critic claims that, upon reflection, we can see that the skeptical case fails for all contexts; Lewis says it fails for all contexts except that of epistemology. Lewis seems to say that the critic's rejection of the argument in *all* contexts shows a failure to appreciate its prima facie force: "if you continue to find it eminently resistible in all contexts, you have no need of any...explanation" of the argument's seeming irresistibility (561). It's hard to see how this is supposed to follow. The prima facie force of an argument is not refuted by pointing out that, on reflection, it turns out to be wrong in all rather than all but one context. Perhaps the emphasis in Lewis's comment is on "eminently" rather than "all," his point being that we reject the prima facie plausibility of the argument by concluding that it is eminently resistible? If "eminently" here means "obviously, even before any reflection or discussion," then Lewis is right; but there is no reason to read the critic as saying this. The central point is that apparent or prima facie irresistibility is a feature of our initial impression of an argument and is entirely unaffected by our final reflective assessment of it. It's very hard to see what grounds Lewis has for saying that his critic simply thinks that there is nothing to explain.

In fact, it would seem that the critic's explanation would be the same as Lewis': that the skeptic's argument appears sound so long as we fail to realize that there may be, in a given context, some skeptical possibilities that we need not take account of. Given that this realization is not immediately obvious, we can see how the skeptic's argument is initially attractive. If we subsequently add a clause that excludes certain possibilities in certain contexts, that does not undermine our explanation or the need for it.

So far the threat of skepticism has emerged from Lewis' denial of Gettier's assumption that justification, and therefore knowledge, is fallible. As we saw, Gettier also assumed that justification transferred from a belief to another logically implied by that belief. Extended to the case of knowledge, the assumption has come to be known as the closure principle: if I know p, and know that $p \rightarrow q$ (and believe q because of this knowledge), then I know q. Whereas Lewis earlier risked skepticism by disagreeing with Gettier's first principle, he now risks it by agreeing with him on the closure principle.

To see how the risk arises, consider G. E. Moore's famous example, I know I have hands. Next, notice that "I have hands" entails that *I am not handless but deceived by a demon about this fact*. Applying the closure principle, it follows that I know I am not being deceived about this point by the Cartesian demon. But I obviously don't know that I'm not being deceived in this way. Therefore, by modus tollens, it follows that I don't know that I have hands – a prototypical skeptical conclusion.

To avoid such conclusions, philosophers such as Fred Dretske and Robert Nozick have claimed that we should abandon closure and allow for cases in which we do not know q even though we know p and know that p entails q. Lewis, however, thinks his contextualist epistemology avoids the skeptical argument without giving up closure. The skeptic's argument, as Lewis formulates it (564), goes like this:

1. "I have hands" implies that I am not a handless being;
2. "I am not a handless being" implies that I am not a handless being deceived by a demon into thinking that I have hands;
3. Therefore, "I have hands" implies that I am not a handless being deceived by a demon into thinking that I have hands;
4. Therefore (by the closure principle), "I know that I have hands" implies that I know that I have hands and am not deceived . . .
5. I don't know that I am not handless and deceived . . .

Therefore (by modus tollens), I don't know that I have hands.

Obviously, we can stop the inference by denying closure (premise 2). But Lewis suggests another route. He notes that an argument can lack validity because "we switch contexts midway" and argues that this is what happens in the above argument: "the context switched midway, the semantic value of the context-dependent phrase 'know' switched with it" (564). Specifically, in the skeptic's argument, the context switches between the premise "I know that I have hands" and the conclusion "I know that I am not handless and deceived." (I assume that by "premise" and "conclusion" Lewis means, respectively, the antecedent and the consequent of [4], the instance of the closure principle.) "I know that I have hands" is true in the context of everyday life, where we properly ignore the demon possibility. But the mention of demons puts us in the context of epistemology, where we do not properly ignore the demon possibility, and, in that context, "I know that I am not handless and deceived" is false. The problem is with premise (4) but not because the closure principle (of which [4] is an instance) is false. Rather, (4) is ill-formed (a "phenomenon of pragmatics" not of logic, Lewis says) because of the switch in contexts. If we avoid the switch by evaluating the conclusion "I know that I am not handless and deceived" in the everyday context in which the premise "I know I have hands" is true, then the conclusion as well as the premise is true.

Here Lewis shows that it is not necessary to deny closure to avoid the skeptic's conclusion. That does not, of course, show that denying closure is not a better or equally good way to avoid the conclusion.

Although arguments are hardly absent from "Elusive Knowledge," they are not the primary engine of its philosophical achievement. For the most part, Lewis argues effectively only against objections to his views, as in the preceding defense of the closure principle. For example, his critique of the rival justificationist view of knowledge is carried by two quick counter-examples, which, as we saw, are hardly decisive. For his central positive theses – the claim that knowledge is infallible and the seven rules for properly ignoring possibilities – he offers no direct arguments. The infallibilism is explicitly presented as simply his intuition, which he tries to nudge us rhetorically into sharing; the rules are supported only by their apparent plausibility and his ability to respond to a few objections to them.

CHAPTER 4

Reflection: pictures, intuitions, and philosophical knowledge

The previous three chapters have a distinctly skeptical conclusion: in three of the most admired and cited examples of recent philosophical argumentation, the arguments did not establish the conclusion intended. This does not, however, mean that Quine, Kripke, and Gettier have not achieved important philosophical knowledge. In this chapter, further looks from different angles will reveal their real cognitive achievements.

QUINE: IMAGINATION AND FRUITFULNESS

Quine's "Two Dogmas" did not provide an effective argument against the claim that there is no analytic-synthetic distinction. Although his discussion was very effective in changing minds, it did not achieve this by the objective force of Quine's arguments. It does not, however, follow that the achievement of "Two Dogmas" was merely sociological or psychological, not cognitive. It was a significant cognitive achievement, although one rather different from what the author and his audience took it to be.

What was this achievement? What did the community of analytic philosophers come to know as a result of Quine's discussion? From sections 1–4 of "Two Dogmas," one thing we learn is that there is no way of defining "analytic" except via a small circle of similar terms ("necessary," "synonymous," etc.). Quine doesn't strictly prove this, but he shows that many of the obvious approaches don't work and leaves readers with a challenge to do better. This sort of "challenge argument," although seldom noted, is particularly prominent (and effective) in contemporary analytic philosophy, where repeated failure to meet a much-discussed challenge is a good reason for thinking that the challenge cannot be met. Knowing that analyticity cannot be defined in essentially different terms means that we must either accept it (or another term in its immediate family) as basic or else reject it. Quine's own radical empiricist presuppositions lead him to reject it, but his result also allows that analyticity could, in principle, be taken as basic – as Kripke does with his appeal to the intuitions about metaphysical necessity implicit in ordinary-language use. What appeared as a proof that there was no intelligible necessity beyond the narrowly logical sense could be just as well taken as a proof that necessity could be accepted only as a basic category.

But is there any need to accept necessity as a basic category? Might there not be an alternative, radically empiricist epistemology for which all statements are revisable in the light of sense experience? Sections 5 and 6 of "Two Dogmas" present just such an alternative. Although they offer little in the way of argument, they sketch a vivid picture of Quine's epistemological holism, especially through the metaphor of a "fabric" (later "web") of beliefs that impinges on experience only at its periphery. Although this picture provides no compelling reason for giving up the analytic-synthetic distinction, it does give a sense of what it might be like to do so. Reflecting on this possibility led many philosophers to suspect that there might be little price to pay for dropping the distinction. In this way, "Two Dogmas" opened up a new range of philosophical possibilities. It was, as Rorty said, an impressive exercise of "imaginative power."

Quine's adumbration of new intellectual possibilities was particularly effective because the received logical positivist view was losing its grip. Even by its own lights, it had failed to sustain, without serious qualification, its youthful commitments to verificationism and reductionism. "Two Dogmas" showed that there was a possibly fruitful alternative to tinkering with the old positivist theses. This alternative was a vision of knowledge in which our acceptance of a statement always depends on the role of the statement – or rather of an entire network of statements – in our project of accounting for the contingent facts. Nothing Quine said showed that this vision was correct or even superior to that of the logical empiricists, but he did show that it was an attractive alternative to positivist orthodoxy.

Given Quine's own pre-philosophical commitments, what he shows in "Two Dogmas" is sufficient to undermine the analytic-synthetic distinction. He comes to philosophy with a conviction that there is no knowledge outside the ambit of scientific inquiry. He rejects what he sees as discredited positivist claims that science can be translated into a purely empirical language (whether that of sense-data or that of everyday objects), and he recognizes that there can be meaningful scientific discourse about any entities, from sets to electrons, so long as this discourse is ultimately tied to the stimuli that impinge on our sense organs. But he is adamant in rejecting any claims that cannot be tied to such stimuli. In this sense, Quine philosophizes from the standpoint of a radical empiricist picture. From this standpoint, the notion of analytic truth will be acceptable only if it can be explicated in broadly behaviorist (stimulus–response) terms. Quine's discussion in sections 1–4 does make it highly improbable that any such explication is forthcoming. But this has no significance for those who do not share Quine's radical empiricist convictions, for which he offers no philosophical defense.

Quine's holistic picture remained attractive, however, even to those who concluded that he was wrong to reject the analytic-synthetic distinction. Consider, for example, Hilary Putnam's discussion some ten years after "Two Dogmas." Putnam thinks that Quine is wrong – indeed, obviously wrong – to deny the analytic-synthetic distinction: "That Quine is wrong I have no doubt. This is not a matter of philosophical argument: it seems to me there is as gross a distinction between 'All bachelors are unmarried' and 'There is a book on this table' as between any two things in the world, or, at any rate, between any two linguistic expressions in the world."[1] But Putnam thinks Quine's error is of little importance, since the analytic-synthetic distinction holds only for mundane cases of no philosophical significance. Quine's claim is correct, he thinks, with regard to "synonymies and analyticities of a deeper nature"; specifically, there are no analytic truths except for the obvious ones formulated by lexicographers or linguists. There are no "deep" analytic truths to be discovered by philosophers, a conclusion supported by the many cases in which apparent conceptual necessities (circular planetary orbits, absolute simultaneity, causal determinism) have turned out to be dispensable (36–7).

But how, we may well ask, does Putnam derive this view of the analytic-synthetic distinction from Quine's critiques in "Two Dogmas" or elsewhere? The view is certainly not established by Quine's arguments against the distinction, which do not discriminate between mundane and philosophical instances of analytic truths. Putnam, in fact, barely alludes to these arguments but instead insists on Quine's "exceedingly important theoretical insight" regarding "the monolithic character of our conceptual system"; in other words, his holism, which, as we have seen, is a vision or picture put forward without benefit of argument. But why does Putnam find Quine's holism so attractive? "With Quine's contribution," he tells us, "we have to

---

[1] Hilary Putnam, "The Analytic and the Synthetic," in his *Mind, Language, and Reality, Philosophical Papers, Volume II*, Cambridge: Cambridge University Press, 1975, 36. [First published 1962.] Further references will be given in the text.

face two choices: We can ignore it and go on talking about the 'logic' of individual words." But, he says, "in that direction lies sterility and more, much more, of what we have already read. The other alternative is to face and explore the insight achieved by Quine ... In that direction lies philosophic progress." For Putnam, then, Quine's achievement was "the discovery of new areas for dialectical exploration" (42). This reaction fits well with what we have seen: that Quine had made intellectual room for – had imagined – a fruitful alternative to the old positivist project.

In a similar vein, Quine's new picture led philosophers to reflect more carefully about the claims of conceptual analysis, reflection that has led to the recent carefully nuanced defenses of analysis by philosophers such as Sosa, Jackson, and Bealer. In this regard, it is worth noting that Kripke's reversal of Quine's strictures against necessity, although it rehabilitated essential properties, did not do so by appealing to conceptual analysis but to metaphysical intuitions.[2] Even when philosophers have firmly rejected Quine's radical empiricist convictions, they have not found it possible to go back to a full-blown endorsement of conceptual analysis. Despite its argumentative limitations, Quine's holistic vision remains a picture to be reckoned with.

KRIPKE AND LEWIS: SYSTEM AND PERSUASIVE ELABORATION

The positive cognitive features of Quine's "Two Dogmas" are present more fully in our case studies of Kripke and Lewis. Kripke's appeals to intuition do not function in isolation from one another, but connect together to form an overall account impressive for its coherence and explanatory power. At the center of the nexus is the "intuitive thesis" – which he also calls the "natural" (5) or "direct" intuition (14) – that names are rigid designators. Given this thesis, it follows that a name denotes its referent in all possible worlds in which it exists, which eliminates Quine's objection to the objective reality of essential properties. Further intuitions about which properties are essential for a given entity (Nixon's humanity, material objects' molecular constitution) give specific content to essentialism. Next, rigid designation combined with essentialism suggests that there are necessary a posteriori truths. This claim faces serious objections, which Kripke resolves by appealing to his intuitive distinctions

---

[2] See Jerry Fodor's deft and engaging formulation of this point in his review of Hughes' *Kripke*, "Water's Water Everywhere," *London Review of Books*, October 21, 2004. Fodor, however, goes on to argue that modal intuitions themselves turn out to be implicitly based on conceptual analysis, so that Kripke does not in fact provide a new alternative to Quinean naturalization.

between, on the one hand, the a priori as epistemological and the necessary as metaphysical and, on the other, epistemological and metaphysical possibility. Kripke's rigid-designation account of names is directly challenged by descriptivism, a challenge that he initially meets by attacking a theoretical formulation of descriptivism with intuitive counterexamples. Kripke acknowledges that in itself such an attack does not refute the descriptivist picture, but he suggests that reflection on the critical dialogue with descriptivism initiated by his attack leads to what we might think of as a "higher-level" intuition that the picture is essentially flawed. All of this fits nicely with Kripke's suggestion, in the Preface, that *Naming and Necessity* roughly recounts some of the complex intellectual process whereby Kripke came to see that his "natural intuition that the names of ordinary language are rigid designators can in fact be upheld" because "the received presuppositions against the necessity of identities between ordinary names were incorrect" (5).[3]

We see, then, that, for all its frank and amiable appeal to informal intuitions, Kripke's account is at the same time a highly complex systematic enterprise, sketching a series of interacting and mutually supporting philosophical pictures on a striking range of topics in metaphysics, epistemology, and philosophy. (Sections we passed over also move into philosophy of mind and philosophy of science; and, as we noted, logic is just below the surface.) This strong systematic character was a major reason Kripke's ideas were so rapidly taken up by so many philosophers. Like Quine's imaginative vision for the preceding generation, Kripke's sweeping architecture of new ideas opened fruitful new spaces for thought.[4] But Kripke's lectures also raise the question of whether a systematic development of ideas provides epistemic support for them. Beyond the excitement of new possibilities, does Kripke's fruitful systematization also offer some good reason for thinking that his conclusions are true?

The mere fact of developing a claim in some detail may serve to persuade us of its plausibility. Since more detail is likely to lead to problems, particularly when ideas are extended beyond their original domain, the more thoroughly and extensively a claim is developed without encountering problems, the more likely it is to be correct. Systematization can, in other words, involve what we might call *persuasive*

---

[3] Kripke's brief account also sketches some early intuitions and reflections on logical identity (not explicit in *Naming and Necessity*) as the ultimate source of his ideas.

[4] We should also note that Quine's work as a whole has strong systematic qualities that weren't apparent from our examination of just one of his essays.

elaboration.[5] This point becomes particularly powerful when we connect it to the distinction, which Kripke introduced and which I have been implicitly invoking here, between philosophical *pictures* and philosophical *theories*. Kripke, as we saw, insists that his concern in *Naming and Necessity* is to show the superiority of a causal picture of proper names, not to establish the truth of a particular theoretical version of this picture. (Indeed, he maintains that any sufficiently specific philosophical theory will be false.) What philosophers typically do is develop, refine, and criticize theoretical formulations of pictures. This, in Kuhnian terms, is *normal* philosophical practice. The viability of a picture depends not on the truth of any of its theoretical formulations but on its resources for generating (and revising in the face of criticism) theories about a wide range of philosophical questions. A capacity for successful theoretical systematization is a striking sign of a picture's viability, and a picture that proves itself viable over a long period of theoretical elaboration must, it is reasonable to think, have some degree of truth and so be worth taking seriously.

The reception of Kripke's work provides a striking example of the power of persuasive elaboration. In *Naming and Necessity*, Kripke presented a picture, in the tradition of the great rationalist metaphysicians from Aristotle through Hegel, that located necessity in reality, not in language or concepts. For analytic philosophy, strongly rooted in an empiricist rejection of idealistic rationalism, this picture had disappeared as a real option; it had ceased to be viable. The effect of Kripke's and others' systematic development of his essentialist ideas was not to show that there were reasons to accept them but to show that there was reason to once again take them seriously. He did not establish that his essentialist theses were true, but that the picture they presented was worthy of attention.

"Worthy of attention," of course, is hardly adequate to the stampede towards necessity that followed Kripke's lectures. To explain the amazing turn-around Kripke effected in analytic philosophy, we need to take account of several factors. First, prior to Kripke there had been substantial work by others leading to similar ideas. Kripke himself mentions Roger Albritton, Charles Chastain, Keith Donnellan, Michael Slote, and Hilary Putnam.[6]

---

[5] Here "persuasion" should not be taken as mere rhetorical effect unrelated to evidence and truth. But the case made by persuasive elaboration cannot, of itself, establish the truth of a picture. This could be done only by showing that some particular theoretical formulation of the picture is true, whereas persuasive elaboration at best shows that there is some plausibility that this might be the case.

[6] Saul Kripke, *Naming and Necessity*, Cambridge, MA: Harvard University Press, 1980, 23 n.2. Scott Soames cites others, as well as listing some articles on the background of Kripke's work (*Philosophical Analysis in the Twentieth Century, Volume II: The Age of Meaning*, 353).

This work provided fertile ground for Kripke's persuasive presentation of the essentialist picture. Further, immediately following Kripke, there were very detailed and closely argued theoretical developments of essentialism. Of particular note was Plantinga's *Nature of Necessity*, published just two years after *Naming and Necessity*, which presents a fully worked out positive case for essentialism, thorough responses to the objections of Quine and others, and ingenious applications of essentialist metaphysics to the philosophy of religion.[7] Even though many of Plantinga's claims remained controversial, the detail and rigor with which he formulated and defended them confirmed the theoretical power of the picture Kripke had delineated. Nor was Plantinga an isolated instance. It is fair to say that, over the last thirty years, many of the most interesting and plausible theories in metaphysics, philosophy of language, and philosophy of mind have been expressions of the essentialist picture.

We may still wonder why a picture so contrary to the entrenched empiricist orthodoxy could so rapidly claim the field in central philosophical subdisciplines. A good part of the explanation was that there was nothing comparable on the empiricist side to the challenging specific theories through which Plantinga and others developed Kripke's picture. Unlike Kripke, Quine himself, in *Word and Object*, developed such a theory, which became the focus of sustained and sometimes brilliant work on the radical empiricist picture. But discussions of *Word and Object* bogged down in questions about just what Quine meant by his key theses regarding the indeterminacy of translation, the inscrutability of reference, and ontological relativity. The typical response to critics was that they had misunderstood Quine, but his defenders could never agree among themselves on how to interpret him. Rather than refining and deepening the empiricist picture, Quineans diffused their energies in exegetical disputes. This was not true of the work of Quine's most distinguished successor, Donald Davidson, who both brilliantly developed and extended the Quinean standpoint and brought it into fruitful contact with Kripkean ideas. But Davidson's work posed even greater exegetical challenges than Quine's, and once again an opportunity to achieve powerful theoretical expressions of the empiricist picture bogged down in disputes about how to understand the master. By contrast, Kripke achieved a kind of philosophical clarity that, even though his arguments were inconclusive, allowed for the continuingly

---

[7] Although his book, *The Nature of Necessity*, was published two years later, Plantinga's treatment seems to have been developed largely independently of Kripke's *Naming and Necessity*.

fruitful development of his ideas, without endless disputes about just what he meant.

Tracing the details of the persuasive elaboration of Kripke's ideas would require a history of much of the last thirty years of analytic philosophy. But David Lewis' "Elusive Knowledge" gives us a suggestive microcosm of the sorts of elements that make for persuasive elaboration. In this article, surrounding and enriching a fairly thin line of argument-cum-intuition, are an ongoing series of elaborations of Lewis' claims – more detailed formulations, connections to other issues, relations to alternatives. For example, after stating his brief definition of knowledge in terms of infallibility, Lewis moves to explanations of just what he means by the key terms. Some of these comments link his epistemology to philosophy of language and metaphysics, delineating his understanding of "proposition" and of "possibility." The comments on possibility also deepen his epistemological position, explaining why his definition cannot refer to just epistemic possibilities and connecting the elimination of possibilities to his understanding of perception and memory as forms of "basic evidence."

Lewis' discussion of his seven rules is particularly detailed. For example, regarding the Rule of Actuality, he explains why the actuality in question must refer to the possible world in which the knower exists, not the possible world in which someone ascribing knowledge to the knower exists. This explanation shows simultaneously that the principle would fail if it were about the ascriber's world and how to avoid the failure by taking the principle to be about the knower's world. Similarly, Lewis implicitly responds to obvious counterexamples to the Rule of Belief (e.g., that a jury might believe that a murder could have been caused by an amazingly trained dog) by reformulating it in terms of "degree of belief" in a possibility. There is a careful explanation of just how the Rule of Resemblance should be applied, focusing on the need to make an ad hoc exception to it into order to avoid the conclusion that radical skeptical hypotheses are not properly eliminated. Some of the rules – the Rule of Method, the Rule of Conservatism – are scarcely relevant to the claims he is making in this article, but Lewis seems to include them for the sake of completeness.

There is also a discussion of how assessments of what is properly eliminated vary depending on whether we are talking about our own knowledge or about that of others; and one of how some knowledge can become better by eliminating possibilities that can but need not be eliminated. Finally, there is a tantalizing concluding discussion of the objection that Lewis' entire position is self-refuting since it is epistemological and so, by his own admission, incapable of achieving knowledge.

He accepts the claim as applied to the "short-hand" language he has used for convenience, but maintains that the problem can be avoided in principle by reformulating, via semantic ascent, the entire treatment in a meta-language – a project Lewis entrusts to the reader.

Occasionally, Lewis' elaborations answer objections, or at least suggest the direction in which to seek an answer. But typically they seem to be elaborations for their own sake. As we noted earlier, since more detail is likely to lead to obvious problems, the more detailed a claim is made without encountering problems, the more likely it is to be correct. Even more important is that elaboration displays the fruitfulness and systematic power of Lewis' position. Quite apart from its truth or falsity, Lewis' contextualism raises a whole series of stimulating questions, such as, Can justification be eliminated from the definition of knowledge? Is it possible to revive the Cartesian idea that knowledge requires certainty? What is the nature of knowledge in the context of epistemology itself? Such questions show the fruitfulness of Lewis' contextualism, quite apart from its final truth or falsity. Contextualism also connects with issues outside of epistemology. We have already seen how Lewis relates its references to propositions' possibilities to issues in metaphysics and philosophy of language. There is also an important connection to logic, since a major motive for Lewis' defending the closure principle is that knowledge is a modal notion (defined in terms of possibility) and closure is a typical theorem of systems of modal logic. Likewise, the objection that we can simultaneously be in different epistemic contexts (and so apparently know and not know the same thing) leads Lewis to the claim, interesting for the philosophy of mind, that there may be different "compartments" in persons corresponding to different contexts in which they exist at a given time. Lewis makes a persuasive case for his contextualist picture by showing how it raises interesting new problems and how it connects to other philosophical domains.

To a lesser extent, the same thing is true of Goldman's early article on reliabilism. Although much less developed than in Lewis' article, beneath the relentless dialectic of counterexamples there was emerging a quite different technique of philosophical persuasion, one that depended less on decisive proofs and refutations and more on the combination of rich detail, fruitfulness, and systematic power that I am calling persuasion by elaboration. It was its capacity for elaboration that made reliabilism, like contextualism after it, into a philosophical picture to be reckoned with.

Important as they may be, the sort of results we have been discussing are still knowledge at a second remove, knowledge about the fruitfulness, viability, or plausibility of a view. In a word, it is knowledge that a view is interesting, not that it's true. Whitehead, of course, famously remarked that "it is more important that a proposition be interesting than that it be true." He, however, immediately added, "But of course a true proposition is more apt to be interesting than a false one,"[8] and our interest in a philosophical view is ultimately tied to it as a source of truth about first-order philosophical questions. What good philosophers have to say is interesting and exciting and leads to other ideas that are interesting and exciting. And no doubt all this interest and excitement somehow makes us better "understand" philosophical problems. But what, we will eventually have to ask, does this have to do with truth and knowledge? Does philosophy offer us a body of substantive *knowledge*, not just stimulating opinions? Are there *truths* that philosophers can confidently present to a curious world as the correct answers to important questions? Do philosophers, compared not just to physicists but even to historians, need to feel like runners-up in a beauty contest? Can we move beyond second-order knowledge about what is interesting to first-order philosophical knowledge? A further look at our case studies shows that there is such knowledge, even though it does not take the form of answers to the standard "big questions."

FIRST-ORDER PHILOSOPHICAL KNOWLEDGE

An initial example is provided by Quine's work on the analytic-synthetic distinction. As we have seen, he did not undermine or refute the distinction. What he did do, via his "challenge argument," was make a good case for thinking that the distinction cannot be drawn without using one or another term from a closely related set of modal terms, such as conceptual inclusion, necessity, self-contradiction, and synonymy. The failure of the philosophical community to meet Quine's challenge gives good reason to think that there are no non-modal definitions of modal terms. We must either reject such terms as a group or accept at least one of them as primitive. Further, Quine provided no good reasons for rejecting modal terms as a group, which is why the project of explicating our intuitive distinction of what is true in virtue of meaning and what is not remains viable in the face of his critique. Indeed, once we take modality as a primitive, we can appeal to Quine's discussion to show that there are a

---

[8] Alfred North Whitehead, *Adventures of Ideas*, New York: Free Press, 1967 (first published 1933), chapter 16.

variety of good definitions of analytic as opposed to synthetic statements: definitions in terms of synonymy, of interchangeability in an intensional language, of broadly logical necessity, and even of conceptual inclusion. Surprisingly, Quine turns out to have made a major positive contribution to philosophical knowledge about the analytic-synthetic distinction.

But what about Quine's proposal, very attractive to some, to replace the analytic-synthetic view of knowledge with a holistic view on which all knowledge-claims are susceptible to rejection on the basis of empirical evidence? Even if this holistic view is correct, the analytic-synthetic distinction would still remain a good approximation to the truth. Statements closer to the periphery of our epistemic web behave very like synthetic truths and statements closer to the center of the web behave very like analytic truths. In fact, however, the status of the analytic-synthetic distinction is in all likelihood much stronger. There is, as Putnam points out, every reason to think that Quine is simply wrong about ordinary analytic truths such as "All bachelors are unmarried" – these are true entirely in virtue of their meaning and there is no sense to our giving them up for empirical reasons (although we might have reason to stop using the term "bachelor" or to use the term in some other sense). But Quine may well be right that there are no non-trivial philosophical truths (e.g., about the nature of knowledge or causality) for which the concept of the predicate is included in the concept of the subject (or which are otherwise true in virtue of their meaning). This, however, is a caution about how far analytic knowledge extends, not about the viability of the analytic-synthetic distinction.

Quine's work, then, is best read not as refuting the analytic-synthetic distinction but as an important step in the long process by which philosophers have clarified and deepened our everyday distinction between claims that are true "by definition" (just in virtue of what they mean) and claims true in virtue of something more than an understanding of their meaning. Due to thinkers such as Leibniz, Kant, Carnap, and even Quine, philosophers know a great deal about the distinction between analytic and synthetic truths. Particularly after Quine, we know that the distinction can be effectively formulated using a variety of modal terms, that it cannot be reduced to non-modal terms, and, to the extent that it may be limited or misleading, we know ways of delimiting the boundaries of its applicability.

Kripke's account of proper names seems a prime candidate for a substantive piece of philosophical knowledge. But although it is widely accepted, it has by no means decisively eliminated the descriptivist alternative. To get a sense of how descriptivists have been able to regroup in the face of Kripke's attack, let us briefly look at John Searle's response to Kripke. Searle notes that Kripke's critique assumed a descriptivist theory for which reference is always achieved through the linguistic device of a definite description. He claimed to refute the theory by counterexamples "designed to show that a speaker will refer to an object in the utterance of a name even though the definite description is not satisfied by that object."[9] Searle's descriptivist theory says that what matters for reference is intentional content, whether or not that content can be formulated as a particular definite description. He responds to the counterexamples by trying to show that, even if reference is not achieved via the definite description, it is still achieved "only because the object satisfies the Intentional content in the mind of the speaker" (250).[10] There may be no single description or even disjunction of descriptions that define the "meaning" of a proper noun, but there will always be some descriptive (intentional) content associated with any instance of the use of the noun.

Consider, for example, the Gödel counterexample. Jones identifies Gödel as "the man who proved the incompleteness of arithmetic," although actually Schmidt proved this. Kripke claims that according to descriptivism Jones is referring to Schmidt when he utters "Gödel," when in fact he is referring to Gödel, despite the failure of the definite description. Searle responds that whom Jones is referring to depends on the particular sentence in which he uses "Gödel." If he says something like, "In line 17 of his proof, I think Gödel is making a mistake," then, if we point out that Gödel isn't the author of the proof, Jones will likely respond that he's using "Gödel" to refer to whoever did the proof. On the other hand, if Jones says something like "Kurt Gödel lived in Princeton" and then finds out that Gödel didn't prove the incompleteness theorem, he isn't likely to say he means that Schmidt (who did prove the theorem) lives in Princeton. He will rather say that he was referring to "the man whom I have heard others call 'Kurt Gödel', regardless of whether he proved the incompleteness of arithmetic" (251). Here Searle invokes what he calls the "parasitic identifying description"; that is, a description in terms of the name given to the referent (250). Such a description is typically what is in play in cases where the causal theorists will maintain that there is reference through a causal chain alone with no essential role for intentional content.

---

[9] John Searle, *Intentionality: An Essay in the Philosophy of Mind*, Cambridge: Cambridge University Press, 1983, 250. Further references are given in the text.

[10] Searle uses the capitalized "Intentional" to signal the technical philosophical use of the term to mean "being about something."

Searle also urges the force of the counterexamples mentioned above – Evans' Madagascar case and Searle's own Nixon-as-bar-stool example – against Kripke's account. But Devitt and others have put forward plausible tweaks of the causal theory to evade these difficulties. The dialectic of counterexamples will continue, but there is no reason to think that anyone will decisively refute either Searle or Kripke. Moreover, there have been other versions of descriptivism, for example from Jerrold Katz and, most recently, from some proponents of two-dimensional semantics, such as Frank Jackson.[11] As things now stand, most philosophers of language accept some version of Kripke's causal account, although there continues to be significant minority support for various versions of descriptivism.

Given this situation, we cannot properly claim that Kripke's causal theory of reference is an established philosophical result. But here we need to be careful to sort out different aspects of Kripke's achievement. His own systematic inclinations have made it easy to think of his claim that proper names are rigid designators as inseparable from his rejection of a descriptivist account of reference in favor of a causal account. In fact, however, one can hold that names are rigid designators while remaining neutral between the descriptivist and the causal accounts of reference. As long as descriptivists don't identify names with definite descriptions (or disjunctions of them), they can agree that names are rigid designators while maintaining that they nonetheless refer (rigidly) only because the referent is described in a certain way, regardless of its role as the origin of a referential causal chain.

Further, in the extended discussions and elaborations following on *Naming and Necessity*, it has been Kripke's intuition that names are rigid designators that has most strongly held up. As it turns out, there are versions of descriptivism that evade Kripke's counterexamples, but they do so only by developing descriptivist accounts that allow names to be rigid designators. If an account holds that a name has a contingent content and so does not apply to its referent in every possible world (in which the referent exists), then the account will fall to Kripkean counterexamples. So, for example, Katz has developed a meta-linguistic descriptivism based on the idea that Aristotle, for example, can be described as having the name "Aristotle." But this is false if it means that

[11] Jerrold Katz, "Names without Bearers," *Philosophical Review* 103 (1994), 1–39; Frank Jackson, "Reference and Description Revisited," in J. Tomberlin (ed.), *Philosophical Perspectives 12: Language, Mind, and Ontology*, Oxford: Blackwell, 1998, 201–18.

Aristotle is named "Aristotle" in all possible worlds, since his parents obviously could have given him a different name. Katz, therefore, puts his descriptive point in the following (world-indexed) way: Aristotle has the name "Aristotle" in our (the actual) world. This world-indexed property (*being named Aristotle in the actual world*) is true of Aristotle in all possible worlds and so will not exclude the thesis that names are rigid designators.

My suggestion, then, is that Kripke's claim that proper names are rigid designators has emerged as a well-established truth from recent philosophical discussions. This was not apparent from Kripke's treatment in *Naming and Necessity* because there the thesis functioned merely as a plausible intuition that led to an attractive alternative to the popular claim that names must have some descriptive content. Kripke did refute via counterexamples one typical theoretical formulation of the descriptivist view, but there was no reason at that point to think that descriptivism could not be reformulated so as to avoid counterexamples. Subsequent discussions have produced such reformulations, but only when the descriptions associated with names allow names to refer to the same object in all possible worlds in which the object exists.

In sum, Kripke's philosophical achievement, like Quine's, involved both the imaginative development of an attractive and fruitful picture and the clarification and deepening of a key philosophical distinction. The picture, counter to Quine's radical empiricist (or naturalist) picture, was that of a world (and our knowledge of it) pervaded by metaphysical necessities. Both pictures remain viable, and there is a significant divide on the contemporary scene between Quinean naturalists and Kripkean metaphysicians. At the same time, Kripke has provided a new and highly effective way of understanding the traditional distinction between names and descriptions, characterizing a name as a rigid designator that refers to its object in all possible worlds in which it exists. This characterization, when separated from the still controversial question of whether successful reference is restricted by some descriptive conditions, has emerged as an established piece of philosophical knowledge.

Gettier epistemology has also added to our knowledge of a key philosophical distinction, in this case, the distinction between knowledge and mere true belief. Traditionally, this distinction has been expressed by defining knowledge as *justified* true belief. Gettier's counterexamples seem to undermine this formulation of the distinction. But, I suggest, this has not been the ultimate outcome of Gettier epistemology. We noticed that some philosophers have suggested the possibility of maintaining the JTB analysis of knowledge in spite of putative counterexamples. Thinking along these lines, I suggest we grant that "Knowledge is justified true belief" is not a completely satisfactory definition insofar as it doesn't catch all of our intuitions about when we know things. (Let us call a definition that is completely satisfactory in this sense a *perfect definition*.) But why should we think that knowledge is the sort of thing that can be specified by a perfect definition? Outside of mathematics, such definitions are quite rare. Knowledge is a very common concept, used in a variety of different contexts, involving numerous complexities. Why should we think that it has a perfect definition any more than *game* or *good* does? At a minimum, it would be presumptuous to claim that we *know* knowledge can be defined in this way. Suppose there is no perfect definition of knowledge – hardly an unreasonable conclusion, given the failure of over forty years of effort following Gettier to produce such a definition. Then it may still be true that "knowledge is justified true belief" is, all things considered, the best available definition of knowledge. It may even be that, as far as definitions go, this is the best one. If this is so – and the Gettier discussions support rather than exclude it – then we don't know that knowledge is not justified true belief; Gettier counterexamples have not established this. All they have established is that, if knowledge is something that can be defined in a way that fits all our intuitions, then knowledge is not justified true belief. But if knowledge is not a concept susceptible to perfect definition, then it may well be justified true belief; that is, that may be the best general characterization of knowledge, although it doesn't fit all our intuitions.[12]

Even if we are not prepared to say we know that knowledge is justified true belief, we certainly do know that for a huge range of cases, including almost all everyday ones, the justified-true-belief definition is correct. The enormous effort made by philosophers to find counterexamples to the definition revealed flaws only in non-standard cases, far removed from what we typically encounter.[13] Apart from Gettier-cases, where justification has in various ways come apart from truth, we can be confident that

[12] Compare: *Webster's Seventh Collegiate Dictionary* defines a chair as "a seat with four legs and a back for one person." My intuition is that there could be chairs with only three legs or with one or two legs fixed into a floor. But I'm willing to agree that these intuitions are not likely to be exactly caught in some other definition and that the dictionary formulation is a correct definition of a chair.

[13] This is not to say that there are no Gettier examples that do occur in everyday life (recall the example of justified true belief formed by looking at a stopped clock that just happens to be showing the correct time when I look at it). The point is rather that such examples are unlike the great majority of our justified true beliefs and that we have no problem in practice separating them from standard examples (even though we cannot provide a general characterization of how they differ).

knowledge is justified true belief. At a minimum, JTB is a widely reliable and useful model of knowledge. There are also other models of knowledge – for example, Goldman's characterization in terms of reliability and Lewis' in terms of certainty that illuminate many cases of knowledge. We know that all of these are good models of knowledge and can use them to answer various epistemological questions. We also know a great deal about the limits of their applicability.

Lewis, for example, has not proved that his contextualist definition of knowledge in terms of certainty fits all of our intuitions about what is and is not knowledge. Any precise formulation of the contextualist picture as a universal theory of knowledge will no doubt be inadequate. Insofar as we are seeking a universal theory, the best Lewis can do is, as we saw, convince us by persuasive elaboration that his picture is sufficiently interesting, fruitful, etc. to be worth continuing to develop. Nonetheless, Lewis has shown that his definition is true for an important range of cases, including, for example, the lottery paradox. How is it that I can have overwhelming justification for the true belief that my ticket will not win the lottery and still not *know* that I will not win the lottery? Because I cannot eliminate the possibility that I might win, and, in this case at least, eliminating this possibility is necessary for knowing. This sounds entirely plausible: it seems intuitively right that I can't know that I won't win a lottery until I've actually lost. Lewis' contextualist model is a perfect fit for the lottery case. Accordingly, we should conclude that, in the light of Lewis' account, we *know* why having justified true belief that I won't win a lottery does not amount to knowing that I won't win. Of course, we may also want to know why, in this case, eliminating the possibility of my winning is necessary for knowledge. Lewis even has an answer for this: I can't ignore the possibility that one of the tickets will win, and this includes the possibility that my ticket will win, which also is intuitively right. So we also know why we need to eliminate the possibility of my winning. Beyond this, there is also an inclination to ask for an explanation of our intuitions in the lottery case via universal principles that apply to all possible cases. Neither Lewis nor anyone else has produced knowledge of such principles. But this doesn't mean that, after reading Lewis, we don't know a good explanation for the lottery paradox.

To sum up the knowledge philosophers have gained from Gettier epistemology: (1) The JTB definition turns out to be generally valid, apart from a few isolable domains in which it does not fit most people's intuitions; although not entirely accurate, it is still clearly the best single definition. (2) There are other definitions (e.g., in terms of certainty and reliability) that apply in an important range of cases, including some where JTB fails. (3) We can provide a reasonably accurate map of the domain of knowledge, showing where JTB fails and explaining why it fails and, in some cases, what definition is preferable. (4) It is at least plausible that Gettier epistemology has shown that knowledge is not susceptible to perfect definition (that is, one that will satisfy all of our intuitions about its subject), so that we should not think that settling for an excellent approximation is a fundamental failure.

To insist that knowledge excludes approximation and incompleteness would require claiming that, for example, physicists don't know anything about matter because they don't know its ultimate constituents, or that chemists don't know that PV = kT because they haven't worked out all the limits on its application. In contrast to the natural sciences, philosophers ignore the knowledge they have achieved because of what we might call the *Philosopher's Fallacy*: the assumption that all genuinely philosophical knowledge must involve ultimate, final understanding – through a perfect definition, an explanation that itself needs no explanation, etc. Given this assumption – which begins with our founder, Socrates – it follows that we have achieved little or no philosophical knowledge. But once we give up this assumption, our discipline turns out to have produced a great deal of knowledge. Giving up the Philosopher's Fallacy does not, moreover, mean giving up the great grand goals of ultimate understanding – to give perfect definitions of knowledge and justice, to discover the ultimate source and meaning of the universe, and so on. It is, rather, to realize that, even if these goals are never reached, there is still a substantial body of philosophical knowledge that our inquiry has discovered.

INTUITIONS AND PHILOSOPHICAL KNOWLEDGE

How does philosophical knowledge come about? Not, our case studies show, from valid deductive arguments from obviously true premises. But then how do philosophers come to know what they know? In the case of what I've called "second-order" knowledge about the intellectual value and viability of certain views, the process is complicated but hardly puzzling. It's a matter of working with a set of ideas or claims and developing them – making them clearer, more precise; deriving conclusions from them, relating them to other issues and views – all for the sake of showing their interest and power. In short, it's a matter of showing what we can *do* with certain ideas. This is what I called the process of persuasive elaboration.

For first-order knowledge, the story is really just more of the same. Kripke starts with the idea that names are rigid designators and produces, as we saw, a complex set of interconnected considerations that develop and apply the idea in various ways, persuading us that it is at least worth taking seriously. As others take the idea up, the case becomes all the more persuasive: more detailed theories are constructed, further objections are neutralized, new domains are illuminated. Eventually, it dawns on just about everybody that there is no defensible alternative to thinking of names as rigid designators. The move from persuasive elaboration to knowledge is seamless.

The move, however, is not always fully visible, as shown by the cases of the analytic-synthetic distinction and of Gettier epistemology. In practice, philosophers frequently assume that a statement they are discussing is analytic or that a belief is knowledge because it is justified and true – bare claims lightly veiled by a modest footnote evoking the myth that Quine or Gettier has shown otherwise. The practice is legitimate because, beyond the mythic proofs of Quine and Gettier, there lie decades of complex elaboration of truth by meaning and of justified true belief out of which the classic distinctions have emerged essentially intact. We blush to say otherwise only because we have not sloughed off overly simple standards of clarity and exactness that are not appropriate to these cases.

Although the mode of philosophical argumentation is complexly non-deductive, its logic is no different from that at work in any other non-deductive argumentative enterprise. Philosophers use the same methods of forging agreement by rational discussion as are used in discussions about which scientific theory to accept, which political proposal to adopt, or where to go on vacation. There is no doubt much to be said about the process of rational consensus formation, but much of it we already know from the multitude of contexts in which we practice it, and, in any case, the procedures are essentially the same in all contexts.[14] Differences enter not in the argumentative structures but in the basic premises, themselves not derived from argument, that anchor the entire process. Such differences are due to the distinctive subject-matters about which different discussions seek knowledge. Philosophers have frequently regarded the fundamental knowledge they seek as requiring grounding in basic premises quite different from those at work in common sense and even scientific knowing. The traditional view presents philosophical

---

[14] Much of what we will see (in chapter 7) Kuhn saying about how scientists achieve consensus and knowledge will apply to philosophy.

knowledge as based on a special sort of a priori intuition that provides distinctive and irreducible philosophical insight into essential conceptual or even ontological structures. Even if we admit that recent analytic work does not follow the traditional deductive model, it might seem that it would require distinctive philosophical premises. If so, it might further seem that any claim to a distinctive body of philosophical knowledge, such as I am putting forward, would have no basis without a full account and justification of the intellectual faculty whereby we know these distinctive premises. My view, however, is that the question of whether there is a distinctive philosophical mode of intellectual insight has no bearing on the question of whether there is a distinctive body of philosophical knowledge. I will develop this view through reflection on the current debate within analytic philosophy between "naturalists" and "rationalists" about the role of intuitions in philosophy.[15]

Our case studies have revealed frequent appeals to what we have called intuitions, although we have often seen reliance on intuitions as a sign of failure to show that a claim is genuinely known. But how exactly should we think of intuitions and their role in philosophical knowledge? Intuitions are often regarded as the data or evidence from which philosophical inquiry begins. This view has roots in the traditional idea that the ultimate premises of philosophical arguments derive from intellectual insights (yielding, for example, self-evident truths). Today, however, few are willing to present philosophically substantive claims as self-evident, and instead we tend to speak of intuitions as "intellectual seemings" (Bealer) or "inclinations to believe" (Sosa), which themselves require evaluation through reconciliation with other intuitions (the effort to achieve "reflective equilibrium"). There is also, in good part because of recent attacks by naturalist philosophers, an effort to justify the use of intuitions in philosophy. Naturalists argue that intuition is not cognitively reliable (or, at least, that we have no reason to think it is), and intuitionists respond with defenses of its reliability (or, at least, the rationality of appealing to it).[16]

Robert Cummins provides an instructive example of one sort of naturalist critique of philosophical intuition. According to him, such

---

[15] For a similar view of philosophical intuitions see Timothy Williamson, *The Philosophy of Philosophy*, Oxford: Blackwell, 2007, 215–25.

[16] See Michael R. DePaul, "Why Bother with Reflective Equilibrium?," in M. R. DePaul and W. Ramsey (eds.), *Rethinking Intuition: The Psychology of Intuition and Its Role in Philosophical Inquiry*, Lanham, MD: Rowman & Littlefield, 1998, 293–309. Robert Audi has recently developed an important defense of philosophical intuitions, particularly for ethics, in *The Good and the Right: A Theory of Intuition and Intrinsic Value*, Princeton, NJ: Princeton University Press, 2004.

intuition is like a telescope: a special means of observation that cannot be legitimately employed until it has been "calibrated" by comparison with a means of observation already accepted as reliable. Just as Galileo demonstrated the reliability of his telescope by showing that it yielded the same observations for ordinary objects viewed at a distance as sense perception did close up, so philosophers need to show that their faculty of intuition gives the same results as some already accepted non-intuitive way of knowing (e.g., scientific theorizing) that can be applied to the same objects. Given this view, Cummins argues that either philosophical intuition cannot be calibrated (if there are no non-intuitive ways of knowing what it purports to know) or it is useless (since the non-intuitive knowledge used in calibration will itself be an entirely adequate substitute for intuition). "Philosophical intuition," Cummins concludes, "is epistemologically useless, since it can be calibrated only when it is not needed."[17]

Our case studies provide an effective response to Cummins' objection. Take the case of Kripke. In some sense, he does "begin" with his intuition that names are rigid designators, and he even uses this intuition in various arguments for important conclusions (e.g., the existence of necessary a posteriori truths). But he is not simply taking for granted this substantive, controversial claim on the basis of his intuition. Rather, he is showing what happens when we make use of the intuition in constructing a philosophy of language and of necessary truth. He "assumes" the intuition only in order to persuasively elaborate it. In this case, the intuition (or, more precisely, the fact that we ought to take the intuition seriously) is the conclusion, not a premise, of his argument. As such, it is not a special mode of observation that requires calibration. There are other intuitions that do genuinely function as unjustified premises in Kripke's argument, but these are claims that are just obvious (more fully, obviously true), such as that Aristotle might not have taught Alexander or that there is a distinction between epistemic and metaphysical necessity. Such intuitions do not need to be legitimated by calibration any more than do obvious sense perceptions.

Someone might still object that these "obvious" premises correspond to intuitions that must surely be based on some special sort of intellectual insight. This may be so, but whether it is or not does not alter the fact that such intuitions are rightly put forward as uncontroversially true. Of

[17] Robert Cummins, "Reflections on Reflective Equilibrium," in DePaul and Ramsey, (eds.), *Rethinking Intuition*, 113–28.

course, philosophers – even more than most others – want to make sure that they carefully examine their commitment to their basic premises, taking very seriously any signs of internal contradiction and any potential counterarguments. But there is no reason that philosophers, any more than anyone else, should have to begin by providing some special justification for claims that they already confidently believe. To ask for such justification is a version of the Cartesian mistake of demanding that we refute skepticism about our basic premises before we are entitled to them.[18] There may be many interesting things to say about the nature of obvious intellectual intuitions, just as there may be many interesting things to say about the nature of obvious sense perceptions. But none of these things need be said before we are entitled to accept the obvious as obvious.

Nor is there any need to characterize the objects of basic philosophical knowledge to establish its existence. There are continuing disputes about whether such knowledge is primarily about language, concepts, or the world itself. My own view is that all three are, in various ways, objects of philosophical knowledge, although most philosophical knowledge is about the world.[19] But my claims about the reality of philosophical knowledge do not depend on any particular view about its object.

Naturalist objections like Cummins' are encouraged by accounts, from rationalists such as Bealer and Sosa, that present philosophical arguments as based on intuitions that are not obvious truths. Bealer, for example, treats philosophical intuitions as "intellectual seemings," in contrast to firm, obvious truths.[20] He then undertakes to show that intuitions so understood nonetheless "qualify as evidence, and the correct explanation of this fact is that intuitions have a strong (albeit indirect and fallible) tie to the truth when the subjects are in suitably good cognitive conditions" (203). But even if we take this argument at face value, the apparent strength of Bealer's thesis is undermined by the condition that those who have intuitions be "in suitably good cognitive conditions." What are these conditions and how do we know that we are in anything like a good approximation of them? Bealer himself admits that he at best establishes "only the possibility of autonomous and authoritative philosophical

---

[18] Timothy Williamson has developed a similar point very effectively in his critique of "judgment skepticism," *The Philosophy of Philosophy*, 225–41.

[19] Williamson has made a good case for this conclusion in *The Philosophy of Philosophy*, chapter 1.

[20] George Bealer, "Intuitions and the Autonomy of Philosophy," in DePaul and Ramsey (eds.), *Rethinking Intuition* 201–39. References will be given in the text.

knowledge, perhaps on the part of creatures in cognitive conditions superior to ours." To the objection that such a possibility in principle does "nothing to clarify the relation between science and philosophy as practiced by *human beings*," he replies that it establishes an ideal status for philosophy and that, to the extent that we approximate the ideal, "we are able to approximate autonomous, authoritative philosophical knowledge." But he offers no assessment of where we in fact are with regard to this ideal, saying only that "I believe that collectively, over historical time, undertaking philosophy as a civilization-wide project, we can obtain authoritative answers to a wide variety of central philosophical questions" (203). Even if Bealer's defense of philosophical knowledge succeeds in principle, it tells us nothing about the status of philosophical achievements to date because we have no reason to think that philosophers' intuitions in fact meet the conditions for authoritative knowledge. But, as our case studies show, good philosophical arguments are based on intuitions in the sense of obvious truths that need no prior justification and ground arguments that conclude to, but do not simply assume, more controversial and interesting intuitions.

Another defender of intuitions, Ernest Sosa, initially characterized them as simply "non-inferential beliefs" regarding abstract propositions, but later weakened this to a formulation in terms of "inclination to believe," on the grounds that we can have an intuition of something we do not and should not believe (e.g., we still have the intuition that two lines in an optical illusion are unequal, even though we know they are equal). In a more recent article, he switches to an occurrent rather than a dispositional formulation, defining an intuition as a "conscious attraction to assent" (to a proposition p) that meets two further conditions: (i) p is "sufficiently understood" and (ii) my attraction to assenting to p is "virtuously based" (i.e., based on a reliable ability). This, of course, requires him to answer questions about whether the faculty of intuition is sufficiently reliable. Sosa responds with a version of Descartes' argument for his criterion of truth: there are some intuitions that are obviously reliable (e.g., that $2 + 2 = 4$), and if intuitions were not generally reliable, then there would be grounds for doubting even $2 + 2 = 4$. But this leaves him open to difficult questions about whether paradigmatically reliable intuitions such as $2 + 2 = 4$ may not have distinctive features that other intuitions lack. Our case studies and the model of persuasive elaboration developed from them show that, rather than take on the burden of such questions, philosophers can start simply with what they are quite sure of.

It may be that, in order to arrive at answers to the great questions of our discipline, we would need intuitions that are not obvious but need some special prior justification. If so, that is unfortunate, since it seems pretty clear that no such justification is forthcoming. I suspect that those who insist on special philosophical intuitions, beyond what is just obvious, are often pushed to that position because they see no other way that philosophy can achieve a distinctive body of knowledge. Our case studies, however, show that this is not so, even though the knowledge is not precisely the sort that many of us would like to have.

The demand for prior justification of philosophical intuition is not the only mode of naturalist critique that requires our attention. The recent rise of "experimental philosophy" has presented empirical data that have been taken to challenge the cognitive authority of philosophical intuitions. The data derive from surveys in which various groups of people are asked to respond to classic analytic intuition pumps such as Gettier or Kripkean counterexamples. The results show that the responses of non-philosophers are sometimes significantly different from the intuitions of philosophers and, in some cases, vary significantly among members of different ethnic, racial, or socio-economic groups. So, for example, when people were asked whether someone in a standard Gettier situation really knows that a friend owns an American car, 74 percent of people from Western cultures agreed with the standard philosophical intuition that she did not, but a majority of Indians (61 percent) and of East Asians (56 percent) said that she did really know, while poor whites were about evenly divided on the question.[21] Similarly, when asked about Kripke's Gödel–Schmidt counterexample to descriptivism, a majority of Westerners said that "Gödel" referred to Gödel whereas a majority of East Asians said it referred to Schmidt (the supposed actual discoverer of the proof).[22]

Essentially, the challenge posed by experiments of this sort is an argument from disagreement. Why should philosophers trust their intuitions when others disagree with them, particularly when this disagreement correlates with epistemically irrelevant variables such as race and class? Don't the results suggest that the agreement of analytic philosophers about such intuitions may be due to the fact that most analytic philosophers come from Western cultures?

---

[21] J. Weinberg, S. Nichols, and S. Stich, "Normativity and Epistemic Intuitions," *Philosophical Topics* 29 (2001), 429–60.

[22] E. Machery *et al.*, "Semantics Cross-Cultural Style," *Cognition* 92 (2004), B1–B12. References will be given in text.

A challenge from disagreement has no force unless there is some reason to think that those who disagree with us are epistemic peers – roughly, people who are in as good a position (have as much relevant knowledge, experience, and cognitive skills) as we are. This suggests the immediate response that those surveyed (typically college undergraduates) are not epistemic peers of trained philosophers who have thought and published about these issues for many years. Interestingly, experimental philosophers often reject this response out of hand as a sign of intellectual arrogance. Regarding Kripke's intuition, for example, Machery *et al.* say:

> We find it *wildly* implausible that the semantic intuitions of the narrow cross-section of humanity who are Western academic philosophers are a more reliable indicator of the correct theory of reference (if there is such a thing . . .) than the differing semantic intuitions of other cultural groups . . . In the absence of a principled argument about why philosophers' intuitions are superior, this project smacks of narcissism in the extreme. (89)

They also suggest that philosophical training and experience are more likely to be a hindrance to having reliable intuitions: "Given the intense training and selection that undergraduate and graduate students in philosophy have to go through, there is good reason to suspect that the alleged reflective intuitions are in fact reinforced intuitions" (89).

The charge of narcissism ("elitism" is sometimes the preferred epithet) will seem absurd unless we keep in mind that the question is not about a special capacity for philosophical intuitions that only those specially trained in the discipline could be expected to have. The point is rather that philosophers are claiming that their intuitions are representative of what most people would think, so that a high level of philosophical sophistication is not relevant. Philosophers are, for example, trying to find out what concepts such as *knowledge* and *naming* mean, and the meaning of a concept is a function of how the corresponding word is used.[23] To say that the Gettier cases are not instances of knowledge is to say that "we" would not say that they are, where "we" refers to most competent speakers of a language.

On the other hand, it would make no sense to ask competent speakers about these cases without making sure that they really understood what they were being asked about, were taking the questions seriously, and had enough time to reflect on the matter. How do we know that the studies cited met these conditions for adequate judgment? One good sign that the conditions were being met would be a convergence of responses to the same

---

[23] Frank Jackson emphasizes this point in his *From Metaphysics to Ethics: A Defense of Conceptual Analysis*, Oxford: Oxford University Press, 1998, 33–4.

view. This could, of course, also occur if some epistemically distorting factors were producing the convergence. But, if we were able to change circumstances in ways we had reason to think would help meet the conditions, and had no reason to think that these changes introduced distorting factors, then convergence would be a good sign that the conditions for adequate judgment were closer to being met. If, for example, when students were given only 30 seconds to answer the survey question, they were split 50–50 on the answer; and, when we subsequently gave them 2 minutes to answer, the split went to 90–10, this would suggest that we were approaching conditions for adequate judgment.

In this regard, it is interesting to note, first, that empirical studies show that students who have had some philosophy (even just one or two courses) are more inclined to give "standard" answers to the survey questions and, second, that, as philosophers well know, those who pursue philosophy as majors and graduate students almost all converge to the standard answers. Accordingly, unless there are good reasons to think that the relevant experiences of philosophy students (thinking more about these sorts of questions, being trained to reflect more carefully and critically, engaging in the back-and-forth of argument, etc.) are likely to distort their judgment, it is reasonable to conclude that the conditions under which people study philosophy are much closer to adequate conditions for making reliable judgments about the survey questions than are the conditions under which the surveys were given.

The standard experimentalist response to this line of thought is the one we have already seen from Machery *et al.*: that there are good reasons to think that philosophical training distorts the judgment of those undergoing it in favor of the standard responses. But on reflection, this is an extraordinarily implausible claim. Philosophy in general encourages sharply critical debate, and professional advancement correlates with ability to challenge entrenched views. There may well be cases in ideologically loaded areas, such as ethics, political theory, and philosophy of religion, where there are important social pressures to adhere to a given line (although, one would think, far less than among a general public that is not inculcated with the critical spirit of philosophy). But what reason is there to think that the analytic profession has a vested interest in insisting that the JTB definition is wrong or that names are rigid designators? If that were so, why were the opposites of both views held for so long?

Lacking evidence of specific distorting factors, the suggestion of bias of judgment by professional training is an engine of self-refuting skepticism, since every discipline (and even ordinary informal thinking) depends on intuitive intellectual judgments. The sciences, including cognitive science, require judgments by trained investigators about whether a given hypothesis has been sufficiently tested, whether the diverse tests supporting a theory are sufficient to make it acceptable, etc. Even in logic and mathematics, the conclusion that a given proof is deductively valid is not itself a result of deductive argument but an intuitive judgment. (What do we say to someone who agrees that modus ponens is a sound principle of reasoning but denies that "All humans are mortal; Socrates is a human; therefore, Socrates is mortal" is an instance of it?) If the mere possibility of distortion by professional training undermines the authority of intuitive judgments, then all intellectual disciplines are in big epistemic trouble.

There remains the experimentalists' suggestion that philosophical intuitions may vary with factors such as ethnicity and class. Given our defense of the authority of the philosophical community's shared intuitions, this becomes less of a problem, since there is no evidence that, within the discipline of analytic philosophy, intuitions about epistemology and philosophy of language differ along ethnic or economic lines. But what should we make of the apparent fact that, in a population of non-philosophers, the intuitions of more affluent Westerners come closer to the intuitions of the community of analytic philosophers? The skeptical suggestion is that East Asians, for example, think in importantly different ways from Westerners, so that to privilege the agreement of Westerners about analytic intuitions is ethnocentric. But the hypothesis of "thinking differently" can cut two different ways. It might mean that the minds of East Asians differ in fundamental ways from the minds of Westerners, which would lead them to respond differently to certain philosophical questions *however they were formulated*. But it might merely mean that there are certain differences in how East Asians process information that made them read and respond to *the specific formulations used in the surveys* in different ways. If so, the conclusion would be that the surveys were ill-designed because they did not take account of distinctive ways in which Westerners and East Asians would interpret and react to a particular formulation of a philosophical question. If, as seems to be the case, East Asians who have seriously studied analytic philosophy don't seem to have different intuitions from those of Westerners, this is reason to think that there are not fundamental differences in this regard and hence to prefer the design-flaw hypothesis. To respond that the intuitions of East Asians who study analytic philosophy are distorted by their training or that they are a minority predisposed to think like Westerners is to, once again, open the door to a self-refuting skepticism about intellectual disciplines.

The failure of experimentalist philosophy to undermine, in a general way, the authority of philosophical intuitions does not mean, of course, that all such intuitions are beyond challenge. One point, noted above, is that some intuitions do not function as premises in arguments but are actually just initial expressions of the conclusions of such arguments (Kripke's intuition that names are rigid designators). Moreover, as intuitions move further from a grounding in everyday practices and come to reflect detached intellectual insights, they often become less compelling. It's hard to see how anyone could seriously challenge the intuition that Aristotle might not have taught Alexander or that merely believing that Jones owns a Ford does not constitute knowledge of that claim. But philosophical reflection itself can and has questioned the authority of widely shared intuitions on topics less closely tied to everyday practices. Indeed, our earlier discussions showed this happening with both the examples exploited by the experimentalists. Weatherson and Lycan suggested the possibility of "walking away" from Gettier counterexamples, and Searle argued for cases in which "Gödel" would refer to whoever proved the incompleteness theorem. Even without appeals to empirical evidence, philosophical reflection itself has raised questions about the authority of these intuitions.

One important reason that some philosophical intuitions are less than compelling is that they are in fact more a matter of evaluative judgment than semantic or ontological insight. Think about what is going on when, for example, I reject the Gettier barn-case as an instance of knowledge. Is this really a matter of my consulting some conceptual structure expressing the necessary and/or sufficient conditions for knowledge? Or my knowing what I or others would say if confronted with actual examples of this sort? I suggest that, on the contrary, what is driving my "intuition" may well be my commitment to "knows" as an *evaluative* characterization, connoting an epistemic achievement, which is not appropriate in this case because I have come by my justified true belief by sheer dumb luck. I don't "see" that my belief that there's a barn isn't knowledge: maybe it is by some standard of adequacy to a Platonic form or to empirical facts about human language-use. The point is that, if this is what knowledge means, then I don't find it particularly important or interesting. Freedom provides another example. It's not that I intuitively know that free actions (as a matter of conceptual definition or de facto usage) are ones for which I am morally responsible. But if there are free acts for which I'm not morally responsible, their freedom is not of moral interest or importance. In such cases, my intuitions are not insights into the intrinsic natures of certain characteristics but expressions of what I (and typically others) find valuable about such characteristics.

Once we distinguish the various roles intuitions can play in philosophical arguments, the skeptical challenge of experimental philosophy dissipates. Intuitions that are utterly obvious, even after critical reflection, are the gold standard. They are not infallible but philosophers are entitled to take them as anchors providing ultimate premises for their arguments. This is just to say that philosophers, like anyone else, can and should start their intellectual inquiries from what they find obviously true. Even these intuitive beliefs may turn out to be wrong: "obvious" does not mean "infallible." But in the face of naturalist critiques, it is crucial to emphasize that there is no Cartesian obligation to first determine the origin of obvious beliefs and then show why this origin guarantees their truth. They need no certification beyond their obviousness. It may be that some such truths will turn out to have a special source that explains their obviousness, and investigating this source may be of interest in its own right; but such investigation has no role in establishing the cognitive authority of the truths that anchor philosophical arguments.

Many philosophical intuitions fall far below this gold standard of the obviously true. One important group, already noted, consists of merely individual inclinations or hunches (mere "intellectual seemings"). Such intuitions are actually the intended conclusions, not the premises, of arguments, a fact obscured because they are often hypothetically "assumed" for the sake of the persuasive elaboration that makes the case for them. A third group of intuitions falls between the obvious and the to-be-proved. These are insights that many (sometimes even most) philosophers find more convincing than mere intellectual seemings, but which are not utterly obvious in the sense that giving them up would undermine practices to which we are deeply committed in our pre-philosophical lives. (Intuitions based on evaluative attitudes rather than objective insights will often fall into this category.) Such intuitions can be reasonable tentative starting points in philosophical discussions, but eventually they need support either by clarifications and distinctions that extract from them an overwhelmingly obvious core or by argument from obvious premises. The three sorts of intuitions were nicely represented in our case study of Kripke. Specific modal intuitions such as "Nixon might have lost the 1968 election" are obvious, "Names are rigid designators" is an intellectual seeming for which Kripke argues by persuasive elaboration, and "'Water is H$_2$O' is necessary a posteriori" is a widely shared intuition that has some but not decisive cognitive authority.[24]

CONCLUSION

Our case studies show a significant body of philosophical knowledge of various sorts, but there is no need to posit a distinctive faculty of philosophical intuition to explain or vindicate this knowledge. Whether such a faculty (or a more general faculty of intellectual or conceptual insight) exists may be a fruitful topic of philosophical or psychological inquiry, but it is not relevant to the question of whether there is a body of philosophical disciplinary knowledge. Global naturalistic critiques of philosophical intuition, including those of experimental philosophy, fail unless they take the self-refuting form of attacks on the cognitive authority of all intellectual disciplines. Responding to these critiques has shown the role (implicit in our case studies) of three quite different sorts of intuitions in philosophical arguments.

I now turn to another set of case studies that will both further illustrate and reinforce the points made so far but will also reveal another domain of philosophical knowledge, a domain corresponding to what I will call (pre-philosophical) *convictions*. I begin with a discussion of religious convictions in the work of Alvin Plantinga, but go on to show in the next chapter that convictions also have an essential role in recent discussions of philosophy of mind and of freedom. In two following chapters I will look, respectively, at the work of Thomas Kuhn and John Rawls, who shed particular light on the role of convictions in philosophy. A final case study will face Richard Rorty's challenge to the claim that there is a body of philosophical truth, a discussion that will further our treatment of convictions in philosophy and also lead to some reflections on the nature of philosophical truth.

---

[24] For a similar view of intuitions, developed from a different direction, see Michael DePaul, "Reflective Equilibrium and Foundationalism," *American Philosophical Quarterly* 23 (1986), 59–69.

PART II

Arguments and convictions

Turning the tables: Plantinga and the rise of philosophy of religion

For at least the first half of the twentieth century, there was no such thing as the philosophy of religion among analytic philosophers. Most analytic philosophers rejected religion as at best rationally gratuitous and at worst meaningless and, in any case, saw no need for serious, prolonged philosophical discussion of its ideas and status. This situation began to change around 1950, as witnessed by the still remarkable volume edited by Anthony Flew and Alasdair MacIntyre, which gathered papers by philosophers (a roughly equal mix of believers and non-believers), all working in the analytic tradition and sharing "a concern with theological questions, and a conviction that these call for serious and particular treatment" through philosophical analysis and argument. The editors noted that they would have liked to described the pieces they collected as essays in "the philosophy of religion," but did not do so because "this expression has become, and seems likely for some time to remain, associated with Idealist attempts to present philosophical prolegomena to theistic theology" (viii). Their title spoke instead of "new essays in *philosophical theology*."[1]

Although the volume represents a new opening to religious questions, it still presents religion as distinctly under siege from analytic philosophy. A dominant issue is whether religious language even meets the standards of meaningful discourse, and although there are several discussions of theistic proofs, no one defends their soundness. Even the essay by the Christian co-editor, Alasdair MacIntyre, attacks arguments from religious experience. By contrast, J. N. Findlay presents his "negative ontological argument" against the existence of God, while the atheist co-editor, Anthony Flew, tries to revive the atheistic argument from evil by deflating the traditional free-will defense. These new analytic philosophers no

---

[1] Anthony Flew and Alasdair MacIntyre (eds.), *New Essays in Philosophical Theology*, London: Macmillan, 1955.

longer ignore religion, but their logical tools are primarily directed towards its critique.

In a period of no more than twenty-five years, the situation was reversed. Philosophy of religion, thoroughly detached from its idealist origins, had become a major subdiscipline of analytic philosophy, and one in which most of the leading contributors were religious believers. Christians, particularly members of various Protestant churches, dominated. The success and the nature of the new enterprise was well represented by the founding, in 1978, of the Society of Christian Philosophers. The Society, along with its journal, *Faith and Philosophy*, quickly became a fertile source of analytic philosophizing with a distinctly positive attitude towards Christian belief, offering new, more rigorous formulations of traditional arguments, subtle logical analyses and defenses of central Christian doctrines such as the Incarnation and the Trinity, and, more generally, developing a vibrant body of analytic thought that understood itself as Christian philosophy. In stark contrast with the situation fifty years ago, there are now prominent philosophers in many major analytic departments who see their philosophical work as, to an important extent, connected to their religious belief. Of the ten presidents of the Society of Christian Philosophers, five have been presidents of a national division of the American Philosophical Association (Alvin Plantinga, William Alston, Nicholas Wolterstorff, Robert Audi, and Eleonore Stump).

This transformation no doubt had important social sources, but it also was an intellectual achievement, forged by the sheer philosophical quality of the work associated with it. In this regard, no contribution was more important than that of Alvin Plantinga, whose 1967 book, *God and Other Minds*,[2] launched a series of striking defenses of religious belief against the standard objections that, without receiving rigorous discussion, had led most analytic philosophers to view religious claims as unworthy of their attention. To get a sense of the nature and effectiveness of Plantinga's arguments, we will look first at his version of the free-will defense against the problem of evil and then at his defense of the reasonableness of religious belief.

THE PROBLEM OF EVIL

The fundamental assertion and consolation of religion is that there is someone worthy of our absolute trust. Unlike lesser beings, God will never betray us through malice or fail us through weakness. He must,

---

[2] Alvin Plantinga, *God and Other Minds*, Ithaca, NY: Cornell University Press, 1967.

accordingly, be all-powerful and all-good. But such unlimited perfection seems inconsistent with the obvious evils of our world. Surely an all-good God would not have wanted, for example, the horrors of the Holocaust, and an all-powerful God would have been able to prevent them. But these horrors did occur; therefore, it would seem, there is no one who is both all-good and all-powerful. God, understood as an object of absolute trust, does not exist.

The traditional response to the above argument from evil is that, although God could have created a world with no evil, such a world would be less good than the world we actually have. For, it is maintained, there are goods that require corresponding evils, and the world is better for having both. Free will is a paramount example: it is much better to have a world with creatures capable of freely choosing moral good, but there is no way for even an omnipotent God to ensure that free creatures will not choose evil. So even a world created by an all-good, all-powerful God may have to contain moral evil.

But is it so obvious that free agents must escape the control of an omnipotent God? Couldn't an omnipotent being cause even a free agent to choose the good? And, even if this is not possible, omnipotence implies omniscience, so why couldn't God simply create only those free agents that he knows will not chose evil? Alvin Plantinga's Free Will Defense is a rigorous and detailed effort to answer such objections and to establish the possibility that our world, with all its evil, was nonetheless created by an all-good, all-powerful God.

Plantinga's discussion[3] is specifically directed at contemporary analytic philosophers, such as J. L. Mackie, who maintained that the existence of evil is *logically inconsistent* with the existence of the Christian God, that a contradiction can be deduced from the assumption that both evil and the Christian God exist. If so, the undeniable existence of evil proves that God does not exist. Responding to this strong version of the problem requires only a proof that a world with both God and evil is logically possible, not that it is actual or even probable. Accordingly, a defense against the objection may appeal to the most outlandish assumptions as long as they are logically possible. This immediately allows Plantinga, in formulating a free will defense, to avoid complex issues about the nature of freedom. Many philosophers are compatibilists, maintaining that free actions are not uncaused but rather caused in specific ways. Plantinga,

---

[3] Alvin Plantinga, *The Nature of Necessity*, Oxford: Oxford University Press, 1974, chapter 10. References will be given in the text.

however, defines free actions as uncaused: "If a person S is free with respect to a given action, then he is free to perform that action and free to refrain; no causal laws and antecedent conditions determine either that he will perform the action, or that he will not" (165–6). He can do this because a successful proof of logical consistency does not require establishing the incompatibilist (libertarian) conception of freedom against compatibilism. It needs only the *possibility* that "what God thought good . . . was the existence of creatures whose activity is not causally determined," whether or not this is "the ordinary use of the word 'free'" (171). Perhaps compatibilism is the correct account of human freedom, perhaps not. Nonetheless, it is logically possible that freedom in Plantinga's libertarian sense is a good and that God wanted to include it in the world. This is all that is needed for the Free Will Defense.

Given the possibility that God wanted a world with freedom in this sense, it is obvious that he could not have excluded evil by causing free agents to always make good choices; an action caused by God, directly or indirectly, would not be free in the relevant sense. But God's omnipotence includes omniscience (or, at least, it includes any knowledge necessary for omnipotence). It would seem, therefore, that God would be able to exclude evil by creating only free agents who, he knows, will always choose the good.

Consider, to use Plantinga's example, the case of Curley Smith, a mayor of Boston who has opposed a proposal by Smedes, the Director of Highways, to build a throughway that would require the destruction of the Old North Church. Smedes offers Curley a bribe of $30,000 to drop his opposition, and Curley accepts. But suppose Curley would have rejected a bribe of only $20,000. If so, God could have made Curley a free agent but avoided evil by seeing that he was offered no more than $20,000. Similarly, for all the free agents that God creates, he could see to it that they are never in circumstances in which their free choices will be wrong.

This line of argument assumes that, for any possible situation in which a free agent makes a choice, God knows what choice that agent would make. Regarding Curley's dealings with Smedes, God knows which of the following is true:

(1) If Curly had been offered $20,000, he would have accepted;
(2) If Curly had been offered $20,000, he would not have accepted.

Based on such knowledge, God arranges the world so that Curley – and anyone else he creates – does not go wrong.

Some philosophers have argued that counterfactual conditionals such as (1) and (2) are neither true nor false, and so could not be known to be true, even by God. If so, then the present objection to the Free Will Defense cannot get off the ground. Plantinga, however, thinks that it is "obvious" that either (1) or (2) is true, although, he says, "I do not know how to produce a conclusive argument for this supposition." (But he does criticize two arguments against the supposition.) Accordingly, Plantinga has to argue that, even though an omniscient God would know how free agents would choose in various situations, this might not enable him to exclude evil.

Why not? A first point is that it is not true that, just because a world is possible, God can create (actualize) it. If, for example, it is true that Curley would accept a $20,000 bribe, then God could not have actualized the specific possible world in which Curley did not accept the bribe; and, if it is true that Curley would not have accepted the bribe, then God could not have actualized the specific world in which Curley did accept the bribe. If Curley is free, then which world is actualized depends partly on him, not just on God. As Plantinga puts it,

there are possible worlds such that it is partly up to Curley whether or not God can actualize them. It is of course up to God whether or not to create Curley, and also up to God whether or not to make him free with respect to the action of taking the bribe . . . But if he creates him, and creates him free with respect to this action, then whether or not he takes it is up to Curley – not God. (184)

But the Free Will Defense needs much more than the mere claim that there are some possible worlds that God could not actualize. It requires further that "among the worlds that God could not actualize are all the worlds containing moral good but no moral evil" (185). How can we show this? Consider once again, Plantinga says, the case of Curley. Regarding Smedes' effort to bribe him, it might be that, no matter what amount Smedes had offered him, Curley would have accepted. Then, no matter what, God could not actualize a possible world in which Curley was offered a bribe by Smedes (in the given situation) and did not accept it. Notice, the point is not that there is no possible world in which Curley does not accept the bribe, just that God cannot actualize such a world, since this is up to Curley. Of course, in such a case, God could see to it that Smedes never offers Curley a bribe: he might, for example, actualize a world in which Smedes does not exist or is rigorously honest. But it is also possible that, *no matter what world God actualizes*, there will be some situation in which Curley will act wrongly. Once again, whether or not this is the case depends entirely on Curley. God, omnipotent though he is, can, if he wants Curley to exist as a free agent, only put Curley in situations in which Curley has moral choices. It is up to Curley to decide what to do in such situations. If, in fact, Curley is sufficiently perverse, there will always be some situation in which he does moral wrong. If this is so, Plantinga will say that Curley suffers from *transworld depravity*. If Curley is transworldly depraved, then there is no world God can actualize that contains Curley as a free agent but no moral evil.

Well, we may say, then an all-good God should not create Curley. But, of course, the problem is that Curley may not be unique; indeed, he may be entirely typical. It may be that any free agent that God could create also suffers from transworld depravity. If so, it is impossible for God to actualize a possible world that has free agents and no moral evil. When he, so to speak, looks out at all the possible worlds, he does of course see many in which there are free agents but no moral evil. He can, certainly, bring about all the aspects of such a world apart from the choices of free agents. But whether the world as a whole (including these choices) turns out to be the actual world depends not just on God but on the free agents. If the agents are all transworldly depraved, then even an omnipotent being cannot actualize a world in which they exist and there is no moral evil. Since this is logically possible, it is logically possible that the actual world contains moral evil even though it is created by an omnipotent God.

One further wrinkle. The Free Will Defense shows merely that moral evil may be unavoidable. But a great deal of evil is not due to the free choices of moral agents. There is also the evil produced by impersonal forces of nature (what is called natural evil). Surely, we may think, God could have eliminated all of this sort of evil. It might, of course, be argued that even natural evil is for the sake of greater goods; for example, to stimulate our appreciation of the world's goods or to help form our characters. Such a response would require a quite different line of argument than the Free Will Defense. Plantinga, however, notes that it is also possible to subsume the problem of natural evil under the problem of moral evil. It is logically possible that, contrary to what most people think, all the evil in the world is the result of evil choices by free agents. Evil spirits (devils), for example, could be the cause of all diseases, earthquakes, etc. Or there might be immensely powerful space aliens behind such things. It is, in short, logically possible that all apparently natural evil is moral evil.

Plantinga's free will defense has been generally accepted as a successful response to the claim that God's existence and the existence of evil are logically inconsistent. J. L. Mackie himself acknowledged that "since this defence is formally possible, and its principle involves no real abandonment of our ordinary view of the opposition between good and evil, we can concede that the problem of evil does not, after all, show that the central doctrines of theism are logically inconsistent with one another."[4] Critics have generally retreated to weaker versions of the objection from evil, maintaining that it is the amount or sort of evil in our world that makes God's existence impossible; or, as is more often argued, that the existence (or amount or sort) of evil makes God's existence improbable. Despite continuing controversies on these issues, Plantinga's proof that there is no logical inconsistency in asserting both the existence of God and the existence of evil remains a model of a successful philosophical argument.[5]

THE REASONABLENESS OF CHRISTIAN BELIEF

Christians believe amazing things, things our ordinary experience does not lead us to expect, things that, if true, should lead us to radical transformations of our lives. As Plantinga puts it: "What is allegedly known is (if true) of stunning significance, certainly the most important thing a person could know" (256).[6] Anyone who reflects on the extraordinariness of the Christian message should appreciate the suggestion of Alexander Kinglake (a nineteenth-century British historian) that into the walls of every Christian church should be carved the motto: "Important if true." Those who do not share the Christian faith naturally respond to professions of it by asking for reasons supporting its truth. Plantinga agrees that no generally compelling reasons are forthcoming. That is, Christians can provide no valid arguments for central Christian doctrines that employ only premises any rational non-believer would have to accept. There is no valid case, from generally acceptable premises, for the truth of Christianity.

Many conclude from this that Christians' beliefs are therefore not reasonable.[7] But this, Plantinga points out, is a *non sequitur*. A belief is not unreasonable simply because it is not held on the basis of sound argument (in Plantinga's terminology, because it is a basic belief). Arguments need premises, and Plantinga, like most analytic philosophers,

[4] J. L. Mackie, *The Miracle of Theism*, Oxford: Oxford University Press, 1982, 154.
[5] For a contrary view, see Keith DeRose, "Plantinga, Presumption, Possibility and the Problem of Evil," *Canadian Journal of Philosophy* 21 (1990), 497–512.
[6] Alvin Plantinga, *Warranted Christian Belief*, Oxford: Oxford University Press, 2000, 256. Further references will be given in the text.
[7] Here I am using "reasonable" in the sense of "not violating any epistemic obligation" ("justified" in standard terminology). We will later consider other relevant senses of "reasonable."

accepts a broadly foundationalist picture on which arguments begin from some ultimate premises that are themselves rationally accepted without argument (in Plantinga's terminology, these are properly basic beliefs).[8] To show that fundamental Christian beliefs are unreasonable, the critic will have to show that they are not properly basic.[9]

There are versions of epistemic foundationalism that would readily entail that Christian beliefs are not properly basic. To cite the most important example, classical foundationalism, formulated by Locke and accepted by many other philosophers, maintains that the only properly basic beliefs are those that are self-evident (like basic mathematical truths), incorrigible (like the cogito), or evident to the senses (like my current belief that I'm seated at a desk). But Plantinga readily refutes classical foundationalism. First, there are clear cases of properly basic beliefs (e.g., memories, the belief that the future will be like the past) that are not self-evident, incorrigible, or evident to the senses. Second, the fundamental claim that only beliefs of these three sorts are properly basic is not itself of any of these three sorts; nor does it seem to be derivable from such beliefs. So by its own standards, the thesis of classical foundationalism is not reasonable.

Critics may, of course, try to formulate other, non-classical criteria for properly basic beliefs that will exclude religious beliefs. But Plantinga maintains that this is a vain enterprise, since it is entirely obvious that Christian beliefs can be properly basic. A first case would be that of someone raised in a closed Christian community, who has been inculcated with a deep commitment to the Christian creed and who sees no meaningful alternatives to this commitment. What fault could there possibly be in believing what everything in my life leads me to believe and which I have never had the slightest reason to question? But next suppose that our isolated believer goes into the greater world, say attends a secular university and studies philosophy. Suppose, "she is aware of the objections people have made to Christian belief; she has read and reflected on Freud, Marx, and Nietzsche (not to mention Flew, Mackie, and Nielsen) and the other critics of Christian belief. . . She thinks as carefully

---

[8] Here "foundationalism" refers to an epistemological view that merely rejects the coherentist view that there are no properly basic beliefs and that justification is a matter of mutually consistent, mutually supporting arguments. This is quite different from the philosophical foundationalism, discussed earlier, that requires philosophical arguments from uncontroversial premises for all controversial convictions.

[9] If we reject this foundationalist picture in favor of coherentism, then showing that Christian beliefs are unreasonable would require the very difficult task of showing that they cannot be supported by a set of mutually consistent, mutually supporting arguments.

as she can about these objections and others, but finds them wholly uncompelling" (100). On the other hand, "she has a rich inner spiritual life" that, without providing anything like good arguments for Christian beliefs, makes these beliefs seem "to her enormously more convincing than the complaints of the critics." Clearly, Plantinga says, such a person is not "going contrary to [epistemic] duty in believing as she does" (100–1). She has every right to continue believing what, even in the face of criticism, continues to seem, after full reflection, compellingly true. The simple point is this: surely it is reasonable to believe what seems true to me given the most careful scrutiny and reflection, even if I have no argument for it; the Christian may well believe in this way; therefore, Christian belief can be reasonable.

Of course, this "epistemic right to believe" conveys only what we might call a subjective rationality, and is consistent with the beliefs in question deriving from an objectively disordered (and, in this sense, unreasonable) cognitive apparatus. Those deranged by drugs or psychosis may have an epistemic right to their insane beliefs. It remains, then, for the critic to maintain that religious beliefs are irrational because they derive from malfunctioning cognitive faculties. This, moreover, is precisely what such critics as Marx, Nietzsche, and Freud have maintained. Believers themselves will not find such claims compelling, but the claims may still be objectively right and, if so, religious beliefs are objectively irrational. Is there any way for believers to exclude this possibility?

The question, in Plantinga's terminology, is whether Christian beliefs are *warranted*. Here he is distinguishing warrant from justification, with the latter referring to (subjective) conformity to epistemic obligations and the former to (objective) proper functioning of cognitive faculties. The move from justification to warrant is intended to resolve the Gettier difficulties in defining knowledge. Plantinga initially introduced warrant as meaning "whatever it is that is needed to transform true belief into knowledge" and eventually argued that a belief has warrant only if it is produced by "cognitive faculties that are functioning properly" (153). He further understands "proper function" as a matter of cognitive faculties operating according to a "design plan" that specifies the "way they are *supposed* to work" (154).[10]

---

[10] Plantinga emphasizes that these characterizations should not be taken to mean that our cognitive faculties must be designed by a conscious agent (e.g., God): "I mean, instead, to point to something nearly all of us, theists or not, believe: there is a way in which a human organ or system works when it is working properly . . .; and this way of working is given by its design or design plan" (154).

The critic will claim that Christian beliefs are not warranted, even if they are subjectively justified. This will be so only if the beliefs are produced through something less than the proper functioning of the Christian's cognitive faculties. Is this the case? Only, Plantinga maintains, if Christian beliefs are not true. If these beliefs are true, it is highly likely that they are the result of the proper functioning of our cognitive faculties. Why so? Because there is, according to Christian belief, an all-powerful, all-good God who is intent on redeeming us from our sins and bringing us to salvation precisely through our belief in the core truths of Christianity. It follows that God intends "that we be able to be aware of these truths." Given this, Plantinga argues, "the natural thing to think is that the cognitive processes that do indeed produce belief in the central elements of the Christian faith are aimed by their designer at producing that belief" (285). But, if our cognitive processes are designed to produce such beliefs, then, when they do produce them, they are functioning properly and the beliefs they produce are warranted.

It follows that Christian beliefs are, in all probability, warranted if they are true (and it can be correspondingly argued that they are not warranted if they are not true). But this means that the question of the rationality of Christian belief is not separable from the question of its truth. Critics cannot, as they so often do, claim that Christian beliefs are unwarranted without also claiming that they are false. Christianity is true if and only if it's warranted. Therefore, there is no room for the standard skeptical claim: "I'm not saying whether Christianity is true or not, just that belief in it isn't warranted." Christianity cannot be challenged epistemologically – by questioning its rationality – but only metaphysically (or theologically) – by questioning its truth. Neither in terms of (subjective) justification nor (objective) warrant is there any case against the rationality of Christian belief. Even without any evidence or proof of their beliefs, Christians can be entirely secure that their beliefs are justified and warranted.

Many readers of Plantinga, although impressed by the subtlety and rigor of his discussion, remain convinced that there must be some sort of sleight-of-hand going on. As noted at the outset, Christians do believe quite amazing things – things many would rejoice to be able to believe, but that they see as too uncertain, too controversial to believe without evidence. How then can we sensibly agree that Christians in no way offend against standards of rationality when they believe such things without evidence or proof? Of course, there are no arguments per se in such a reaction, and those that immediately spring to mind are not easy to formulate effectively. Often, for example, people maintain that

Plantinga's position allows any belief at all, no matter how bizarre, to be properly basic. If Christian beliefs are properly basic, then why, to cite the example that became famous, isn't the belief (à la Charlie Brown) that there is a Great Pumpkin who gives candy to children on Halloween also properly basic? But, as Plantinga points out, his claim that Christian beliefs are properly basic does not imply that any other beliefs are properly basic: "This objection, of course, is plainly false. To recognize that *some* kind of beliefs are properly basic ... doesn't for a moment commit one to thinking all *other* kinds are" (344). The fact that Christians regard their beliefs as properly basic does not logically require them to accept belief in the Great Pumpkin as properly basic.

Critics are likely to respond that the above formulation does not do their point justice. Michael Martin, for example, agrees that the Christian is not committed to accepting just any belief as properly basic but still maintains that those holding bizarre beliefs (e.g., voodooists) can just as legitimately as the Christian maintain that their beliefs are properly basic.[11] Plantinga calls this objection "Son of Great Pumpkin." Following his response to it will help us appreciate both the nature of Plantinga's epistemology of religious belief and the complexity of the issues it raises.

As Plantinga understands it, we can formulate Martin's argument as follows:[12]

(1) If Christians can legitimately claim that their fundamental beliefs are properly basic, then voodooists could legitimately claim that their fundamental beliefs are properly basic.
(2) Voodooists cannot legitimately claim that their fundamental beliefs are properly basic.
(3) Therefore, Christians cannot legitimately claim that their fundamental beliefs are properly basic.

Following Plantinga, we note that "properly basic" may refer either to justification or to warrant. If it refers to justification, then the problem is that premise (2) is false: "obviously the voodooists could be within their intellectual rights in thinking what they do think (if only by virtue of cognitive malfunction); hence they could be justified" (346). So if the objection is to be sound, we must take it to be referring to warrant. But in addition to this specification, we need to know what is meant by "legitimately claim." "There seem," Plantinga says, "to be three salient

---

[11] Michael Martin, *Atheism: A Philosophical Justification*, Philadelphia: Temple University Press, 1990.
[12] I've made some non-essential changes in Plantinga's formulation to make it consistent with the terminology we have been using.

possibilities: claim *truthfully*, claim *justifiably*, and claim *warrantedly*" (346). If "legitimately claim" is taken to mean "truthfully claim," then premise (1) fails to be true. For it may be true that Christian beliefs are warranted whereas voodoo beliefs are not (e.g., our cognitive faculties may be designed to lead to basic belief in the Christian God but not in fundamental voodoo tenets). If so, the antecedent of (1) can be true and the consequent false; hence (1) is false. If "legitimately claim" means merely "justifiably claim," then, as we have seen above, (2) will be false, since voodooists can be within their intellectual rights in claiming that their beliefs are properly basic. So, for the argument to work, we must take "legitimately claim" to mean "warrantedly claim."

Reformulating the argument in line with the preceding paragraph, we get:

(1) If Christians can warrantedly claim that their fundamental beliefs are properly basic with regard to warrant, then voodooists could warrantedly claim that their fundamental beliefs are properly basic with regard to warrant.
(2) Voodooists cannot warrantedly claim that their fundamental beliefs are properly basic with regard to warrant.
(3) Therefore, Christians cannot warrantedly claim that their fundamental beliefs are properly basic with regard to warrant.

But, Plantinga points out, it is entirely possible that Christian beliefs be true and arrived at via the reliable processes of, say, an innate *sensus divinitatis*, whereas voodoo beliefs are false and arrived at by faulty cognitive processes. If so, the antecedent of (1) will be true and the consequent false; this possibility shows that premise (1) is false, so the argument fails.

Once again, critics may feel that Plantinga has not refuted their *real* point, which has been obscured by the formulation imposed on it. Specifically, Plantinga has taken the objection to be that the claims made on behalf of Christian belief are not legitimate. But perhaps the point is rather that any belief could be defended as legitimate by an argument similar to that which Plantinga has used to defend Christian belief. This wouldn't mean that Christian belief was illegitimate, but it would show that its legitimacy gives it no advantage over any other belief. As Plantinga points out, even this does not quite make the critic's point, since there are some beliefs that could not be defended in the way he defends Christian beliefs. This is obviously true of the belief that no beliefs have warrant and also, Plantinga maintains, of other beliefs that raise doubts about our cognitive faculties, such as Humean skepticism or philosophical naturalism. He does, however, concede finally that the critic might well be correct with regard to at least a certain class of religious beliefs. In particular, it would seem that apologists for many rivals of Christian belief could, following Plantinga's approach, construct a model of proper belief formation that, given the truth of their beliefs, would make it highly probable that these beliefs are warranted. "Probably," Plantinga concedes, "something like that is true for the other theistic religions: Judaism, Islam, some forms of Hinduism, some forms of Buddhism, some forms of American Indian religion" (350).

It seems, then, that what Plantinga has provided is not merely a defense of Christianity (in most of its sectarian varieties) but a defense of virtually any religion that has a strong (even if unargued for) sense of the truth of its fundamental doctrines and supports a claim that a powerful being has appropriately designed our cognitive capacities. To make the point vivid, suppose an epistemologist with all Plantinga's knowledge, skill, and subtlety, committed not to Reformed Christianity but to a core set of conservative Islamic doctrines, writes a book titled *Warranted Islamic Belief.* This book is identical with Plantinga's *Warranted Christian Belief,* except that all references to Christian faith, theology, and practices are replaced by corresponding references to the writer's Islamic sect. It is so successful that similar volumes (from other hands) follow, including *Warranted Roman Catholic Belief, Warranted Hindu Belief,* and perhaps eventually even *Warranted Jehovah's Witnesses Belief* and *Warranted Aztec Belief.* Such texts would provide precisely the defense of their preferred beliefs that Plantinga's provides of the standard core of Christian beliefs. So to the extent that Plantinga's book supports the warrant of Christianity, these books would support the warrant of, for example, conservative Islamic views on the status of women, Catholic views on papal infallibility, and perhaps even Jehovah's Witnesses' views on blood transfusions and Aztec views on the need for human sacrifice.

But why should any of this bother Plantinga or other Christians who rely on his defense? They can admit that rival beliefs are warranted and still reject them as false, given their own commitment to Christianity, which they are entirely entitled to claim is both warranted and true. What harm is there in admitting that false beliefs can be warranted? Maybe what is obvious (to us) is that the beliefs are false, not that they're unwarranted. On the other hand, Christians who maintain that any of these rival beliefs are unwarranted cannot consistently assert that their own beliefs are warranted in virtue of Plantinga's argument.

In any case, what is most questionable about Plantinga's defense of Christianity is his usual assumption that Christians find their beliefs "obviously," "clearly," or "compellingly" true. At one point, having repeated this characterization, he notes its idealized nature. Most of the language in the main text is typically robust: "For the person with faith (at least in the paradigmatic instances), the great things of the gospel seem clearly true, obvious, compelling. She finds herself convinced – just as she does in the case of clear memory beliefs or her belief in elementary truths of arithmetic" (264). But the parenthetical qualification raises a question that Plantinga addresses in a crucial footnote to the passage:

Again, in the paradigmatic cases; but of course the fact is the conviction and belief involved in faith come in all degrees of firmness. As Calvin puts it, "in the believing mind certainty is mixed with doubt" and "we are troubled on all sides by the agitation of unbelief." In typical cases, therefore, as opposed to paradigmatic cases, degree of belief will be less than maximal. Furthermore, degree of belief, on the part of the person who has faith, typically varies from time to time, from circumstance to circumstance. (264, n.43)

What does Plantinga's defense of the rationality of belief do for these typical cases of belief "mixed with doubt" and "troubled on all sides by the agitation of unbelief"? Suppose, for example, I occasionally feel a compelling conviction that "the great things of the gospels" are true, but also occasionally experience them as claims I hope are true but have no real confidence in, and most often view them with a complex mixture of belief and doubt. In such a situation – which is surely very common – belief is not a matter of confidently asserting what is utterly clear to me. In terms of certainty, there is, in contrast to Plantinga's paradigmatic case, little similarity to clear memories or self-evident mathematical truths. Nor is our typical believer's epistemic situation one that could not be improved by the support of philosophical or historical arguments from plausible premises. There may well be historical facts and even metaphysical principle of which the believer is more certain than the articles of faith. For such cases, it's hard to see how Plantinga could claim that the believer's faith is "obviously" justified. Particularly given the importance of the claims, it might well seem, even to the believer, that it would be better to withhold belief until there is greater certainty. But even for those who decide that belief is appropriate, faith will, contrary to the paradigmatic cases, be something like a "leap in the dark" (263).

The point is not that the typical believer who remains steadfast despite doubts is necessarily irrational in doing so. There are no decisive criteria for how much doubt is consistent with rational belief or for how strong convictions ought to be in matters of supreme importance. But it is surely not implausible to think that many believers are allowing hope to get the better of epistemic responsibility or that many who do believe rationally should still hold their faith with epistemic "fear and trembling." Plantinga's defense shows that the fully confident, paradigmatic believer can be unperturbed by the skeptic's call for evidence and argument. Showing that belief can, in an ideal case, be immune to skeptical objections does not show that believers in general should not be moved by such objections.

Nonetheless, philosophical critics of religion have lessons to learn from Plantinga's defense. He does make a strong case for the claim that religious belief per se, even in full-blooded doctrinal form, need not be epistemically deficient. The paradigmatic believer may well be immune to the standard evidentialist objections. Plantinga's defense against such objections turns out to be very like his free will defense: against critics who maintain that basic Christian belief of any sort is irrational, it establishes the logical possibility of rational basic Christian belief.[13] What the critic can still maintain is that Plantinga's defense may well not protect from epistemic criticism those, like most of us, whose belief is mixed with doubt. But, although the faith of less than paradigmatic believers is open to skeptical objections, such believers may still have evidence and arguments that make it rational for them to assert at least some of their religious beliefs. Such "real-world" faith is precarious and engaged in intellectual and spiritual inquiries similar to those of non-believers who are open to the possibility of attaining religious truth.

It is also important to note that the paradigmatic religious belief needed to profit from Plantinga's defense is not achieved simply by being strongly certain about what one believes. Such strength of belief, as Plantinga makes clear, must also be maintained in the light of a careful and honest examination of the modern case against belief, insofar as the believer is (or should be) aware of it. A dogmatist who refuses serious engagement with alternatives and challenges is not a paradigmatic believer. Nor is paradigmatic belief achieved merely by wholeheartedly committing oneself to a life of faith. It is one thing to have made a pragmatic decision to live as if I am certain, quite another to enjoy the reality of such certitude. Finally, those who have paradigmatically certain belief about generic theistic beliefs may be far less certain about core Christian beliefs and even less certain about the beliefs (transubstantiation, the nature of Church authority, etc.) that

---

[13] Assuming that there are at least some believers who come close to Plantinga's paradigm, it also establishes the instantiation of this possibility, at least in a few cases.

divide Christians into distinct sects. Paradigms of theistic belief may be fairly common, but paradigms of Christian or still more of, say, Roman Catholic belief are likely to be far less so.

By focusing on the uncommon paradigmatic cases, Plantinga makes a strong case in principle against the strong claim that Christian belief cannot be rational. But this strategy also leaves a misleading impression of polarization between believers and non-believers. There is a world of difference between Plantinga's idealized believers, combining robust faith with honest and subtle reflection on skeptical challenges, and dogmatic non-believers (of whom Plantinga finds all too many actual examples), who think any form of religious commitment is irrational. But between these extremes – in what I would call the domain of honest inquiry – are a large and particularly important group of both believers and non-believers whose main concerns Plantinga does not address.

CONCLUSIONS

Plantinga's transformation of the philosophy of religion makes fully explicit the role of convictions in philosophical inquiry. Convictions are basic beliefs with two distinctive features. First, unlike standard examples of basic beliefs, they are neither self-evident (obvious to anyone who understands them) nor incorrigible reports of inner experience but substantive, controversial claims that are central in our conceptions of ourselves and have a guiding role in our lives. Second, although they are basic beliefs and so not justified by evidence or argument in any ordinary sense, our commitment to them is not just a matter of their seeming obviously true when we think about them. Rather, they strike us as arising naturally out of experiences we have had, have maintained themselves in the face of various challenges, and are central for our way of life. Philosophy has often, especially since Descartes and Locke, seen itself as the critic or arbiter of such convictions, demanding that their proponents give good reasons for their truth or else, on pain of intellectual irresponsibility, withdraw assent from them. Plantinga refutes this standard view by showing that the only plausible defenses of it are based on dubious epistemological assumptions, such as classical foundationalism. I think that he does, in fact, establish in principle the point that convictions can be epistemically in order independent of philosophical scrutiny – and, more relevantly, that, even when they require philosophical defense against potential defeaters, they need not require positive philosophical justification.

Plantinga's position does not depend on unique features of religious belief or on the fact that he himself is a committed Christian. It requires only that we give up traditional foundationalist claims that convictions require grounding in a narrow range of basic truths that are self-evident or otherwise philosophically impeccable. Without these claims, a wide variety of convictions can be readily recognized as properly basic. Our next three chapters look at further examples of the role such convictions play in philosophical discussions.

CHAPTER 6

Materialism and compatibilism: two dogmas of analytic philosophy?

Some positions widely held by analytic philosophers seem obviously false. Materialism, for example, seems to deny our overwhelming sense that our conscious experiences have qualitative features (what they are like for us) that make them something beyond quantifiable states and events in our brains and nervous systems. Likewise, compatibilism seems to deny the obvious fact that we are free in the sense of not being determined by external causes to act as we do. The primary source of both puzzling doctrines is science. We incline towards materialism because scientific accounts seem to require that consciousness be nothing beyond matter. Given a complete set of the relevant scientific laws, it would seem that we could derive every truth about consciousness. We can maintain the obvious truth that we are conscious, but only by agreeing that, despite our distinctively qualitative experience of consciousness, it is in the end nothing beyond quantitative material processes.

Science is likewise the source of our backing away from our common-sense view of freedom. There seems to be good reason to think that scientific laws determine everything about us, including our free actions. Given a complete set of scientific laws, it would seem that we could derive every truth about our free actions. In order to save the apparently obvious truth that we are free, it seems we must accept the implausible idea that freedom can somehow be compatible with complete scientific determinism. In either case, however, we could equally respond by simply denying that science provides a complete account of consciousness or freedom. The fact that analytic philosophers so often tend to embrace materialism and compatibilism shows the strength of their commitment to the completeness of scientific accounts.

In recent years, this commitment has been challenged by powerful philosophical arguments against both materialism and compatibilism. There are now serious cases for dualism (the claim that consciousness is something beyond its material correlates) and for libertarianism (the claim that free actions cannot be caused). In this chapter, I discuss David Chalmers' zombie argument against materialism and Peter van Inwagen's consequence argument against compatibilism. As in our first three case studies, we will reflect on the role of argument and intuition, but also, as in our previous case study on Plantinga, on the role of pre-philosophical convictions.

NAGEL AND THE CHALLENGE TO MATERIALISM

One of the earliest challenges to materialist orthodoxy was Thomas Nagel's article, "What Is It Like to Be a Bat?," which opened by accusing contemporary philosophers of giving consciousness "little attention" or, when they did discuss it, getting "it obviously wrong" (435).[1] What materialist philosophers missed about consciousness was, according to Nagel, its "most important and characteristic feature." This is its "subjective character," the fact that "an organism has conscious mental states if and only if there is something that it is like to *be* that organism – something that it is like *for* the organism" (436). Trying to understand consciousness entirely through the physical categories of natural science, philosophers exclude this subjective character. This is because subjectivity (Nagel even uses the Sartrean language of "the *pour-soi*") "is essentially connected with a single point of view," which "an objective, physical theory will abandon" (437) in its insistence on what Nagel later called a "view from nowhere."

Nagel uses the bat to show that the experiences of an organism are accessible only to those who are able to share its perceptual point of view. To the extent that bats perceive the world through a system of echo-location quite dissimilar from our seeing or hearing, we can, in principle, form no conception of what their experience is like for them; we quite literally can have no idea of what it is like to be a bat. In view of this, Nagel says, it is hard to see how there can be an objective, physical account of the bat's experience as such. "If the facts of experience – facts about what it is like for the experiencing organism – are accessible from only one point of view, then it is a mystery how the true character of experiences could be revealed in the physical operation of that organism," since "the physical operation" is, by definition, something that "can be

---

[1] Thomas Nagel, "What Is It Like to Be a Bat?," *The Philosophical Review* 83 (1974), 435–50, 435. Further references will be given in the text.

observed and understood from many points of view and by individuals with differing perceptual systems" (442). The usual scientific strategy – for example, in studying the optics of the rainbow or the neurophysiology of vision – is to eliminate subjective elements to arrive at an entirely objective reality. But when our intended "object" is subjective experience itself, this strategy makes no sense: "If the subjective character of experience is fully comprehensible only from one point of view, then any shift to greater objectivity – that is, less attachment to a specific viewpoint – does not take us nearer to the real nature of the phenomenon: it takes us farther away from it" (444–5).

Nagel is far from proving that there can be no complete physical explanation of consciousness or even that conscious experiences are not identical to physical states or processes. As Jaegwon Kim has recently noted, there is not sufficient clarity in Nagel's key concepts to sustain solid conclusions about the nature of subjectivity: "Nagel does not explain . . . in what sense phenomenal experience is 'subjective', and in what sense and why, a single 'point of view' is associated with each subjective phenomenon – or indeed what a 'point of view' really is."[2] Nor, correspondingly, is it clear just how subjectivity would contrast with or exclude objectivity.

Kim's comment is, as he says, more a remark about the "confusing way" philosophers often use these terms than a specific criticism of Nagel. And Nagel himself emphasizes that firm conclusions about whether consciousness is ultimately physical will have to await a better understanding of what such a claim might mean. "At the present time the status of physicalism is similar to that which the hypothesis that matter is energy would have had if uttered by a pre-Socratic philosopher. We do not have the beginning of a conception of how it might be true" (447). This does not mean we should reject the claim that consciousness is physical: "it would be a mistake to conclude that physicalism must be false" (446); and Nagel even allows for the possibility that we could have evidence that consciousness is physical even if we don't "really understand" what this would mean (448). The ultimate point of Nagel's seminal article is not to refute the physicalist reduction of the mental to the physical but to remind us that any such reduction will have to be carried out with full recognition of the distinctively subjective nature of our experience.

Nagel's animadversions made a strong impression, but most analytic philosophers, like Nagel himself, were reluctant to challenge the

---

[2] Jaegwon Kim, "The Mind-Body Problem at Century's Turn," in Brian Leiter (ed.), *The Future for Philosophy*, Oxford: Oxford University Press, 2004, 146.

ontological priority of natural science and argue that the claims of the mental showed the incompleteness of materialist accounts of the mind. Recently, however, a good number of philosophers have overcome this reluctance and have offered powerful arguments against physicalism (materialism)[3] that have attracted a great deal of attention. We will look carefully at David Chalmers' formulation of the zombie argument.

CHALMERS AND THE ZOMBIE ARGUMENT

Chalmers' zombie argument is a key element in the general argument against materialism that he develops in *The Conscious Mind*.[4] He states the general argument as follows:

1. In our world, there are conscious experiences.
2. There is a logically possible world physically identical to ours, in which the positive facts about consciousness in our world do not hold.
3. Therefore, facts about consciousness are further facts about our world, over and above the physical facts.
4. So materialism is false. (123)

By materialism Chalmers means "the doctrine that the physical facts about the world exhaust all the facts, in that every positive fact is entailed by the physical facts" (124).[5] Earlier, he explains physical facts as those expressed in terms of physical properties, which he in turn understands as "the fundamental properties that are invoked in a complete theory of physics" (33). He cites as examples of such properties "mass, charge, spatio-temporal position" and, in general, the properties of whatever physics winds up taking as its fundamental entities. He emphasizes that his use of "physical" applies only to "fundamental" ("micro-physical" or "low-level") properties, not to "such high-level properties as juiciness,

---

[3] I will use "materialism" and "physicalism" interchangeably.
[4] David Chalmers, *The Conscious Mind*, Oxford: Oxford University Press, 1996. References will be given in the text. Although Chalmers has offered later, more refined versions of the argument, this version has been most influential. A zombie argument was formulated as early as 1974 by Robert Kirk. See, for example, his "Zombies v. Materialists," *Proceedings of the Aristotelian Society*, Supplementary Vol. 48 (1974), 135–52.
[5] Why does Chalmers not simply say that for materialism "every fact [not just every positive fact] is entailed by the physical facts"? Because the positive physical facts alone might not exclude the existence of entirely non-physical things (angels, immaterial ectoplasm). Excluding such non-physical things would then require a further materialist assertion that the physical facts are all the facts there are. Since Chalmers does not claim that there are separate immaterial things (that is, he is not a substance-dualist), his denial of materialism need not entail that non-physical substances exist. Therefore, the materialism that his dualism rejects need not be taken to deny the existence of non-physical substances.

lumpiness, [or] giraffehood." He also notes that "if physics changes radically, the relevant class of properties may be quite different" from those of current physics. But this, he says, will not affect his argument against materialism (33).

Given this definition of materialism, we can flesh out the end of Chalmers' argument:

1. In our world, there are conscious experiences.
2. There is a logically possible world physically identical to ours, in which the positive facts about consciousness in our world do not hold.
3. Therefore, facts about consciousness are further facts about our world, over and above the physical facts.
4. If materialism is true, there are no further facts about our world, over and above the physical facts.
5. Therefore, materialism is not true.

Premise 1 is beyond dispute, as long as it means merely that thoughts, feelings, perceptions, etc. exist, without assuming whether they are physical or not. Premise 2 says that a world exactly like ours (that is, physically identical to ours) but without consciousness is logically possible. By this Chalmers means that we can conceive of such a world; that is, we can describe the world without falling into contradiction (asserting or implying both p and ~p).

The soundness of the argument turns on premise 2, which can also be stated in terms of the notion, central to much recent philosophical discussion, of *supervenience*. One property (or set of properties) B is said to supervene on another property (or set of properties) A when the occurrence of A brings with it the occurrence of B. So, for example, the mathematical property of *being rectangular* supervenes on the property of *being a square*; similarly, in a gas, the physical property of having a specific temperature supervenes on the physical properties of having a specific pressure and a specific volume. In the first case, the supervenience is logical (B follows A in virtue of logical laws), in the second the supervenience is natural (B follows A in virtue of laws of nature). There is strong scientific evidence that the mental naturally supervenes on the physical. Premise 2, however, implies that the mental does not logically supervene on the physical.

The zombie argument is one of Chalmers' main ways of making a case for premise 2.[6] He defines a zombie as "someone or something physically

---

[6] Other arguments for (2) include the inverted spectrum argument and the knowledge argument, made famous by Frank Jackson.

identical to me (or to any other conscious being), but lacking conscious experiences altogether" (94). A zombie so defined may engage in mental activities or be in mental states in what Chalmers calls a purely "psychological" sense. Here "psychological" refers to any mental activities or states that do not of themselves involve conscious experience, merely the instantiation of certain structures or the performance of certain functions.[7] If, for example, seeing A is defined in terms of the impingement of photons on the retina, etc., then seeing is a structural psychological state. If believing p is defined (very roughly) as a tendency to act, in appropriate circumstances, as if p is true, then believing p is a functional psychological state. These are not, however, in Chalmers' terminology, *phenomenal* states: not states that involve consciousness. There may be disputes about just what should be understood as psychological as opposed to phenomenal, and Chalmers allows that most of what we include in the domain of the mental has aspects of both. There are, for example, purely psychological aspects of thinking, paying attention, and perceiving; that is, aspects of these mental activities that can be defined in structural or functional terms. But there are also aspects of mental life (including aspects of thinking, paying attention, and perceiving as they occur in us) that are phenomenal. Zombies have no mental life in this sense.

Scientific efforts to explain the psychological aspects of consciousness deal with what Chalmers calls the "easy problems" – not because they are simple or trivial but because they require only the sort of structural and functional models that have already been successfully developed by neuroscientists. The "hard problem" is to explain phenomenal consciousness. On Chalmers' view, the problem is distinctively hard because it will not yield to resources continuous with current neuroscience but will require a whole new level of scientific theorizing, one that accepts phenomenal consciousness (or some other phenomenal reality from which consciousness can be derived) as fundamental and discovers the laws that connect it to the physical world. A solution to the hard problem will, he maintains, explain why zombies are not naturally possible but merely logically possible.

If zombies are logically possible, then the mental does not logically supervene on the physical and premise 2 is true: there is a possible world physically identical to ours but without consciousness. Chalmers agrees

---

[7] "Psychological," accordingly, connotes the third-person standpoint of an objective, scientific psychology.

that, in all likelihood, zombies are not physically possible. It is very probable that there are natural laws connecting physical states and mental states in virtue of which no being could in fact have my exact physical constitution and not be conscious. Accordingly, Chalmers agrees that consciousness naturally supervenes on the physical. His claim is just that such connections are not logically necessary, so that zombies are logically possible and premise 2 is true.

How do we know that zombies are logically possible? According to Chalmers, the possibility is "obvious," just like, he says, the possibility of a mile-high unicycle. Of the possibility of the unicycle he says, "It just seems obvious . . . the description certainly appears to be coherent." If someone suggests that the notion is not logically possible, "there is little we can say, except to repeat the description and assert its obvious coherence. It seems quite clear that there is no hidden contradiction lurking in the description." "I confess," he goes on to say, "that the logical possibility of zombies seems equally obvious to me" (96). Chalmers agrees that "in some ways an assertion of this possibility comes down to a brute intuition," but it seems to him that "almost everybody . . . is capable of conceiving of this possibility" (96). The burden of proof, accordingly, should lie on those who claim (usually, he says, to save a philosophical theory) that zombies are not logically possible.

Chalmers goes even further to claim that, apart from his (and others') beliefs about this case, "in general, a certain burden of proof lies on those who claim that a given description is logically *impossible*." There is, he says, "a natural assumption in favor of logical possibility," unless there is a "reasonable analysis of the terms in question" that suggests a notion is contradictory (96). So, even if we allow, as we should, that our belief in the possibility of zombies could turn out to be wrong, we can appeal to the failure of anyone to meet the challenge of proving that zombies are not possible.

Chalmers also sees a role for certain "indirect arguments, appealing to what we know about the phenomenon in question and the way we think about hypothetical cases involving these phenomena" (96). In the unicycle case, for example, we might "describe a series of unicycles, each bigger than the last" or imagine that everything around me, including my unicycle, suddenly became a thousand times larger.

In the zombie case, Chalmers puts forward indirect arguments based on hypothetical examples of "nonstandard realizations" of psychological (functional) properties. We can imagine, for example, that the structure of my brain and central nervous system is realized in a different material form, say silicon-based rather than carbon-based chemicals. More radically, we might imagine that this structure is realized on a huge macroscopic scale, by, for example, the population of a large country such as China constructing a mega-isomorph of my brain by having one person simulate the behavior of each of my neurons. Chalmers notes that there has been controversy over whether such non-standard realizations would be conscious. Would, for example, there be a "group mind" that emerged from the Chinese simulation of my brain? Regardless of what we might conclude about this, Chalmers' claim is that it seems obvious that those who defend a negative answer are, at least, "expressing a coherent possibility." If so, consciousness is not supervenient on non-standard physical structures. But then why think that it is supervenient on standard biochemical structures? It follows that a zombie is logically possible.

As Chalmers admits, these "indirect arguments" are "in a sense . . . all appeals to intuition" (97). Agreeing that a non-standard realization of my brain could occur without consciousness seems as much a matter of brute insight as is agreeing that zombies are possible. But Chalmers maintains that the non-standard realizations have the value of "eliminating a source of conceptual confusion." Because we so closely associate the standard biochemistry of our brains with consciousness, it is easy to assume that there is a conceptual connection between them, that I could not, logically, have the neural structures I do without being conscious. Thinking about non-standard cases makes it easier to see that physical structure does not logically require consciousness.

Given our reflections in chapter 4 about intuition, we should not assume that Chalmers' endorsement of the intuition that zombies are possible involves an appeal to a special philosophical faculty that needs prior certification. Nor should we assume that it is a mere intellectual seeming that needs further support to be a fully-fledged properly basic belief. It is a belief Chalmers presents as entirely obvious and so proper to hold. Like almost any belief, it might turn out to be wrong, but that mere possibility is no reason to deny it cognitive authority. Our belief that there could be a zombie is, Chalmers says, like our belief that there could be a mile-high unicycle: seen as true simply by reflecting on the proposition it asserts.

MATERIALIST RESPONSES: DENYING
THE ZOMBIE INTUITION

The zombie argument (or similar arguments) has convinced quite a few philosophers. Of those who don't accept it, a few deny the zombie intuition (premise 2); most, however, accept the intuition but say that, even with it, the argument does not prove its conclusion (is not logically valid). Those who deny the intuition typically agree that the claim *seems* obvious. It's not that they simply don't see what he's getting at, a case of "Can't you just see that the witness is lying?" versus "No, she seems entirely sincere to me." They do not claim that they can detect contradictions in the idea of a zombie, nor do they deny that they themselves feel the force of the suggestion that zombies are logically possible. Even Daniel Dennett, the most vehement critic of the zombie intuition (or, as he calls it, the "Zombic hunch"), says "I can feel the tug as well as anybody else."[8] He agrees that (phenomenologically, so to speak) zombies *seem* to be logically possible, just as, over three hundred years after Galileo, the sun still *seems* to move around the earth. But, he maintains, the seeming is illusory. In particular, he anticipates

a day when philosophers and scientists and laypeople will chuckle over the fossil traces of our earlier bafflement about consciousness: "It still *seems* [they will say] as if these mechanistic theories of consciousness leave something out, but of course that's an illusion. They do in fact explain everything about consciousness that needs explanation." (43)

It seems clear that Dennett and other critics in the first group (e.g., John Perry and Thomas Nagel) reject the zombie intuition because they accept materialism. They in effect argue: if zombies are possible, then materialism is false; but materialism is true, so zombies are not possible. The question we need to ask is, why do they hold materialism to begin with? Do they have convincing philosophical arguments for it or do they hold it as a pre-philosophical conviction?

As a matter of fact these critics do offer two sorts of arguments for materialism. One, suggested by Dennett in the discussion cited above, is an appeal to the (anticipated) explanatory success of science. Dennett cites in particular the success of computer models of mind, in virtue of which "we are quite certain that a naturalistic, mechanistic explanation of consciousness is not just possible; it is fast becoming actual." In the face of this explanatory success, he maintains, the force of the long-standing intuitions about the irreducibility of the mind will fade away: "If you are patient and open-minded, it will pass" (43). But, even supposing we have reason to think that there will someday be a naturalistic explanation for consciousness (e.g., via an exact computer simulation of the mind), why

---

[8] Daniel Dennett, "The Zombic Hunch: Extinction of an Intuition?," in A. O'Hear (ed.), *Philosophy at the New Millennium*, Cambridge: Cambridge University Press, 2001, 37. Further references in text.

should we think that this explanation will prove that consciousness *logically* supervenes on matter? Science explains on the basis of logically contingent laws, so how could a scientific explanation of consciousness show anything more than that consciousness *nomologically* supervenes on matter? What we have reason to believe is that science itself could well establish a complete correlation between the physical and the mental, but this does not imply a logical reduction of the one to the other.

The second, and more impressive, argument for materialism comes not from the fact that science may be able to explain the mental, but from the fact that it will in all likelihood be able to explain all material facts. This is a powerful argument because we have every reason to think that mental states and events cause (and hence explain) many aspects of the material world. When, to use John Perry's example, I eat a chocolate chip cookie, the taste sensation causes me to say, "Boy, was that good!" This is a clear case of a mental event (my feeling of taste) producing a material effect (the production of sounds). But we have excellent reason to believe that there is (or will eventually be) a complete scientific explanation, in purely materialistic terms, of my utterance "Boy, was that good!" Unless my taste of the cookie is identical with (or at least logically supervenient on) the material causes that produce my utterance, there is no way of understanding how it can cause that utterance.[9] It seems that the only way around this argument is to deny that the mental has causal effects and accept epiphenomenalism: the view that consciousness exists but has no causal role in the world.

Responding to this suggestion, Chalmers agrees that his position leads to a picture that "looks *something* like epiphenomenalism" but notes that "the very nature of causation is quite mysterious, and it is possible that when causation is better understood we will be in a position to understand a subtle way in which conscious experience may be causally relevant" (150).[10] This response seems disappointingly obscurantist, appealing to the "mysterious" nature of causation and the corresponding possibility that we may one day develop an understanding of causation that will allow the mental to be causally relevant. But a similar appeal to mystery is implicit in his critics' rejection of the zombie intuition.

[9] Unless we invoke the ad hoc assumption of causal overdetermination, based on the possibility that my utterance has two separate causes, each sufficient for its occurrence.

[10] In a similar vein, he also suggests that our intuitions against epiphenomenalism may not "translate into compelling arguments" so that "it may turn out the sort of epiphenomenalism this position implies is only counterintuitive, and that ultimately a degree of epiphenomenalism can be accepted" (150–1).

For example, Thomas Nagel, writing almost twenty-five years after "What Is It Like to Be a Bat?," invokes, like Perry, the causal role of the mental in support of physicalism (materialism): "mental phenomena . . . occupy causal roles, and it has been one of the strongest arguments for some kind of physicalism that those roles may prove upon investigation to be occupied by organic [and therefore physical] processes."[11] But how can he reconcile this conclusion with what he admits is "the powerful intuition" that zombies are possible? The only course, he says, is to maintain that, given the case for physicalism, "the powerful intuition that it is conceivable that an intact and normally functioning physical human being could be a completely unconscious zombie is an illusion – due to the limitations of our understanding." But he emphasizes that "those limitations are real." It is not merely, as Dennett suggests, that we need to discard antiquated modes of thought in favor of what science has discovered. Rather, "we do not at present possess the conceptual equipment to understand how subjective and physical features could be both essential aspects of a single entity or process" (342). Accordingly, Nagel says, "what we need is not a reductionist or eliminative revision but an expansionist one." The expanded concept of mind will be one that "will permit subjective points of view to have an objective physical character *in themselves*." Our current concept of the mind has "no room for a necessary connection with physiology." What we need is a "successor concept of mind which will both preserve the essential features of the original and be open to the discovery of such connections" (343).[12]

Nagel conjectures that, in terms of such a concept, mental states would "have a tripartite essence – phenomenological, functional, and physiological." Our problem, of course, is that we currently cannot conceive of how all three of these elements could be essential for the mind. As things now seem to us, the physiological/functional elements are clearly separable from the phenomenological: this is the heart of the intuition that zombies are possible. But, given the causal case for materialism, this intuition must be wrong; the fact that we have it proves only that we need a more adequate conception of the mind. Nagel's appeal to a possible new concept of the mind is on a par with Chalmers' appeal to a possible new concept of causation. In both cases we have an

---

[11] Thomas Nagel, "Conceiving the Impossible and the Mind-Body Problem," *Philosophy* 73 (1998), 342. Further citations given in text.
[12] Nagel had earlier suggested this line of thought at the end of "What Is It Like to Be a Bat?"

argument *ex mysterio*, and there is no more reason to invoke mystery regarding the mind than there is to invoke it regarding causation.

As Nagel points out, there are intuitions so strong that it makes no sense to talk of overcoming them. No future developments in science could lead us to give up our belief that the number 379 has no biological parents. The zombie intuition is not that compelling. But there is no reason to think that the currently "inconceivable possibility" that the mind is physical is any less bizarre and mysterious than Chalmers' suggestion that, even given a complete physicalist explanation of the world, there is room for a causal role for the irreducibly mental. In both cases there is an appeal to a possibility that we literally cannot conceive.

There is, in short, no compelling case for materialism that those who accept the logical validity of the zombie argument can use to counter decisively the force of the zombie intuition. They can show that maintaining the zombie intuition and avoiding epiphenomenalism requires a commitment to a mysterious future change in how we conceive of causation. But their own argument commits them to a similar mysterious change in our concept of consciousness. Why prefer one mystery to the other? Simply in terms of the intellectual intuitions involved, it is hard to see why anyone would insist on the unrevisability of our concept of consciousness rather than our concept of causation, or vice versa. It would make more sense to conclude that we are in no position to decide between materialism and anti-materialism. We might not expect Dennett *et al.* to accept Colin McGinn's suggestion that the human mind is incapable, in principle, of understanding the relation of mind and body.[13] But we would expect them to acknowledge that we are, at least at present, unable to understand the relation and so become agnostic in the debate over materialism.

I suggest that a good explanation of why this has not happened is that these philosophers (like some of their anti-materialist opponents) come to the debate with pre-philosophical convictions. The milieu of materialism does not encourage avowals of such convictions, but Valerie Gray Hardcastle, for example, is refreshingly frank: "I am a committed materialist and believe absolutely and certainly that empirical investigation is the proper approach in explaining consciousness. I also recognize that I have little convincing to say to those opposed to me." She simply has, she says, "total and absolute faith that science as it is construed today will someday explain [consciousness] as it has explained the

---

[13] Colin McGinn, "Can We Solve the Mind-Body Problem?," *Mind*, New Series, 98 (1989), 349–66.

other so-called mysteries of our age."[14] Daniel Stoljar suggests why this may be a rather widespread attitude in his preface to a discussion of arguments for physicalism: "The first thing to say when considering the truth of physicalism is that we live in an overwhelmingly physicalist or materialist intellectual culture. The result is that, as things currently stand, the standards of argumentation required to persuade someone of the truth of physicalism are much lower than the standards required to persuade someone of its negation."[15] As a conviction pervading the intellectual air so many of us breathe, it is not surprising that a commitment to materialism is able to trump a mere intuition.

MATERIALIST RESPONSES: ACCEPTING THE ZOMBIE INTUITION

The most common materialist response to the zombie argument is to accept the zombie intuition but deny the logical validity of the argument. Here by far the most popular case is based on Kripke's views on necessity. The zombie intuition is that there is nothing in our concept of a zombie that excludes its existence; there is, in other words, no a priori argument from the definition of a zombie (a being physically identical to me but without consciousnesss) for the necessary non-existence of such a being. But this intuition concerns only the *a priori* possibility of zombies. There is a parallel intuition that it is possible for water not to be composed of H_2O. But according to Kripke, there are also a posteriori necessary truths (like "Water is H_2O") that are not apparent from mere conceptual analysis but are discovered by empirical investigation. If "zombies are impossible" is such a truth, then we of course cannot discover it by a priori intuition. Like "Water is H_2O," its denial will seem to be possible, even though it is not.

Thinking along these lines leads us to distinguish two sorts of possibility: possible in the (epistemic) sense of *conceivable without contradiction* and possible in the (ontological or metaphysical) sense of *existing in some possible world*. Chalmers admits the need for such a distinction, which he expresses as that between *conceivability* and *metaphysical possibility*. Putting this in the terms of Chalmers' argument, even if there is a logically possible world physically identical to ours but without consciousness, it does not follow that the facts about consciousness are not all physical

---

[14] Valerie Gray Hardcastle, "The Why of Consciousness: A Non-Issue for Materialists," in Jonathan Shear (ed.), *Explaining Consciousness – The "Hard Problem,"* Cambridge, MA: MIT Press, 1997, 61.
[15] "Physicalism," *Stanford Encyclopedia of Philosophy* (online), http://plato.stanford.edu/entries/physicalism/

facts. The logical possibility of such a world may reflect simply the content of our concepts, not the metaphysical nature of the reality those concepts refer to. The zombie intuition shows that zombies are conceivable but not that they are metaphysically possible. Therefore, Chalmers' argument, as he admits, requires another premise, one connecting the conceivability established by the zombie intuition and the metaphysical possibility required to refute materialism. Adding this premise (and restricting ourselves to the zombie case), we get:

1. In our world, there are conscious experiences.
2. Beings physically identical to us but not conscious (zombies) are logically possible.
3. If such beings are logically possible, then they are metaphysically possible.
4. If such beings are metaphysically possible, then the facts about consciousness are further facts about our world, over and above the physical facts.
5. If materialism is true, there are no further facts about our world, over and above the physical facts.
6. Therefore, materialism is not true.

Kripke himself argued that while "Water is H_2O" is necessary a posteriori, a typical materialist claim such as "Pain is the firing of C-fibers" is not.[16] According to Kripke, "Water is not H_2O" is conceivable because "water" in the sense of "the primary potable liquid on our planet" could, in some other world, not have H_2O as its molecular composition. Because of this, we can form a conception of water that is not H_2O. Nonetheless, given that, in our world, this liquid is H_2O, it is true in all possible worlds that such is the composition of this very liquid. But the denial of the necessary truth, "Water is not H_2O", is conceivable only because something can seem to be water (have all the observable attributes of "the primary potable liquid on our planet") and yet not be water. In the case of pain, Kripke argued, this necessary condition does not hold: if something seems to be a pain, it is a pain. Nothing can have all the observable attributes of, say, "the feeling I have when I hit my thumb hard with a hammer" and not be a pain. Accordingly, if pain were the firing of C-fibers, there could be nothing that had all the observable attributes of pain but was not the firing of C-fibers. We would, therefore, know a priori that pain was the firing of C-fibers. Since we don't know this, pain is not the firing of C-fibers.

The above line of argument can, more generally, be applied to "To be conscious is to be in physical state P," resulting in the conclusion that consciousness cannot be reduced to any physical state, from which it

---

[16] Saul Kripke, *Naming and Necessity*, Cambridge, MA: Harvard University Press, 1980, 153–4.

would follow that zombies are metaphysically possible if they are conceptually possible. In *The Conscious Mind* (146–9), Chalmers has developed and refined this Kripkean argument by developing it in the context of "two-dimensional semantics." The notion of "two-dimensions" of meaning comes from reflecting on just why claims such as "Water is not H_2O" are conceivable but not metaphysically possible. On Chalmers' analysis, this is because a term like "water" has two meanings (intensions). The first meaning (the primary intension) concerns what the term means in the actual world. Roughly, this is "the dominant clear, drinkable liquid in rivers and lakes here on Earth" (or, as Chalmers puts it briefly, "watery stuff"). But, given Kripke's line of thought, this liquid is (we have learned from experience, a posteriori) necessarily composed of H_2O molecules. Accordingly, there is another meaning (the secondary intension) of water, which applies not only to the actual world but also to possible worlds other than the actual one: "substance composed of H_2O." The key point is that, in other possible worlds, there might be "watery stuff" that is not composed of H_2O. Such a substance will not be water because it is not composed of H_2O. It is the existence of these two different meanings of "water" that makes the claim "Water is not H_2O" conceivable but not metaphysically possible. In the first meaning (primary intension) of the term (water = watery stuff), "Water is not H_2O" is conceivable; that is, there is no contradiction in thinking that the dominant, clear, drinkable liquid on Earth is not H_2O. But in the second meaning (secondary intension) of the term (water = substance composed of H_2O), the statement is necessarily false: a substance that was the dominant, clear, drinkable liquid in its world, but was not composed of H_2O, would not be water in this sense.

The two-dimensionality of meaning opens the door to the possibility that phenomenal concepts (e.g., pain) may have different primary and secondary intensions. For example, the primary intension of pain is something like "qualitatively painful feeling," but the secondary intension might be "firing of C-fibers." That is, we might discover that in fact pain is the stimulation of C-fibers, just as we have discovered that water is H_2O. But Chalmers argues that for phenomenal concepts primary and secondary intensions are the same. For water the two intensions are different because there are possible worlds in which there is a dominant clear, drinkable liquid that is not water (although it looks and feels like water, it is not composed of H_2O but of some other molecules). In the case of pain and other phenomenal concepts, however, if something is a qualitatively painful feeling, then it is pain. Whereas something can have the same phenomenal appearance as water and not be water, nothing can have the same phenomenal appearance as pain (that is, feel like pain) and not be pain.

Two-dimensional semantics has been the focus of increasingly complex debates in recent years, partly because of its relevance to the mind-body problem but also because of its intrinsic interest as a development of Kripke's views on language and necessity. For purposes of evaluating the zombie argument, the basic point is that, to establish the falsity of materialism, we need not only the conceivability of zombies but also their metaphysical possibility. On the other hand, to say that zombies are conceivable but not metaphysically possible requires holding that there is, even for phenomenal concepts such as *being in pain* and *being conscious*, a distinction between appearance and reality. This conflicts with our strong intuition (call it the phenomenality intuition) that being conscious (e.g., being in pain) is no different from appearing to be conscious (e.g., appearing to be in pain). So, although the zombie intuition alone is not sufficient to refute materialism, the combination of the zombie intuition and the phenomenality intuition is.[17]

Like the zombie intuition, the phenomenality intuition is not utterly compelling. It is, for example, possible to develop, as Brian Loar has done, an account of phenomenal concepts that makes room for a distinction between an appearance/reality distinction on even the phenomenal level.[18] It may even be possible – though this remains to be seen – to develop such an account to a point where we could plausibly see ourselves adopting it and giving up the phenomenality intuition. But the fact remains that the phenomenality intuition is something we believe far more than we do alternative accounts of phenomenal concepts. For us to reject the latter in favor of the former requires that we have some other belief that alters the epistemic balance. As in the case of efforts to reject the zombie intuition, the only plausible candidate is a pre-philosophical conviction that materialism is true.

In suggesting that contemporary materialists may trump strong intuitions with pre-philosophical convictions, I am not indicting them for epistemic irresponsibility but merely pointing out the epistemic limits of even strong intuitions. Although there are some such intuitions

---

[17] Here I am following the common view of the argument. Chalmers himself argues that the phenomenality intuition is not necessary and that the zombie intuition alone is sufficient. See his "The Two-Dimensional Argument Against Materialism," in his *The Character of Consciousness*, Oxford: Oxford University Press, forthcoming (a draft is available on Chalmers' website at http://consc.net/papers/2dargument.html).

[18] Brian Loar, "Phenomenal States (Revised)," in P. Ludlow, Y. Nagasawa, and D. Stoljar (eds.), *There's Something about Mary*, Cambridge, MA: MIT Press, 2004, 219–39. For Chalmers' response see, in the same volume, "Phenomenal Concepts and the Knowledge Argument," 269–98.

that we could never give up (e.g., that numbers do not have parents), there are seldom if ever disputed philosophical issues that can be settled by intuitions that cannot be overcome. This is particularly so when it is a question of a purely "theoretical intuition" – one that may be close to intellectually compelling but is not a conviction rooted in the Humean practices that make us the persons we are before we are philosophers. Such intuitions may rightly be set aside for the sake of such convictions. Another example of the priority of convictions over intuitions occurs in recent debates about freedom.

THE DEBATE OVER FREEDOM

Determinism certainly seems inconsistent with being able to do otherwise than I do. To say that an action is determined is to say that it has been causally produced by something other than itself. This alone might seem consistent with the ability to do otherwise: perhaps my action was caused by my choice, which I might have made differently, or by my character, which my choices might have formed differently. But determinism asserts that every event (including, therefore, every cause) is caused by something outside it. This immediately leads to a causal chain going back in time indefinitely, so that even if the immediate causes of my action are "internal" choices or traits that seem to allow my doing otherwise, the chain at some point extends to a point well before I even existed. Given determinism, it follows, for example, that there were causes operating ten million years ago that produced my present action. If so, none of my choices, character traits, or other features made any ultimate difference as to whether I performed the action. Given the state of the world ten million years ago, along with the causal laws governing its development from that point, I couldn't have acted otherwise than I did.

Of course, the above informal line of thought skates blithely over issues that have been fiercely contested, in particular the questions: Just how should determinism be defined? and, In exactly what sense does freedom require the ability to act otherwise? The soundness of any argument that determinism implies that I cannot do otherwise than I did depends on precise answers to these questions.[19] Beginning in the 1960s and 1970s,

---

[19] We should also note that even if it is shown that determinism implies that I cannot do otherwise, this shows that determinism excludes freedom only on the assumption that freedom requires my being able to do otherwise. This assumption has been challenged by Harry Frankfurt's much-discussed article, "Alternate Possibilities and Moral Responsibility," *Journal of Philosophy* 66 (1969), 829–39. Frankfurt's challenge is supported by counterexamples such as the following: A

several philosophers, including David Wiggins, Carl Ginet, Charles Lamb, and Peter van Inwagen, formulated the consequence argument (also called the "standard argument," the "incompatibility argument," and the "unavoidability argument") with significantly more rigor than had been achieved before, leading to a vigorous and fruitful revival of discussions of freedom and determinism.[20] We will focus on van Inwagen's influential version of the argument.[21]

VAN INWAGEN'S CONSEQUENCE ARGUMENT

A particular merit of van Inwagen's argument is his deftness in avoiding issues that are not essential to the consequence argument. For example, he defines determinism in terms of the *state of the world* at a given time and the *laws of physics*. But he avoids entangling complications by allowing *state of the world* to be understand in any way that (i) makes the state at one time *logically* entail nothing about states at other times and (ii) requires that an observable change in the way things are entails a change in the state of the world (186). He similarly avoids an analysis of *laws of physics* by merely insisting that, regardless of how we understand such laws, "if any one can . . . render some proposition false, then that proposition is not a law of nature" (193).[22] As to the vexing case of being able to do otherwise, van Inwagen avoids a full analysis of the notion and, as we shall see, builds his argument only on claims about this

---

political party has hired a neuroscientist to ensure that Kathy votes for their candidate. The neuroscientist rigs things so that, when Kathy is in the voting booth, if there is any preliminary indication that she might not vote for the candidate, outside electronic impulses will cause her to vote as the party wishes. As it turns out, Kathy has decided on her own to vote for the candidate and does so. Accordingly, the neuroscientist never does anything to her brain. Such cases are often presented as showing that a person (such as Kathy) can be morally responsible for something that she could not have done otherwise. If we take freedom by definition to require the ability to do otherwise, then the Frankfurt counterexamples try to show that moral responsibility does not require freedom. If, however, we use "freedom" in a full-blooded moral sense that involves moral responsibility, then the Frankfurt examples suggest that freedom does not require being able to do otherwise. Given this sense of freedom, showing that compatibilism excludes freedom requires showing both that compatibilism excludes being able to do otherwise and (contra Frankfurt) that freedom requires the ability to do otherwise. We will bracket Frankfurt's challenge and look only at the argument that compatibilism excludes the ability to do otherwise.

[20] Van Inwagen notes that C. D. Broad had produced a comparable version of the argument some thirty years earlier in his Knightbridge Inaugural Lecture (1933).

[21] I discuss the argument as van Inwagen develops it in "The Incompatibility of Free Will and Determinism," *Philosophical Studies* 27 (1975), 185–99. References will be given in the text. See also van Inwagen's monograph, *An Essay on Free Will*, Oxford: Oxford University Press, 1983.

[22] In the same vein, van Inwagen talks of propositions (as in this claim about laws) but requires no specific understanding of them except that they have their "usual features" such as being either true or false and obeying the standard laws of logic (see 185).

ability that he argues will have to be entailed by any adequate analysis. These minimal claims, he maintains, are sufficient to make his argument.

Van Inwagen's definition of determinism in terms of "state of the world" and "laws of physics" is as follows:

(a) For every instant of time, there is a proposition that expresses the state of the world at that instant.
(b) If A and B are any propositions that express the state of the world at some instants, then the conjunction of A with the laws of physics entails B. (186)

He develops the consequence argument by applying this definition to a case that is a paradigm of what we would ordinarily call a free action. For concreteness, he chooses the case of a judge who does not raise his hand at a time T, when this will lead to a defendant being punished. (The idea is that raising his hand would, by the conventions of the court, have granted clemency.) Van Inwagen assumes that the circumstances of this non-raising of the hand are ones that correspond to our idea of an entirely free decision: the judge was not constrained physically or mentally, he had reflected fully on all relevant considerations, etc.

To apply determinism to this case, let P denote the state of the world at T, the time at which the judge (J) does not raise his hand, and let P_0 denote the state of the world at T_0, where T_0 is an instant of time prior to the birth of J. Also, let L be the conjunction of all laws of physics. Then, from the definition of determinism, we get the first premise of the consequence argument:

(1) If determinism is true, then P_0 & L entails P.

Van Inwagen next notes that "if J had raised his hand at T, then the world would have been in a different state at T from the state it was in fact in" (191). (This follows from condition (ii) on the meaning of *state of the world*.) Obviously, if the world is in a different state than that expressed by P, then P is false. This yields van Inwagen's second premise:

(2) If J had raised his hand at T, then P would be false.

The rest of the premises of van Inwagen's argument make use of a peculiar idiom he introduces, he says, as merely a linguistic convenience. The idiom is: "J was able to render proposition P false."[23] In simple cases,

---

[23] In his 1975 article, van Inwagen uses "could have rendered," etc. instead of "was able to render," etc. Here I follow his later practice of substituting the latter for the former, which he says is less

this readily translates into something quite ordinary. Thus, "He was able to render the proposition *that he did not reach Chicago by midnight* false" = "He was able to reach Chicago by midnight." But there are cases – including claims made by the consequence argument – where there is no simple action that we can substitute for "rendered P false"; that is, there is no simple way of stating the content of the proposition that expresses what someone was able to do. For example, van Inwagen's argument needs to talk about a situation in which J was able to *render the conjunction of P_0 and L false*. There is no ordinary English expression for doing something that is such that, if J does it, then the conjunction of P_0 and L is false (there is no equivalent here of *reaching Chicago by midnight*). In such cases, van Inwagen has to use the "render-false" idiom.[24]

The next premise, then, is:

(3) If (2) is true, then if J was able to raise his hand at T, J was able to render P false.

This, van Inwagen says, is true simply because (2) entails that "there is, if J was able to raise his hand, at least one condition sufficient for the falsity of P that J was able to produce" (192).

The rest of the premises of the argument are as follows:

(4) If J was able to render P false, and if the conjunction of P_0 and L entails P, then J was able to render the conjunction of P_0 and L false.
(5) If J was able to render the conjunction of P_0 and L false, then J was able to render L false.
(6) J was not able to render L false.

Given (1) through (6), van Inwagen has the materials to draw his conclusion that

(7) If determinism is true, J was not able to raise his hand at T.

The basic reasoning of the argument is as follows:

From (2) and (3), we get:

(A) If J was able to raise his hand at T, then J was able to render P false.

---

misleading. Cf. his "Freedom to Break the Laws," *Midwest Studies in Philosophy* XXVIII (2004), 344, n. 17.

[24] The render-false idiom is just a linguistic convenience and does not of itself introduce any substantive hidden assumptions into the discussion. But it does involve an ambiguity that Lewis tries to exploit in his criticism of the consequence argument. However, this ambiguity also lurks in ordinary talk about capacities to do otherwise.

From (5) and (6), we get:

(B) J was not able to render the conjunction of P_o and L false.

From (B) and (4), we get:

(C) Either J was not able to render P false OR the conjunction of P_o and L does not entail P.

Now suppose that determinism is true:

> Then, from (1) we get: The conjunction of P_o and L entails P.
> From this and (C) we get: J was not able to render P false.
> From contraposition of (A) we get: If J was not able to render P false, then J was not able to raise his hand at T.
> From this we get: J was not able to raise his hand at T.
> Therefore, (7) if determinism is true, J was not able to raise his hand at T.

This seems to be a valid argument, and we have already seen van Inwagen's case for the truth of premises (1)–(3). Van Inwagen regards (4) and (5) as instances of general analytic truths. The generalization of (4) follows from elementary logical considerations (cf. 192). The generalization of (5) seems likewise obvious: J surely can't render false a proposition solely about his past, so to render false the conjunction of this proposition with a second requires rendering the second false.

Finally, van Inwagen argues that (6) is a conceptual truth given the meanings of "can" and "law": if someone can do something that would render a proposition false, that proposition, even if it happens to be true, cannot be a law of nature. So, to use van Inwagen's example, it might be true that nothing travels faster than light. But if a physicist can build an accelerator that would produce particles moving faster than light, then the fact that nothing travels faster than light is just a contingent feature of the world, due (perhaps in part) to the fact that the physicist happens not to build this accelerator. But no such merely contingent fact can be a law of nature. Given the truth of (1)–(7), it seems that the consequence argument is sound.

LEWIS' RESPONSE

David Lewis argues that van Inwagen's argument fails because "was able to render false" has two meanings, a weaker and a stronger.[25] If we use the weaker meaning, then (6) is false; if we use the stronger meaning, then

---

[25] David Lewis, "Are We Free to Break the Laws?," in his *Philosophical Papers, Volume II*, Oxford: Oxford University Press, 1986, 291–8. All references are given in the text.

(5) is false. In either case, the argument is unsound. Lewis defines the general notion of an event's making a proposition false as follows: "an event would falsify a proposition iff, necessarily, if that event occurs, then the proposition is false" (297). But there are two ways this can happen. I am able to render a proposition false in the *weak sense* "iff I was able to do something such that, if I did it, the proposition would have been falsified (though not necessarily by my act, or by any event caused by my act)." By contrast, to render a proposition false in the *strong sense* means that my action, or an event caused by it, caused the proposition to be false: "I could have rendered [was able to render] a proposition false in the strong sense iff I was able to do something such that, if I did it, the proposition would have been falsified either by my act itself or by some event caused by my act" (297). Lewis agrees that it is absurd to think that he can, in the strong sense, break a law of nature (render it false): he cannot cause, directly or indirectly, the law to be false. But he sees no absurdity in the weak sense: it may well be that there are things that he could do, which, if he did them, a law of nature would turn out to be false (would be broken).[26]

If we run the argument using the strong sense of "was able to render false," then, Lewis thinks, (6) is true, since we obviously cannot cause a law of nature to be false; but then (5) is false, since its truth requires J's causing a law to be false when the condition specified in its antecedent is fulfilled. On the other hand, if we use the weak sense of "was able to render false," then (5) is true, since J was able to render L false (without *causing* it to be false) under the condition specified; but (6) is false.

Van Inwagen, in his response to Lewis, does not argue against Lewis' contention that his argument is invalid if "was able to render false" is taken in either the strong or the weak sense. Rather, he maintains that there is another sense of "was able to render false" for which the argument is valid. The sense is this: "An agent was able to render a proposition false if and only if he was able to arrange things in a certain way, such that, his doing so, together with the whole truth about the past, strictly imply the falsity of the proposition."[27] Substituting this definition, (6) becomes:

---

[26] A theological example (not from Lewis) might illustrate the point. Even though I can't cause the law of gravitation to be suspended, it might be that God, by his own free choice, unconstrained by me, decides that, if I perform a certain action (say jumping from a bridge), he will temporarily suspend gravitation to save me from injury.

[27] Van Inwagen, "Freedom to Break the Laws," 346. This, as van Inwagen notes, is the definition he gives of "able to render false" in *An Essay on Free Will*. Although this definition had not been published when Lewis was writing his critique, van Inwagen tells us that he had cited it in correspondence with Lewis ("Freedom to Break the Laws," 345).

(6*) J was not able to arrange things in any way such that his doing so, together with the whole truth about the past, strictly implies the falsity of L.[28]

Lewis notes this definition, but thinks it does nothing to help van Inwagen's argument. It amounts, he says, to the claim that an agent (say, J) "could not have arranged [was not able to arrange] things in any way such that [J] was predetermined not to arrange things in that way." To this Lewis says: "It is uninstructive to learn that the soft determinist [compatibilist] is committed to denying Premise 6 thus understood."[29] Lewis suggests that understanding van Inwagen's argument via this definition makes him unable "to make his premises defensible without circularity."[30] Van Inwagen is – justifiably, I think – puzzled at Lewis' claim that using (6*) as a premise renders his argument circular. It may well be that Lewis finds this premise implausible or unjustified. But circularity does not arise from using premises that one's opponent may disagree with. As van Inwagen says, "The question should be: How plausible are these premises?"[31]

Why might Lewis find (6*) implausible? It's hard to imagine that he has some direct reason for thinking that we are able, even in the weak sense, to render laws of nature false. He agrees that, even though I am not able to break (causally) a law of nature, my rendering a law false would be associated with a "law-breaking event," a "divergence miracle" (240) that would precede my act of rendering the law false. But Lewis does not have, apart from his acceptance of compatibilism, evidence for the possibility of such miracles. It seems clear that Lewis finds the key premise of the consequence argument implausible just to the extent that he finds compatibilism plausible.[32] More precisely, if, as Lewis seems to agree, van Inwagen's argument entails that compatibilism is false and all its premises except for (6*) are true, then, if compatibilism is true, then (6*) is false. Given this, we can, van Inwagen says, characterize the "dialectical situation" in which he and Lewis find themselves. Van Inwagen says that (6*) is obviously true; Lewis responds that compatibilism entails that (6*) is false. As a result, van Inwagen's argument "enables compatibilists like Lewis . . . to measure the price" of remaining compatibilists; namely, "the philosopher who believes in the possibility of free agents in a possible

---

[28] Here I have slightly revised the wording to match van Inwagen's statement of the premise in "Freedom to Break the Laws," 348.
[29] Lewis, "Are We Free to Break the Laws?," 296, n.5.   [30] Ibid., 296.
[31] Van Inwagen, "Freedom to Break the Laws," 348.
[32] Presumably, Lewis is not willing to accept the consequence argument and still maintain compatibilism by denying, à la Frankfurt, that freedom requires being able to do otherwise.

world, must believe that a free agent in a deterministic world is able to arrange things in such a way that one's so arranging them, together with the whole truth about the past, strictly implies the falsity of at least one law of nature."[33]

It is initially hard to think that there is epistemic parity here between van Inwagen and Lewis. Just in itself, the denial of (6*) is highly counter-intuitive. The only scrap of plausibility it has comes from the fact that it is a weaker claim than the claim that free agents are able directly to cause laws of nature to be false. But, apart from the connection of the denial of (6*) with compatibilism, there is no tug to believe it. Lewis' entire case against (6*) rests on his belief that compatibilism is true – a conviction due, presumably, to his intuitive commitment to the possibility of an action's being both free and causally determined. But compatibilism, surely, is a highly disputed philosophical position. Any intuition that it is true at best amounts to a personally compelling insight – if not just an inclination to believe or even a mere hunch. It falls quite a distance short of the ideal of the plainly obvious. By contrast, the premises of van Inwagen's conse-quence argument, even (6*), are far more compelling (or at least follow from principles that are far more compelling).

But Lewis might well respond that the above argument misrepresents his intuitions. He could agree that compatibilism is not obvious in the following sense: it is not obvious *how* freedom and determinism are logically consistent. But he could still assert that it is obvious that: (a) we are free; and (b) all our actions are (or may be) causally determined. (a) and (b) entail that compatibilism is true, even if we don't see how it can be.[34] Lewis' claim that (a) and (b) are obviously true (or follow from

---

[33] Ibid. Van Inwagen tries to tighten the screw one more turn. He notes that "it is entirely plausible . . . to define a miracle as an event or state of affairs whose occurrence would be inconsistent with the whole truth about the past and the laws of nature," from which it follows that "it is entirely plausible to define the *ability* to perform a miracle as the ability to bring about an event or state of affairs whose occurrence would be inconsistent with the whole truth about the past and the laws of nature." From this he concludes that the price of compatibilism can also be measured this way: "free will in a deterministic world . . . strictly implies the ability to perform miracles" (349). He further illustrates his point with a biblical-style scenario, in which "Elijah, who is currently in Jerusalem, claims that he is able to be in Babylon ten minutes from now." But it is not clear that this is any heavier burden than Lewis has already assumed. It does not, as van Inwagen's use of "perform" and "bring about" (along with his evocation of biblical miracles) may suggest, show that he must hold that we are able to *cause* miracles. Lewis need only agree that what we do can "lead to" miracles in a sense parallel to Lewis' weak sense of "rendering a law of nature false." The only miracles relevant are the "divergence miracles" that Lewis has already acknowledged.

[34] In a similar vein, if we could prove the existence of God from entirely obvious premises, then, since evil obviously exists, it would be rational to conclude that the existence of God and the existence of evil are compatible, even though we may not be able to see how.

obvious truths) can be upset only by showing that they conflict with other truths equally or more obvious. In particular, he would maintain, (6*) is less obvious than (a) and (b). Accordingly, van Inwagen's argument does not require him to give up compatibilism.

Van Inwagen doesn't consider this particular line of response for Lewis, but he does agree that the consequence argument is not rationally compelling. It is not a "knock-down argument," one that forces assent on the pain of irrationality. Indeed, van Inwagen agrees with Lewis that, in philosophy, there are no knock-down arguments. Rather, a philosophical argument at best allows us to "measure the price." What van Inwagen's argument does establish is that one price of compatibilism is accepting that free agents have the ability to arrange things so that laws of nature would turn out false.

The further question is whether this price is too much to pay. This question, Lewis maintains, is not one we can settle by philosophical argument:

> But when all is said and done, and all the tricky arguments and distinctions and counterexamples have been discovered, presumably we will still face the question which prices are worth paying, which theories are on balance credible, which are the unacceptably counterintuitive consequences and which are the acceptably counterintuitive ones. On this question we may still differ. And if all is indeed said and done, there will be no hope of discovering still further arguments to settle our differences.[35]

So we are left with our "intuitions" about what prices are worth paying. But, Lewis says, no philosophical intuition has the status of "unchallengeable evidence." Intuitions and, a fortiori, the theories based on them are "simply opinions." No doubt our "tricky arguments and distinctions and counter-examples" will have excluded some positions as simply unacceptable (logically inconsistent, incompatible with claims we are utterly incapable of giving up), but there will remain a range of theories that have not been eliminated by the give-and-take of philosophical discussion. Lewis calls these points of "equilibrium." "Our common task [as philosophers] is to find out what equilibria there are that can withstand examination," but, once this argumentative task has been carried out, "it remains for each of us to come to rest at one or another of them." This can be achieved only by "intuition," in Lewis' sense of opinion: "once the menu of well-worked-out theories is before us, philosophy is a matter of opinion."

---

[35] David Lewis, "Introduction," *Philosophical Papers, Volume I*, Oxford: Oxford University Press, 1983, x.

Here van Inwagen demurs. Why, he asks, should I prefer the equilibrium points corresponding to my intuitions, when I know that other philosophers, at least as intelligent, careful, and informed, see things differently? In other words, since my philosophical peers disagree with my assessment of the relevant arguments, isn't it obvious that our disagreement is due to non-epistemic differences such as the contingencies of genetic dispositions, upbringing, and subsequent life-history? This leads van Inwagen to conclude that it is hard "to explain how (in the light of pervasive and irresoluble philosophical disagreement) anyone can be justified in believing anything of philosophical consequence."[36]

On the question of the metaphilosophical significance of their dispute about freedom, Lewis and van Inwagen offer, respectively, two degrees of despair. For Lewis, philosophy is simply a "matter of opinion," with each philosopher determining which equilibrium-points in philosophical discussion support his or her opinions. But van Inwagen is even more skeptical, urging that, since my opinions differ from those of equally reliable thinkers, I am not even entitled to them.

Their skepticism is plausible as long as our intuitions amount to nothing more than "opinions," which is often the case. But, as we have seen, some philosophical intuitions are also *convictions*: not just basic beliefs but basic beliefs that are rooted in practices central to our conceptions of ourselves.

If we take seriously, as we should, Hume's injunction, "Be a philosopher, but first be a man," it follows that convictions have priority over the project of philosophizing. Indeed, it is hard to see how the very impulse to philosophize could be warranted by anything other than pre-philosophical convictions. But even apart from the self-referential argument that seems implicit here, the refutation of classical foundationalism opens the door to epistemic standing for a wide range of convictions. This doesn't mean that convictions are in principle immune to philosophical refutation. The rigor of philosophical examination may show some to be unacceptable (self-contradictory; inconsistent with other, stronger convictions; contrary to common-sense truths, etc.). But philosophy can also serve to clarify, refine, systematize, and otherwise improve the epistemic status of pre-philosophical convictions.

The point here, however, is that a conviction is not a mere opinion, unsustainable when faced with the disagreement of epistemic peers. Convictions may – and sometimes must – be given up. But, because of

---

[36] Van Inwagen, "Freedom to Break the Laws," 343.

their central status in my life and their deep roots in my experience, the case for giving them up needs to be particularly compelling, typically involving the emergence of new convictions. In any case, merely learning that I have epistemic peers who do not share my convictions is not justification for renouncing them. On the contrary, doing so would result in a loss of *epistemic integrity* by giving up beliefs at the core of my identity simply because I realize that there are alternatives to them.

CONCLUSION

So far, we have been treating convictions as those of an individual or of a restricted subgroup such as Christians or Enlightenment intellectuals. But there are convictions that are far more widely shared. For example, virtually all of us engage in the practice of holding people (ourselves and others) responsible for what they do. Consequently, philosophical results about convictions deriving from this practice will have a much more general validity than those concerning, say, specific religious beliefs.

This practice of holding people responsible is very deeply rooted. Even when we conclude that certain forms of causal determination are inconsistent with freedom, our immediate reaction is to say that, in such cases (e.g., mental illness, alcoholism) *we should not* hold people so determined responsible. Facing the prospect of a total lack of freedom, we are still gripped by the incoherent conclusion that, then, it would be *irresponsible* to hold anyone responsible. It seems clear that we are simply and irrevocably committed to the practice of holding people responsible.

From this standpoint, then, there is simply no question of whether we should or should not hold people responsible for what they do – we're going to do this no matter what. Perhaps we can take this very result as an important piece of philosophical knowledge. Couldn't it be plausibly claimed that one outcome of philosophical anti-foundationalism, applied to the case of freedom, has been that the practice of holding responsible is in order even without philosophical justification? Are there any philosophers working on the topic who would deny this?

Beyond this, it would also seem that philosophers are in a position to assure us that, regardless of whether our actions turn out to be entirely determined causally, there is no logical inconsistency in continuing our practice of holding people responsible for what they do. The discussion between van Inwagen and Lewis shows that compatibilism remains a consistent alternative, even in the face of the strongest argument for incompatibilism. Even van Inwagen, faced with conclusive proof that there are no coherent non-determinist accounts of freedom (e.g., the agency theory, according to which free agents are uncaused causes of their actions), would presumably conclude that compatibilism is true. His current view, that "free will remains a mystery," seems to reflect only his uncertainty as to whether there is some viable non-deterministic account.[37] Philosophy has provided, then, the intellectual resources for maintaining the intellectual integrity of our practice even if causal determination is found to be total.

Even more important is the philosophical contribution to our understanding of the distinction between causation and compulsion. Our practice of holding one another responsible depends on this distinction, since it is obvious that there are some cases in which the manner in which an action is caused excludes moral responsibility and others in which it does not. Philosophers from Aristotle to Hume to Frankfurt have provided rich resources for understanding the meaning and applications of this distinction. No one has a completely adequate theory explaining what sorts of causes result in a compulsion to act that excludes moral responsibility. But our ability to think intelligently about difficult cases (neurosis, character defects, etc.) will be greatly impeded if we are not familiar with the results of philosophical discussions of these issues.

More generally, philosophical reflection has discovered various models of free action: freedom as non-necessitated decision, freedom as spontaneous choice, freedom as self-determination (autonomy), freedom as determination by higher-order desires, etc. None of these models has been established as a generally true account. Each model has difficulty making sense of certain cases. No single account can explain all our intuitions about particular cases of free or unfree action. It is precisely because philosophers have focused on the difficult cases – the ones that question the universal validity of our various models of freedom – that they seem to have made no progress on the problem of freedom. But this is a false appearance, based on what I have called the Philosopher's Fallacy. Each of the philosophical models of freedom is a correct account of a wide range of cases, even if none can be extended universally. The same is true of any particular set of laws of nature with which scientists work. Depending on our needs and interests, there will almost always be a philosophical account of freedom that will apply to the case confronting us. We philosophers tend to think of our models of freedom as incidental

---

[37] See Peter van Inwagen, "Free Will Remains a Mystery," in Robert Kane (ed.), *The Oxford Handbook of Free Will*, Oxford: Oxford University Press, 2002, 158–9.

artefacts, constructed as preliminary sketches of the final, universal theory that is our only real goal. In fact, we should think of these models as our primary achievements, with the dream of a universal theory just a guiding idealization that need never be realized for our discipline to have achieved a substantial body of knowledge about freedom. It may even turn out that the ideal itself is incoherent and that what appear to us as merely partial or preliminary insights are all the truth there is on this topic.

CHAPTER 7

Was there a Kuhnian revolution? Convictions in the philosophy of science

It is by now a banality that Thomas Kuhn's book on scientific revolutions itself precipitated an intellectual revolution.[1] Certainly, the book has had a startlingly wide influence. As John Zammito says, "no other work in the history of philosophy of science has been so widely read, discussed, or appropriated by the entirety of the literate public" (52).[2] And even beyond the literate public, we may think, noting that "paradigm" has become part of standard business babble or – as I serendipitously read in today's newspaper – that a rock star earnestly avows that her new album is a "paradigm-shift" for her.

But the question remains of where, if anywhere, Kuhn's effect was deep enough to be judged truly revolutionary. Certainly not in the history of science, where Kuhn himself purported to be offering nothing that historians had not known and been practicing since Koyré. Not even, it might seem, in philosophy of science, to which Kuhn intended his book to be a contribution. There he undeniably created a major stir, but, as Zammito notes, "by 1980, it is fair to say, Kuhn had become a marginal figure for the philosophy of science" (53). More than twenty-five years later the judgment of marginality seems reaffirmed. The grand Kuhnian issues of rationality and truth are no longer central to the discipline. Most of the best philosophy of science consists of highly specialized discussions in the conceptual foundations of specific disciplines, particularly physics, biology, and cognitive science. Nor is this because the big questions Kuhn raised have been decisively settled. The challenge to science's cognitive

[1] Thomas Kuhn, *The Structure of Scientific Revolutions*, second edition, Chicago: University of Chicago Press, 1970 [first published 1962]. All references will be given in the text.
[2] John H. Zammito, *A Nice Derangement of Epistemes: Post-Positivism in the Study of Science from Quine to Latour*, Chicago: University of Chicago Press, 2004. Further references will be given in the text.

authority associated with his work continues to flourish in the new discipline of social studies of knowledge (SSK), where the *irrationality* of science is often taken as an unquestioned starting-point. Philosophers of science, however, despite occasional forays into journalistic discussions of the "science wars," no longer seem to view the challenge with urgency. In this chapter, I ask how this has happened and what it says about Kuhn's impact on philosophy of science and, more generally, about the role of argument in philosophy of science. The answers lead, once again, to the role of pre-philosophical convictions.

KUHN AND HIS EARLY CRITICS

Kuhn himself well illustrates the sense of crisis his book provoked:

I was talking to a . . . friend and colleague whom I knew, from a published review, to be enthusiastic about my book. She turned to me and said, "Well, Tom, it seems to me that your biggest problem now is showing in what sense science can be empirical." My jaw dropped and still sags slightly.[3]

Kuhn's was not the only jaw that dropped in 1962 after he published *The Structure of Scientific Revolutions*. Many readers, particularly among analytic philosophers, were stunned by what they saw as his all-out assault on the rationality (empirical or otherwise) of science. Israel Scheffler[4] spoke of "Objectivity under Attack" (title of chapter 1) and included Kuhn as a major example of "current attacks" that raise the question of "whether scientific objectivity is not, after all, an illusion, whether we have not, after all, been fundamentally mistaken in supposing empirical conceptions capable of responsible control by logic and experience." In the wake of Kuhn (along with Paul Feyerabend and N. R. Hanson), "the question before us becomes, in short: How, if at all, is scientific objectivity possible?" (8). More bluntly, Imre Lakatos famously said: "*In Kuhn's view scientific revolution is irrational, a matter for mob psychology.*"[5] There quickly developed a widespread enterprise of "refuting" Kuhn and "saving" the rationality of science.

It is by no means clear that this was a fair reaction to Kuhn's book, which certainly does not present itself as an attack on the rational or empirical character of science. Most of the discussion is couched as a

---

[3] Thomas Kuhn, "Reflections on My Critics," in I. Lakatos and A. Musgrave (eds.), *Criticism and the Growth of Knowledge*, Cambridge: Cambridge University Press, 1970, 263, n.3

[4] Israel Scheffler, *Science and Subjectivity*, Indianapolis: Bobbs-Merrill, 1967. References will be given in the text.

[5] *Criticism and the Growth of Knowledge*, 178, Lakatos' italics.

challenge to the "concept" or "image" of science implicit in scientific textbooks and positivist philosophy, an image that Kuhn finds inconsistent with that revealed by recent work in the history of science. The largest part of *Structure* consists in his sketch of an alternative "image" of science, illustrated by a good number of succinct case studies from the history of physics and chemistry, designed to formulate what is needed in science beyond observations and inferences from them.

Broadly, according to Kuhn, what is needed are answers to questions such as "What are the fundamental entities of which the universe is composed? How do these interact with each other and with the senses? What questions may legitimately be asked about such entities and what techniques employed in seeking solutions?" (3–4). The answers are provided by a *paradigm* (an exemplary past scientific achievement) that guides the *normal science* (further work in the manner of the paradigm) carried out in a given domain. The paradigm, however, provides not a set of explicitly formulated propositions but a body of "tacit knowledge" (a term Kuhn borrows from Michael Polanyi, *Structure*, 191) derived from scientists' accepting a previous scientific achievement as a model for their scientific work. This acceptance is typically brought about through the education that forms scientists as competent practitioners in their discipline.

In one sense, commitment to a paradigm is a dogmatic attitude that seems to arbitrarily exclude alternatives. But, Kuhn maintains, it is precisely this dogmatism that produces new, eventually revolutionary ideas. To the extent that our paradigmatic view is, as it will always be, not sufficient for answering our questions about nature, applications of it will encounter resistance – what Kuhn calls *anomalies*. Of course, scientists will repeatedly make the application work, looking for flaws in equipment, experimental design, mathematical derivations – anywhere except the paradigm's guiding vision. Logically there can never be a decisive *proof* that a paradigm has failed: there is always the possibility that further efforts will resolve the anomalies. But at some point (that of *crisis*, in Kuhn's terminology), it will become reasonable for scientists to consider rejecting key elements of their approach and seek a new way of looking at their scientific world: a new paradigm. If a new paradigm is developed and replaces the old one, we have a scientific *revolution*.

Kuhn's critics were most disturbed by two of his claims: that rival paradigms resisted evaluation by standards neutral to the paradigms themselves and that changes of paradigm involve gestalt switches in how scientists see the world. Israel Scheffler summarized the first point (and connected it to the second): "evaluative arguments over the merits of alternative paradigms are vastly minimized, such arguments being circular, and the essential factor consisting anyway not in deliberation or interpretation but rather in the gestalt switch" (78). Close readers of Kuhn will note that, like many others, Scheffler is inattentive to the details of Kuhn's formulations. For example, Kuhn, after noting what he calls the circularity of arguments in paradigm disputes, goes on to say:

> The resulting circularity does not, of course, make the argument wrong or ineffectual. The man who premises a paradigm when arguing in its defense can nonetheless provide a clear exhibit of what scientific practice will be like for those who adopt the new view of nature. That exhibit can be immensely persuasive, often compellingly so.

He goes on to explain that this is why we must, in order to understand scientific revolutions, "examine not only the impact of nature and of logic, but also the techniques of persuasive argumentation effective within the quite special groups that constitute the community of scientists" (94).

Scheffler ignores these qualifications, presumably because he thinks the "persuasive argumentation" Kuhn has in mind can be only "mere persuasive displays without deliberative substance" (Scheffler, 81). This is because he thinks that Kuhn allows proponents of rival paradigms no "shared standards" that could provide premises for arguments that do not beg the question against their opponents. Arguments for paradigms can be only circular self-justifications: "each paradigm is, in effect, inevitably self-justifying, [so that] paradigm debates must fail of objectivity" (84).[6] On the other hand, in the very passage Scheffler quotes in support of this interpretation, Kuhn says only that arguments over rival paradigms are "partially circular" (109), a point he has earlier explained by noting that, although the parties to a paradigm debate do share "premises and values," these are "not sufficiently extensive" to produce arguments that are "logically or even probabilistically compelling" (94). But are arguments that are short of "compelling" necessarily "mere persuasive displays without deliberative substance"?

As to Kuhn's claim about gestalt switches, Hilary Putnam describes it as "the thesis that terms used in another culture, say, the term 'temperature' as used by a seventeenth-century scientist, cannot be equated in meaning or

---

[6] Lakatos offers a reading almost identical to Scheffler's: "There are no rational standards for their [rival paradigms'] comparison. Each paradigm contains its own standards. The crisis sweeps away not only the old theories and rules but also the standards which made us respect them. The new paradigm brings a totally new rationality. There are no super-paradigmatic standards" (Imre Lakatos, "Falsification and the Methodology of Scientific Research Programmes," *Criticism and the Growth of Knowledge*, 178).

reference with any terms or expressions we possess. As Kuhn puts it, scientists with different paradigms inhabit 'different worlds'. 'Electron' as used around 1900 referred to objects in one 'world'; as used today it refers to objects in quite a different 'world'."[7] Kuhn in fact is more circumspect:

In a sense I am unable to explicate further, the proponents of competing paradigms practice their trades in different worlds. Practicing in different worlds, the two groups of scientists see different things when they look from the same point in the same direction. Again, that is not to say that they can see anything they please. Both are looking at the world, and what they look at has not changed. But in some areas they see different things. (150)

Kuhn also notes the more usual view, that rival scientists literally see the same things but interpret them differently. Of this view he says that it

can be neither all wrong nor a mere mistake . . . It is an essential part of a philosophical paradigm . . . [that] has served both science and philosophy well. Its exploitation . . . has been fruitful of a fundamental understanding that perhaps could not have been achieved in another way.

His suggestion, however, is that, nonetheless, in the light of recent developments in disciplines from philosophy to art history, this "traditional paradigm is somehow askew" (121).

It may well seem that a sensible, sympathetic reading of Kuhn would have taken him to be raising questions about our understanding of scientific rationality, particularly suggesting the need to take account of factors other than the strict canons of deductive and inductive logic. Is there more to scientific rationality than sheer logicality? Are there viable conceptions of rationality that might allow for psychological factors such as intuitive gestalt switches or sociological factors such as consensus? Even when Kuhn's rhetoric is at its most incautious, he always introduces qualifications showing that he envisages modification, not eradication, of received notions of scientific rationality. One might object that he never works out in any detail an alternative conception of scientific rationality and that, lacking this, we can't know whether his modifications of received notions would be plausible or even coherent. But Kuhn does not present himself as a philosopher offering a new theory of scientific reason but as a historian pointing out how even exemplary scientific work doesn't fit standard philosophical models.

Such an irenic reading of Kuhn, however accurate regarding his actual views, nonetheless ignores the fraught context in which his book appeared. This is apparent in Dudley Shapere's review, which notes that

[7] Hilary Putnam, *Reason, Truth, and History*, Cambridge: Cambridge University Press, 1981, 114.

Kuhn's "view reflects widespread and important tendencies in both the history and philosophy of science today" (389). This remark introduces a discussion of Kuhn on incommensurability, from which Shapere concludes that, despite Kuhn's own resistance, his view leads inevitably to a irrationalist relativism for which "the decision of a scientific group to adopt a new paradigm is not based on good reasons; on the contrary, what counts as a good reason is determined by the decision." Immediately upon drawing this conclusion, Shapere comments that "a view such as Kuhn's had, after all, to be expected sooner or later from someone versed in the contemporary treatment of the history of science" (392). A bit earlier in his review, Shapere pointed out that Kuhn's notion of paradigm "incorporated" Norwood Russell Hanson's claim that facts are "theory-laden" and Paul Feyerabend's notion of "meaning variance from one theory or paradigm to another." These ideas, Shapere maintains, lead to Kuhn's disquieting conclusions about relativism and irrationality.

Shapere, then, like other informed philosophers, read Kuhn's book as a particularly effective element in an ongoing historical and philosophical assault on the rationality of science. They typically appreciated the effectiveness of Kuhn's critique of positivist philosophy of science, which, ignoring the radical nature of revolutions, saw science as the continuous accumulation of new truths by the application of established empirical methods. Some, like Shapere, even understood that Kuhn himself did not intend to undermine scientific rationality. But critics saw Kuhn's rejection of the positivist model of rationality as a slippery slope to irrationalism if there were no satisfactory alternative account of scientific reason. The sharp effectiveness of Kuhn's critique of positivism, combined with the hesitant vagaries of his gestures towards an alternative account, provoked a sense of panic beyond anything Kuhn's text in isolation would have likely produced. The ensuing responses, although often misleadingly presented as a matter of "refuting Kuhn," were in fact the effort of the philosophical community to maintain its confidence in the cognitive authority of a science that it could no longer understand in terms of the positivists' accumulationist model.[8]

A central trait of analytic philosophy is precisely its respect for the cognitive authority of science – and not just science as an epistemic ideal but as an existing practice. Understanding the nature of scientific

---

[8] Recent work by Michael Friedman and others has seriously challenged the long-held assumption that Kuhn's ideas were in fact diametrically opposed to those of sophisticated positivists (particularly Carnap). See, for example, Michael Friedman, "Kuhn and Logical Empiricism," in Thomas Nickles (ed.), *Thomas Kuhn*, Cambridge: Cambridge University Press, 2003, 19–44.

knowledge had, from the beginning, been a major concern of analytic philosophers, and the logical positivists had developed a detailed account of scientific methodology. Kuhn's challenge to this account was especially discomfiting because it confronted the positivist account of science with the actual scientific practice that positivist philosophers of science held in such cognitive esteem. That practice, he maintained, even at its best, contradicts the positivist picture of science as the gradual accumulation of empirical truth through logically conclusive reasoning from uncontroversial observations. The positivists were especially vulnerable at this point because, although they accepted the cognitive authority of the scientific practices Kuhn appealed to, their philosophy of science was more based on a priori logical and epistemological principles than on close attention to the actual workings of these practices.

The most direct response to Kuhn would have been to argue against his critique on historical grounds: to show that the history of the best science did fit the accumulationist model. But to this extent at least, Kuhn – following the work of Koyré and other founders of the new historiography of science – had the history right, and no one seriously offered a historical defense of positivist philosophy of science. What was often argued was (at least implicitly) that if the positivist view is false, then science can only be an irrational enterprise, its conclusions following not from evidence and reasoning but from blind psychological and sociological forces. But this line of argument, given that actual science did *not* fit the positivist model, was unwittingly complicit with the skeptical conclusion that science was irrational – a view later taken up with a vengeance by certain historians and sociologists. The collision between stubborn positivists, who denied the consequent to deny the antecedent, and facile skeptics, who asserted the antecedent to assert the consequent, constituted the unfortunate episodes labeled the "science wars."

The fact remains that Kuhn – aided of course by many others arguing in the same vein – did refute the positivist account of science. Even so severe a critic of Kuhn as Shapere makes this clear:

In attacking the "concept of development-by-accumulation," Kuhn presents numerous penetrating criticisms not only of histories of science written from that point of view, but also of certain philosophical doctrines (mainly Baconian and positivistic philosophies of science, particularly verification, falsification, and probabilistic views of the acceptance or rejection of scientific theories) which he convincingly argues are associated with that view of history.[9]

---

[9] Dudley Shapere, "The Structure of Scientific Revolutions," *The Philosophical Review* 73 (1964), 383.

As John Zammito puts it, citing, Ronald Giere's obituary for Kuhn: "it was the difficult achievement of Kuhn's *Structure* to 'shame' philosophers of science into 'dealing with *real* science'" (53).[10]

Despite this achievement, Kuhn's main failure, writing for philosophers but as a historian, was that he did not offer a philosophically sophisticated account of the nature of whatever it is that "real science" requires beyond the application of methodological directives to observed data. He tells us that the key feature of "real science," in contrast to positivist accounts, is "the insufficiency of methodological directives, by themselves, to dictate a unique substantive conclusion to many sorts of scientific questions" (3). Merely making careful observations and deriving logical (inductive and deductive) conclusions from them (what is ordinarily meant by "scientific method") does not result in uniquely justified answers to scientific questions. Accordingly, although "observation and experience ... drastically restrict the range of admissible scientific belief ... they cannot alone determine a particular body of such belief" (4).

The question Kuhn does not answer with sufficient detail and clarity is: What, besides "observation and experience," does determine the decision to accept a given scientific theory? Sometimes Kuhn suggests – as in comments inspired by Polanyi's notion of "tacit knowledge" – a moderate objectivist view of justification as a shared judgment among a community of trained investigators. At other times, he hints – as when he can't resist quoting Planck's infamous claim that new theories are finally accepted only when their opponents have all died off – at a radical subjectivism that would reduce scientific results to personal prejudices. The problem was that philosophers were already acutely aware of the internal philosophical failings of the positivists' accumulationist account of science. Hanson and Feyerabend had made a strong case against the central assumption that observation was independent of theoretical commitment, and Wilfrid Sellars had raised even deeper objections to the idea that experiences of any sort could be the foundation of epistemological legitimacy. Wittgenstein's later philosophy, then becoming very influential, similarly called foundationalist epistemology into question. At the same time, philosophers were increasingly aware that historians of science were presenting case studies that bore little resemblance to the positivist view of science. Kuhn presented a strikingly effective historical case against positivist philosophy of science without offering a philosophically

---

[10] Ronald Giere, "Kuhn's Legacy for North American Philosophy of Science," *Social Studies of Science* 27 (1997), 497.

adequate alternative. Moreover, the alternative picture of science Kuhn did suggest could be readily taken in an irrationalist direction. All this made it easy for philosophers to focus on Kuhn's book as a challenge to the rationality of science.

Discussions of Kuhn typically centered on his notion of "incommensurability," in terms of which Kuhn expressed both of the two theses (discussed above) that disturbed his critics. He claimed that rival scientific theories were incommensurable in the *semantic* sense that, even though they used the same linguistic expressions (e.g., mass, force), these expressions had different *meanings*, so that there was no shared language in which their competing claims could be expressed. He also used the term in an *epistemological* sense to express his claim that there were no shared *standards* by which we could decide which of two competing theories was preferable. In both cases, philosophers saw Kuhn's claims as leading to fundamental problems for our commitment to science as a rational activity.

The semantic problem of incommensurability arose from the following simple consideration: if, as Kuhn seemed to suggest, revolutionary changes in science involved changes in the fundamental meanings of basic terms, then it would seem that there could be no genuine conflict between successive paradigms. Newtonians said "Mass does not vary with velocity," while Einsteinians say "Mass varies with velocity." But if, as Kuhn maintained, the term "mass" has a different meaning in the two statements, then there is no contradiction in what the alleged rivals say; that is, they are not really rivals. But then how can we say, as we surely must, that there is a rational basis for rejecting the Newtonian view in favor of the Einsteinian view? Or at least that the Newtonian and the Einsteinian views cannot both be true? As Philip Kitcher put it: "During . . . those episodes which Kuhn calls 'scientific revolutions' scientists . . . are unable to communicate. Both sides lack the ability to express, within their own language, the assertions of the rival theory." The result is a "situation in which the presuppositions of debate break down."[11] Without meaningful debate, how can scientific conclusions be rationally justified?

---

[11] Philip Kitcher, "Theories, Theorists and Theoretical Change," *The Philosophical Review* 87 (1978), 520. Further references will be given in the text.

Kitcher's influential response to Kuhn is an excellent example of the philosophical reaction to Kuhn's claim about semantical incommensurability, which Kitcher designates as the thesis of *conceptual relativism* ("the doctrine that the language used in a field of science changes so radically during a revolution that the old language and the new language are not intertranslatable" [520]. According to Kitcher, Kuhn (like Feyerabend) has supported conceptual relativism with impressive and detailed examples of historical case studies (of, for example, the transition from Newtonian to relativistic dynamics or from phlogiston theory to Lavoisier's theory of combustion). But his historical care is not matched, Kitcher says, by his confused and misleading philosophical understanding of meaning.

Like most analytic philosophers, Kitcher approaches meaning in terms of Frege's distinction of reference and sense. Roughly, reference is what a term denotes whereas sense is what a term expresses about what it denotes. Although meaning seems to involve both reference and sense, "many philosophers have felt uncomfortable with the notion of sense, and have urged the benefits of doing as much semantics as possible within the theory of reference" (521). Kitcher follows this path – particularly since nothing in Kuhn's writings provides "a legitimate heir to the Fregean notion of sense."[12] He accordingly formulates Kuhn's thesis in terms of reference, specifically, as the claim that "for any two languages used in the same scientific field at times separated by a revolution, there are some expressions in each language whose referents are not specifiable in the other language" (521). His working assumption, then, is that he can meet the challenge of conceptual relativism simply on the level of reference. (If that turned out not to be correct, he could still try to take account of sense in addition to reference.)

To carry out his project, Kitcher reflects on how we would construct a "theory of reference" for a scientific language, particularly one now superseded, such as Aristotle's physics. The simple, very general answer is that we would, for each primitive expression-type *e* of Aristotelian physics, construct a correlation of the form: "In the language of Aristotelian physics, *e* refers to ———— ," where the blank would be filled in by an expression-type in current (scientific) English that has the same reference as (is co-referential with) *e*. The correlations would constitute a complete theory of reference for Aristotelian physics in the sense that we could determine from them the reference of any Aristotelian primitive term. In

---

[12] Scheffler was the first to suggest discussing the meaning of scientific terms via their reference, and most other analytic philosophers have, like Kitcher, followed his lead.

reading an Aristotelian text, we could determine the reference of any (primitive) linguistic token we encounter by finding the corresponding type in our table of correlations and seeing what the corresponding English expression refers to.

This simple model assumes, however, that all the terms of Aristotelian physics are context-free: that their reference doesn't depend on the context in which tokens of them are used. If there were, for example, indexical terms, such as "I" or "now," we could not determine reference from our correlations, since a given correlation would always yield a fixed referent, whereas the referent of an indexical varies with context of use (e.g., with whether Spassky or Fischer said, "I resign"). If there are such terms, we would have to use a context-sensitive theory rather than the simple context-insensitive theory. This might seem to pose no problem for our discussion, since scientific theories are typically formulated in entirely general terms, with no essential use of demonstratives, personal pronouns, ambiguous expressions, etc. Kitcher, however, argues that, at least when we are dealing with superseded scientific theories, we need to allow for the possibility of context-sensitive expressions.[13]

He develops the point through a discussion of phlogiston theory, the eighteenth-century theory, superseded by Lavoisier's oxygen theory, of how combustion (burning) occurs. As developed by proponents such as Priestly, phlogiston theory assumed that a flammable substance contained phlogiston, which was emitted when the substance burned. The emitted phlogiston was absorbed by the surrounding air. So, for example, when we burn a sample of mercury, the residue is a red powder (the "red calx" of mercury, what we now call mercurous oxide), which the theory regards as mercury with the phlogiston removed (dephlogisticated mercury). Priestly performed experiments that showed that heating the red calx transforms it back into mercury, meaning that heating reverses the process of combustion and makes the calx reabsorb the phlogiston from the air. The result is air that is itself dephlogisticated; Priestly isolated dephlogisticated air and even breathed it himself, noting the refreshing nature of the experience.

Modern theory, of course, accounts for combustion in a reverse manner, assuming that combustion involves a burning substance's absorbing

---

[13] Indeed, Kitcher maintains that we will not be able to handle the relevant context-sensitive expressions by merely adding simple general characterizations such as "'I' refers to whoever produced the token 'I'." An adequate theory of meaning requires more than just a few tweaks on the context-independent approach.

something (oxygen) from the air, not emitting it. The experiment in which heated red calx turns into mercury is a matter of the calx emitting the oxygen that it had absorbed in combustion. What Priestly called "dephlogisticated air" is simply the element oxygen.

From one point of view, it would seem that phlogiston theory was correct to some extent and that, for example, when Priestly isolated what he called "dephlogisticated air," he had in effect discovered oxygen. Or, even if we think his theoretical confusion about whether burning sub-stances emit anything denies him this discovery, we might at least agree that "dephlogisticated air" in fact refers to oxygen, so that phlogiston theory was able to single out this important chemical substance, although under an incorrect description. On the other hand, we might note that "phlogiston" means "that which is emitted from a substance during combustion" and argue that, since nothing is emitted during combustion, "phlogiston" does not refer – there is no such thing. Further, if there is no such thing as phlogiston, there is no such thing as "air from which phlogiston has been removed," so that "dephlogisticated air" does not refer either.

Kitcher suggests that both interpretations are correct and can be accommodated if we give up the idea that our theory of reference for phlogiston theory must be context-independent. Rather, we can develop a context-sensitive theory, according to which some tokens of "dephlogisticated air" refer and others do not. Kitcher suggests we for-mulate our theory in terms of the causal theory of reference.[14] As Kitcher puts it, "the central principle of the [causal] theory is . . . that the referent of a token of an expression is the entity that figures in the appropriate way in the correct historical explanation of the production of that token" (525). So, for example, the token "Socrates" refers to the individual it does because it is at the end of a causal chain of which the first link was the naming of that individual back in ancient Greece.

Thinking in terms of the causal theory, we will reasonably think of some of Priestly's uses of "dephlogisticated air" as referring to oxygen.[15] When, for example, he breathed the gas he had isolated by heating red calx of mercury and commented on its refreshing qualities or when he observed that dephlogisticated air allowed for more lively and complete burning of a

---

[14] Kitcher cites work by Donnellan, Kripke, Putnam, and Devitt. We have discussed Kripke's approach in chapters 2 and 4.
[15] Although Kitcher agrees that most uses of "phlogiston" itself are non-referring, he argues that in some cases the term refers to hydrogen (534).

substance, it seems clear that his comments were appropriately caused by the oxygen produced by his experiments and so referred to oxygen. On the other hand, when, in a more theoretical mode, Priestly maintained that the burning of mercury produced dephlogisticated air, his claim was not appropriately caused by oxygen and in fact had no referent.

Kitcher concludes that scientific expressions will not in general have a unique reference; rather different tokens of an expression will refer differently (or not at all) depending on the context of the token's use. Correspondingly, he introduces the notion of the *reference potential* of an expression; that is, the set containing the various events that can, depending on context, appropriately cause use of a particular expression. Reference potential, Kitcher suggests, allows us to understand how conceptual change (even radical conceptual change) is possible in science without loss of communication between successive theories. For example, the reference potential of the expression "dephlogisticated air" contains at least two different appropriate causes for uses of the expression: the burning of mercury and the heating of red calx of mercury. In the context of the first cause, "dephlogisticated air" was used to refer to the gas that results when we remove from air the phlogiston emitted by the burning of the mercury. In the context of the second cause, "dephlogisticated air" was used to refer to the gas that results from heating the red calx of mercury. The crucial assumption of phlogiston theory was that in both contexts "dephlogisticated air" referred to the same gas. This is the precise sense in which the observations of phlogiston chemists were "theory-laden." Later chemists, such as Lavoisier, held a contrary theory: that combustion involved the absorption of a substance (oxygen) from the surrounding air, not the emission of a substance (phlogiston) from burning mercury. Given Kitcher's account, phlogiston chemists such as Priestly and oxygen chemists such as Lavoisier can communicate with one another. They can, in particular, agree that "dephlogisticated air" and "oxygen" refer to the same physical entity and trace their disagreement about the reference of "phlogiston" to the fact that the one theory holds that combustion requires the emission of a substance whereas the other holds that it requires the absorption of a substance.

As Kitcher notes, reference potential corresponds roughly to what Frege had in mind in speaking of sense as opposed to reference. Each element in the reference potential corresponds to a particular "meaning" through which we refer to an entity. Thus, "dephlogisticated air" in some cases refers to what is described as *the result of removing phlogiston from the air* and in other cases to *the result of heating the red calx of mercury.*

Consider a theoretical term that initially has a reference potential = {A, B}. Further development might lead to new experimental or theoretical ways of fixing the term's referent, so that the reference potential becomes {A, B, C, D}. Still further developments (e.g., new experimental data) might, however, eliminate some of the elements of the reference potential, which might eventually be reduced to {C, D}. In such a case, we would have complete change of "meaning" for the theoretical term, even though its reference remains the same. As in the phlogiston example, this constancy of reference would allow communication among scientists at every stage of the process of radical conceptual change. This, Kitcher concludes, refutes the thesis of conceptual relativity.

The above discussion is in effect a response to the following line of argument, suggested, but not endorsed, by Kuhn:

1. Rational choice between rival theories requires shared meaning between the terms of the theories.
2. In typical cases, there is no such shared meaning.
3. Therefore, the choice between rival theories is not rational.

Kitcher in effect begins by revising (1), taking into account the distinction of sense and reference. His suggestion is that shared reference (even without shared sense) is all that is necessary for rational choice. That is,

1* Rational choice between rival theories requires shared reference between the terms of the theories.

Given this, the argument for conceptual relativism requires a stronger second premise:

2* In typical cases, there is no shared reference.

Kitcher then presents a typical case (the move from phlogiston- to oxygen-theory) in which there *is* shared reference. Specifically, he sketches a causal theory of reference on which some (but not all) uses of phlogiston terms have the same reference as uses of oxygen terms. Given the adequacy of this theory, he concludes that premise 2* is false.

Kitcher's response has some obvious limitations. He has, for example, by no means established the adequacy of his version of a causal theory of reference. He can perhaps rely on previous work by Kripke *et al.* to support the general idea that reference is fixed through causal chains. But his own particular version of such a theory – involving, for example, the context-dependent reference of scientific terms and the notion of reference potential – is only roughly sketched and supported by nothing more than its apparent plausibility as applied to a particular case. Further, a critic of Kitcher might reject his revisions of the argument's premises and insist that the historical evidence shows that mere reference (or merely partial shared reference) is not typically sufficient to allow rational adjudication of rival theories. However, Kitcher's response to the problem of semantic incommensurability is no weaker that other major responses by Putnam, Enç, Devitt, and Nola, among others.[16] Like Kitcher, they sketch some version of a causal theory of reference and suggest how it can allow for shared reference across rival theories. Further, despite lingering doubts and discussions, most philosophers of science seem to have accepted some such approach as an adequate defusing of the challenge of semantic incommensurability.[17] Certainly, there is here nothing like the sense of urgency displayed in the immediate wake of Kuhn's book.

THE PROBLEM OF EPISTEMIC INCOMMENSURABILITY

The question of epistemic incommensurability posed a further challenge to scientific rationality. Even if rival theories describe the world in the very same language, it doesn't follow that this is sufficient to support a rational choice between them. The two theories may, for example, operate with quite different standards for evaluating common evidence; moreover, even given shared standards, different scientists may disagree as to how to apply them to particular situations. The basic difficulty is that – to use the term Kuhn sometimes employed – the final choice of a theory is a matter of *judgment* by individual scientists. Such judgment will be informed by evidence and arguments, but in the end it is not determined by them, since equally competent and fair-minded scientists may be aware of the same evidence and arguments but make conflicting judgments about which theory to accept.

Philosophers of science responding to Kuhn – most notably, Imre Lakatos, Stephen Toulmin, and Larry Laudan – constructed complex models of scientific change, designed to improve on Kuhn's simple picture of paradigm–anomaly–crisis–revolution. They succeeded in providing more nuanced and historically realistic accounts of scientific methodology. But no one was able to get around the ultimate need to

---

[16] See Zammito, *A Nice Derangement of Epistemes*, 65–71, for a survey of this literature.

[17] The doubts often concern the applicability of causal theories of reference to theoretical entities (given that they are unobservable and so can't be designated ostensively). For a sense of the recent directions of the discussion, see Paul Hoyningen-Huene and Howard Sankey (eds.), *Incommensurability and Related Matters*, Boston: Kluwer, 2001, particularly the editors' introduction.

supplement methodology with judgments that are not determined by methodological rules. Laudan, for example, located the rational preferability of a scientific theory in its "problem-solving effectiveness" compared to alternative theories.[18] Making decisions about comparative problem-solving effectiveness required, he maintained, assessing the number of problems a theory solved, the number it generated without being able to solve, and the relative "weight" (significance) of these problems. The language here suggests the deployment of an algorithm, given precise, objective numerical assignments of the relevant parameters. In fact, of course, as critics hastened to point out, no such precision or objectivity was forthcoming, and the decision about which theory to prefer had to be based on the personal judgments of individual scientists as to how the various evaluative factors should be assessed.

The need to appeal to such judgments was singled out as the point of attack by historians and sociologists arguing, generally under a Kuhnian banner, against the rationality of science. Typically, the argument was tied to the general epistemological issues raised by the underdetermination of theory by data (the fact that, for any set of data, there are many mutually inconsistent theories that entail all the data) and the Duhem–Quine thesis (discussed in chapter 1). So, for example, Andrew Pickering:[19] "It is always possible to invent an unlimited set of theories, each one capable of explaining a given set of facts. Of course, many of these theories may seem implausible, but to speak of plausibility is to point to a role for scientific judgment . . . Such judgments are intrinsic to theory choice, and clearly entail something more than straightforward comparisons of predictions with data" (5–6). Further, Pickering notes, when an experiment seems to have refuted a theory, "the determined critic can always concoct some possible, if improbable, source of error which has not been ruled out by the experimenters." Accordingly, once again "a judgment is required, that enough has been done by the experimenters to make it probable" that the experiment actually refutes the theory (6–7).

According to Pickering, scientists themselves (not to mention philosophers of science) explain these judgments "retrospectively": scientists' "having decided upon how the natural world really is, those data which supported this image were granted the status of natural facts, and the

---

[18] Laurens Laudan, *Progress and Its Problems: Toward a Theory of Scientific Growth*, Berkeley: University of California Press, 1978.

[19] Andrew Pickering, *Constructing Quarks: A Sociological History of Particle Physics*, Edinburgh: Edinburgh University Press, 1984. References will be given in the text.

theories which constituted the chosen world-view were presented as intrinsically plausible." But, of course, such an account of what scientists are doing is "circularly self-defeating: the explanation of a genuine decision cannot be found in a statement of what that decision was" (404). Pickering's project was to understand the true, sociological causes of scientific judgments. According to him, these causes are the "opportunistic" realizations by groups of scientists that endorsing a particular judgment would, given the resources available to them, open up opportunities for further scientific work. Although Pickering does allow for some experimental constraints on scientists' judgments, any such constraints leave the judgments underdetermined. The final determination comes from scientists' preference for "a communally congenial representation of reality"; that is, a view of reality that fits with their theoretical and experimental resources. Physical reality (e.g., the existence of quarks) is "constructed" by scientific judgments made for the sake of developing or maintaining practices that allow scientists to make fruitful use of their theories and experimental apparatus. What we call "physical reality" is a contingent product of the goals of the scientific community and has no authority over anyone who does not share those goals. In particular, "there is no obligation upon anyone framing a view of the world to take account of what twentieth-century science has to say" (413).

The problem of incommensurability – in both its semantic and its epistemic form – was, in the immediate wake of *The Structure of Scientific Revolutions*, seen as a critical challenge to the rationality of science, one that demanded an immediate circling of the philosophical wagons. The sense of urgency continued through the 1960s and 1970s, when the project of "refuting Kuhn" was high on the philosophical agenda. Even though there never seemed to be a decisive response, interest in the topic gradually decreased, and today discussions of incommensurability and the rationality of science continue only in a much muted form. At the same time, outside of philosophy, critiques of the rationality of science have flourished, with many historical and sociological studies simply starting from the assumption that science has no privileged status as a rational enterprise.

Loss of interest in the issues of incommensurability was not due simply to weariness with a difficult struggle or a faddish turn to new topics. It arose, rather, from a profound, though mostly implicit, transformation in the view philosophers of science held about both their own enterprise and that of science. The initial intensity of efforts to save the rationality of science from Kuhnian assaults involved the assumption that science could be accepted as a rational activity only to the extent that its rationality was underwritten by philosophical analysis. The idea behind Lakatos' "methodology of scientific research programmes," for example, was to provide philosophical norms for judging when it was rational to accept scientific theories. (In writing "case histories" of scientific discoveries, Lakatos sometimes altered the account to conform with his "rational reconstruction" of events and consigned what had actually happened to a footnote.) Eventually, however, most philosophers of science realized that they were not comfortable with the role of legislating norms for science, which seemed to have at least as much prima facie cognitive authority as philosophy. Some, like Laudan, proposed starting from their "pre-analytic intuitions" that certain historical episodes were obviously cases of good science and deriving general accounts of scientific method from the actual practice of good science. But such accounts, precisely because they began from quite uncontroversial examples and aimed at such a high level of generality, yielded little that was not already part of the common sense of scientific practice. Eventually, most philosophers of science decided that there was not much of interest to say about the meaning or rationality of science in general and turned to more complex and engaging issues arising in quite specific areas of scientific practice. As a result, philosophers of science now do most of their work as philosophers of quantum mechanics, of evolutionary theory, of cognitive science, etc., increasingly bringing their analytic skills and historical sensibilities to bear on substantive conceptual problems that arise directly from the practice of particular scientific subdisciplines. They are now less observers and adjudicators of science and more fellow-practitioners with scientists.

This now dominant attitude towards philosophy of science has been called "naturalistic," a term here expressing an acceptance of science on its own terms, without any need of grounding it in norms established by independent philosophical reflection. From the naturalist standpoint, challenges to the rationality of science are not irrelevant, but they are much more easily dealt with. How reasonable it is to reject challenges to a belief depends on the degree of reasonable certainty we have in the belief. My degree of reasonable certainty that the Apollo missions to the moon were, contrary to some claims, not hoaxes is very strong; however, my belief that Neil Armstrong himself (as opposed to the NASA publicity department) devised the words he uttered on taking the first step onto the moon is only moderately strong. Reading in a reputable newspaper that a scientist who worked at the time for the Apollo program has said that he helped stage the "moon-landing" in Houston is not likely to make me doubt the belief, since I can easily think of various scenarios, far more probable than the claim being made, that would explain away the scientist's testimony. But if I read a similar report claiming that Armstrong did not invent his famous statement, I might well doubt my belief. A higher antecedent probability requires stronger evidence to produce reasonable doubt. Naturalistic philosophers of science see themselves as having a high degree of reasonable certainty about the rationality of science. As a result, the standards are fairly low for dissolving doubts about this rationality.

Semantic incommensurability, for example, posed a challenge to scientific rationality by suggesting that rival theories might not share enough meanings to allow them to be rationally compared. But this challenge was met for naturalist philosophers of science once they saw that there were plausible accounts of meaning that seemed able to eliminate the inconsistency. This wasn't the end of work on semantic commensurability, but what continued was primarily a matter of trying to find a fully satisfactory theory of scientific meaning and reference for its own sake, not for the sake of refuting skeptical arguments about the rationality of science.

Epistemic incommensurability, as we have seen, seemed to pose two challenges to scientific rationality. On the one hand, there was the apparent need for a general model of scientific development that would eliminate the questions about rationality raised by Kuhn's model. But this problem dissolved given the new view that there was nothing interesting to say about science at the general methodological level. Kuhn's paradigm model, for example, operated at a level too far from actual scientific practice to pose a serious challenge to that practice. On the other hand, there was the claim that the judgments whereby scientists accept one theory rather than another are caused by irrational sociological factors. Most naturalistic philosophers of science found their antecedent confidence in the rationality of science sufficient to ignore such claims, particularly given the philosophical naiveté of their proponents, who typically assumed that there were no rational alternatives to the old positivist views of scientific rationality and put forward global skeptical theses that were self-refuting. Those who paid more attention to social studies of science acknowledged that social factors are at work in the scientific world, but asked how case studies such as that of Pickering could ever hope to prove that these factors are indeed the final determinants of scientific judgments. They also noted that the irrational judgments of individuals might well contribute to the rationality of the whole community: acceptance of a newly dominant theory might, for example, gain further support by the continuing vain efforts of a rear-guard supporting the old theory. Lacking decisive demonstrations of the irrationality of scientific judgments, naturalist philosophers of science were justified in continuing to maintain their antecedent commitment to the rationality of science.

CONCLUSION

The ultimate impact of Kuhn on the philosophy of science was to show that philosophers' commitment to the rationality of science was a matter not of philosophically justifiable belief but of a *conviction*, prior to philosophical discussion, rooted in our practice (as cognitive producers or consumers) of scientific inquiry. The positivist account of scientific rationality presented itself as based on a priori philosophical analysis. Kuhn and others showed that this account did not fit the de facto practice of even the best scientific work. Philosophers' immediate reaction was to seek a new philosophical basis for science. They never found one, but gradually realized (at least implicitly) that none was necessary: they came to philosophy already committed to the view that science was a model of rational inquiry. Accordingly, all they needed to meet the Kuhnian challenge was to show that it offered no decisive refutation of their antecedent conviction. Thus, the challenge of semantic incommensur-ability was met by showing the possibility of accounts of scientific meaning that allowed for communication between rival theories, even if no such theory was ever worked out in compelling detail. Similarly, the challenge of epistemic incommensurability was met not by providing a full epistemological account of the legitimate role of personal or communal judgments in science, but by pointing out the inadequacies of particular arguments that scientific judgments have sociological causes. Philosophy of science became an instrument for defending and developing our pre-philosophical conviction of science's cognitive authority, not for philosophically grounding that authority. This was the Kuhnian revolution in philosophy of science.

Here we also find the response to a common objection to Kuhn's suggestion that philosophy of science can learn from the history of sci-ence; namely that all history will reveal is what scientists have done in fact, whereas philosophy is concerned with what they ought to do. This objection wrongly assumes that practices have normative status for us only to the extent that we can support that status by appeal to philosophically established standards. In fact, however, it can be proper for us to begin from convictions that certain practices (or, better, certain instances of a practice) are normatively appropriate, even, perhaps, exemplary. Given such convictions, we may be able to formulate general norms from reflection on those practices, but in any case there is no need for prior philosophical certification of those norms or of the practices based on them. In particular, given the well-established cognitive authority among us of certain instances (paradigms) of science, we are justified in taking such historical instances as the pre-philosophical basis for our philosophy of science.

This Kuhnian point is, in principle, no different than the point we saw Plantinga making about religious convictions. There may be people (e.g., Plantinga's "paradigmatic believer") committed to the rightness of religion in the same way that philosophers of science are typically committed to the rightness of science. As we shall see, reflection on John Rawls' theory of justice leads to a similar point about ethical and political convictions tied to the practices of our democracy. The same basic idea, moreover, lies behind the now standard response to general epistemological skepticism, implicit, for example, in Lewis' (ultimately Wittgensteinian) claim that we are more certain of our everyday knowledge than we are of the premises of skeptical arguments challenging that knowledge. The result of the Kuhnian discussion converges with that of discussions in other philosophical subdisciplines, all showing the legitimacy of beginning philosophical inquiry from substantive pre-philosophical convictions. One of the most important recent pieces of philosophical knowledge has been that philosophical knowledge itself is not required to legitimate the epistemic claims implicit in well-established human practices. Philosophy itself has led to the rejection of philosophical foundationalism.

This is not to say that philosophers have refuted foundationalism as a thesis about the structure of human knowledge. It remains quite plausible – though still controversial – to think that our system of beliefs at any given time can be usefully divided into beliefs that are properly basic (are legitimately held without argumentative justification) and those that are derived from properly basic beliefs. The same is not true of the idea that all – or even a key subset – of our properly basic beliefs must be revealed as such through *philosophical* inquiry. This is the view that I have labeled (and rejected) as "foundationalism about philosophy" or "philosophical foundationalism."

We have also seen how Kuhn – and the discussions following upon his work – established the irreducible role of judgment in the epistemology of science. Scientific knowledge is typically, if not always, based on the shared judgment of experts in a field that a particular conclusion is appropriate given all the relevant data and arguments. Even though there is no compelling *logical* proof (deductive or inductive) of the conclusion, the conclusion is still rationally justified (or even required). The rationality of science involves an element of judgment that is not expressible as a logically sound argument. This view was strongly suggested by Kuhn's historical account of scientific practice and has been sustained by the failure of all subsequent efforts to provide an entirely logical model of scientific rationality. Our case studies show that the role of argument is similarly limited in philosophy and that the justification of philosophical conclusions, like those of empirical science, essentially involves the judgment of the philosophical community.

CHAPTER 8

Conviction and argument in
Rawls' A Theory of Justice

There is no doubt that John Rawls' *A Theory of Justice* effected a major transformation in philosophical thinking about political and ethical topics.[1] It is often noted that he revived the enterprises of political philosophy and normative ethics, both of which had languished under the earlier analytic regimen of meta-analysis. He also reversed the polarity of discussions in normative ethics. When his book appeared, utilitarianism was the dominant view among analytic ethicists, but, as Samuel Scheffler notes, "utilitarianism's predominant status has been open to serious question ever since *A Theory of Justice* set forth his powerful alternative vision."[2]

Our concern in this chapter is with the philosophical means whereby Rawls achieved his transformation of ethical and political thought. How did he make his case for his theory of justice and what can we learn about the nature of philosophical inquiry from Rawls' achievement? Unlike our previous case studies, this one deals with a lengthy book and our relatively brief foray will hardly put us in a position to judge what specific philosophical knowledge he has or has not achieved. We will, however, find a deeper understanding of how convictions can function in philosophical argument.

THE ORIGINAL POSITION AND ITS CONSTRAINTS

The ultimate goal of *A Theory of Justice* is to establish the truth of two principles, together expressing a conception of justice that Rawls argues should regulate the basic political, social, and economic structures of

---

[1] I am interested in Rawls' original formulation of his arguments and so will cite the first edition: John Rawls, *A Theory of Justice*, Cambridge, MA: Harvard University Press, 1971. All references will be given in the text.
[2] Samuel Scheffler, "Rawls and Utilitarianism," in Samuel Freeman (ed.), *The Cambridge Companion to Rawls*, Cambridge: Cambridge University Press, 2003, 453.

society. Rawls refines his statement of the two principles as his discussion progresses, arriving at the final formulation only about halfway through the book. This formulation (omitting one qualification we will not need to worry about) is as follows: (1) "Each person is to have an equal right to the most extensive system of equal basic liberties compatible with a similar system of liberty for all"; (2) "Social and economic inequalities are to be arranged so that they are both: (a) to the greatest benefit of the least advantaged . . . and (b) attached to offices and positions open to all under conditions of fair equality of opportunity" (302). Rawls also stipulates the priority of the first principle over the second: there can be no deviation from equal rights for the sake of a better distribution of social and economic goods.

Rawls' argument for these principles begins in what he calls the "original position" from which determinations of how to order a society are made. This way of talking evokes the contract tradition of Locke, Rousseau, and Kant, with which Rawls explicitly associates his view. In Rawls' contract theory, however, the original position is no postulated historical "state of nature." Rather, it is a purely hypothetical situation in which a group of people, deliberating under precisely specified conditions, are imagined to choose principles of justice to regulate a society in which they will all live.

Nor is the deliberation within the original position a matter of negotiating a compromise among parties with conflicting interests. Rawls characterizes the parties to the original position as all having the same knowledge and desires, so that what is rational for anyone to decide is rational for all. As Rawls emphasizes, his talk of an original position is simply a vivid way of expressing a set of conditions that he maintains must be met by a set of principles (a "theory of justice") adequate for a just society. These conditions specify the permissible premises in any argument for a theory of justice. In principle, we could drop the image of a group deliberating and simply present the corresponding argument: "To say that a certain conception of justice would be chosen in the original position is equivalent to saying that rational deliberation satisfying certain conditions and restrictions would reach a certain conclusion" (138). Accordingly, "At any time we can enter the original position, so to speak, by. . . arguing for principles of justice in accordance with these restrictions" (19).

Rawls generally retains the image of the original position because, he says, it is "more economical and suggestive, and brings out certain essential features that otherwise one might easily overlook" (138). On the other hand, the image misleadingly suggests that developing a conception of justice is a matter of negotiation and compromise and can disguise the fact that Rawls is, in the end, simply offering a complex set of arguments for his theory. Despite the elegance and convenience of the original-position picture, understanding Rawls' case sometimes requires focusing on what he is asking us to assume rather than what people in the original position would decide.

Rawls formulates his assumptions about the original position (and hence his view of what premises are allowed in arguments for principles of justice) in sections 22–5. The first set of assumptions concerns "the circumstances of justice" (section 22), that is, the conditions, both objective and subjective, under which a society requires principles of justice. Such principles set rules for human cooperation and so are appropriate only when such cooperation is both possible and necessary (126). The most important objective circumstance of justice is the existence of "moderate scarcity": "natural and other resources are not so abundant that schemes of cooperation become superfluous, nor are conditions so harsh that fruitful ventures must inevitably break down" (127). The main subjective circumstance is the fact that, as Rawls puts it, "the parties [in the original position] take no interest in one another's interests" (127). Here we may be tempted to object that there is no reason to assume that the parties would have such an egoistic attitude. But this is a case where the original-position picture can be misleading. Rawls' point is not about the overall attitudes of any real or possible people but about the logic of disputes that appeal to principles of justice. "Justice," he tells us, "is the virtue of practices where there are competing interests and where people feel entitled to press their rights on each other" (129). Consequently, for an appeal to justice to make sense, we must assume that there is a conflict between two or more persons' interests and that none of the parties accept subordinating their claims to those of others. In general, I may be the most altruistic of mortals, but when I make claims in the name of justice, I am asserting my interests (even if they are my interests in the welfare of someone else) in opposition to the interests of others.

Properly understood, Rawls' assumptions regarding the circumstances of justice should be uncontroversial. Questions about justice always concern conflicts among people involved in cooperative endeavors. When there is no point to cooperation, either because the resources available are so great as to make it unnecessary or so small as to make it fruitless, or because there are no conflicts among our interests, then there is no place for principles of justice. So, if principles of justice are required, then the circumstances of justice must obtain.

A second set of assumptions corresponds to what Rawls calls "the formal constraints of the concept of right" (section 23). These are conditions that Rawls sees as applying to all ethical principles, not just those of justice. They specify that any ethical principle meet the formal conditions of generality (formulablity "without the use of what would be intuitively recognized as proper names," 131); universality (hold "for everyone in virtue of their being moral persons," 132); publicity (be known to all as universally accepted in the society); ordinality ("impose an ordering on conflicting claims" by moral persons, 133–4); and finality (serve "as the final court of appeal in practical reasoning," 135). Rawls insists that he does not derive these conditions from conceptual analysis (of, e.g., the concept of right or of morality), maintaining that he "avoid[s] an appeal to the analysis of concepts at crucial points of this kind" and that "a definition cannot settle any fundamental question" but must be judged by "the soundness of the theory that results" from it (130). He does, however, speak of the conditions as "natural," by which he seems to mean that they express functions that we expect moral principles to fulfill. He further notes that they are "suitably weak" to the extent that "they are satisfied by the traditional conceptions of justice," such as utilitarianism and intuitionism, which are the main rivals of his two principles. The formal conditions do, however, have at least one substantive effect: they eliminate all versions of egoism, which either require reference to some particular individual whose interests are privileged or, if they are formulated to authorize all persons to advance their interests as they please, fail to order conflicting claims (135–6). Accepting the formal conditions involves an intuition that egoism is not a viable ethical standpoint, a view widely but not universally shared among those who think about such matters.

Accepting the formal conditions also seems to beg the question against the critiques of abstract, general ethical theory developed by existentialists from Kierkegaard to Sartre and, in a different vein, by historically oriented analytic philosophers such as Bernard Williams and Alasdair MacIntyre. Rawls might, however, respond that the focus of these critiques is not on the form as such of general theories but on alleged deficiencies in the content of these theories. His project, he could then maintain, is to develop a theory that does not have the deficiencies the critics think affect all general ethical theories. Assuming the formal constraints is simply part of the project of developing such a theory, the specific content of which he will subsequently need to defend against existentialist and historicist criticisms. So far, then, Rawls' argument needs to invoke, beyond obvious, uncontroversial assumptions about morality, an intuition that egoism is false and a promissory note to show that his eventual theory of justice does not fall to existentialist and historicist critiques.

The most discussed constraints on the original position are those Rawls presents as constituting a "veil of ignorance" that excludes all specific information about the abilities and status of any individual contractor in the society being formed. According to Rawls, such information would introduce a fundamental unfairness by allowing individuals to support principles that would likely benefit them simply because of contingent features that have nothing to do with justice. Accordingly, in the original position, "no one knows his place in society, his class position or social status, nor does he know his fortune in the distribution of natural assets and abilities, his intelligence, strength, and the like" (137; an almost identical passage occurs on p. 12). Beyond this, no one knows "his conception of the good, the particulars of his rational plan of life, or even the special features of his psychology such as his aversion to risk or liability to optimism or pessimism" (137). The parties are also ignorant of any specific historical information about the nature of the society in which they will live (e.g., its degree of cultural or technological development, its geographical location and resources). The veil of ignorance does not, however, exclude any knowledge of *general* truths of psychology and the social sciences.

Rawls presents the veil of ignorance as, like the formal constraints, a "natural" condition on the derivation of principles of justice (137, n.11). Specifically, he thinks of the veil as following immediately from "the idea of the original position," which is "to set up a fair procedure so that any principles agreed to will be just" (137). This corresponds to his characterization of his theory as one of "justice as fairness," meaning not that he defines justice *as* fairness but that he derives the principles of justice from conditions that assure fairness in their formulation. Given the goal of fairness, "if a knowledge of particulars is allowed, then the outcome is biased by arbitrary contingencies . . . The arbitrariness of the world must be corrected for by adjusting the circumstances of the initial contractual situation" (141).

Rawls notes, however, that some may object to the veil, maintaining that it is irrational not to allow the principles of justice to "be chosen in the light of all the knowledge available" (139). To this he offers two lines of response. First (in section 24), he argues that excluding specific knowledge is an essential simplification "if one is to have any theory at all" (139). But why not just conclude that Rawls' theoretical project may be impossible to carry out? A more substantive response, developed in section 40, is based on a "Kantian interpretation of the original position" (139). The interpretation concerns Kant's notion of autonomy as the source of morality. On Rawls' reading of Kant, a person acts "autonomously when the principles of his action are chosen by him as the most adequate possible expression of his nature as a free and equal rational being." Acting in this way in turn requires that "the principles he acts upon are not adopted because of his social position or natural endowments, or in view of the particular kind of society in which he lives or the specific things he happens to want" (252). Such principles would lead to non-ethical, heteronymous action (that is, action directed by desires or interests other than those of a free, rational agent as such). The veil of ignorance is designed precisely to eliminate all possibility of heteronomy in our choice of principles of justice. In Kantian terms, "the original position [is] the point of view from which noumenal selves see the world." Noumenal selves have the freedom to choose however they like, but "they also have a desire to express their nature as rational and equal members of the intelligible realm with precisely this liberty to choose" (255). By eliminating everything except conditions corresponding to our precise status as free, rational agents, the veil of ignorance ensures a choice of principles of justice in accord with this desire of the noumenal self. Of course, this defense of the veil of ignorance is no stronger than the Kantian premise, that autonomy is the source of morality, on which it is based. We will return to the question of how, if at all, Rawls is entitled to this premise.

The last set of constraints on the original position concerns the rationality of the parties involved. Rawls requires that they be rational in the standard sense of economists and other social theorists: "in choosing between principles each tries as best he can to advance his interests" (142). It is important to emphasize that this constraint does not amount to a metaphysical assumption about the nature of human beings or of human rationality. Contrary to some critics, Rawls does not begin from the assumption that we are or should be simply instruments for the calculated fulfillment of our desires. The assumption of instrumental rationality has merely methodological significance. An assumption of contractors who are totally benevolent towards one another and fully informed about the particulars of each person's place in society would, Rawls points out, also, in principle, lead to principles of justice that are entirely fair. But there would be intractable questions about the relative strength of different benevolent desires and insurmountable complications in taking account of so much particularized knowledge, so that in practice the "morally more attractive assumptions" (149) would lead to a dead-end. By contrast, "the combination of mutual disinterest and the veil of ignorance achieves the same purpose as benevolence" (combined with total knowledge): forcing "each person in the original position to take the good of others into account" (148). But disinterest plus ignorance has the advantage of working in practice to produce acceptable principles of justice.

Rationality alone, of course, yields no conclusions without some interest that it is employed to advance. There is no sense to employing rational means unless there are some desired goods that we take as ends. Accordingly, Rawls needs to specify some common goods sought by everyone in the original position. Individuals have, of course, quite different specific conceptions of the ultimate good (corresponding, for example, to commitments to a Christian religion or to a secular humanism). But Rawls notes that any plausible end (ultimate good) requires a standard set of natural and social primary goods as necessary means to achieving it. "Greater intelligence, wealth and opportunity, for example, allow a person to achieve goods he could not rationally con-template otherwise" (93). More fully, Rawls sees primary goods as "things that every rational man is presumed to want," including social goods such as "rights and liberties, powers and opportunities, income and wealth" (as well as "self-respect") and natural goods such as "vigor, intelligence, and imagination" (62). The principles of justice are chosen as best satisfying, given the veil of ignorance, our desire to attain these primary goods.

ARGUING FOR THE TWO PRINCIPLES OF JUSTICE

Given the assumptions required for reasoning from the original position, Rawls' next step is to develop arguments from these assumptions for his two principles. Although such arguments would ideally be strictly deductive, Rawls recognizes that he will often have to be content with non-deductive, probabilistic arguments. He also allows that there is little chance of his establishing the absolute correctness of his principles. In theory, it might be possible to define standards that must be met by an optimal set of principles of justice and then show, without specific reference to any alternatives, that Rawls' principles meet these conditions. But, practically speaking, Rawls thinks that the case for his principles will always have to be made through explicit comparison with alternatives. Much, then, depends on our decision as to which are the apparently viable alternatives, and Rawls' case will always be open to attack by the presentation of a better alternative. He thinks, however, that he will have done enough if he has shown his theory's superiority to views included under four traditional headings: Classical Teleological Conceptions of Justice (including utilitarianism and perfectionism), Intuitionistic Conceptions, Egoistic Conceptions, and "Mixed Conceptions" (combining elements of his conception and a utilitarian version of the Classical Teleological Conception). Since Rawls' main concern is to show the superiority of his view to that of utilitarianism, we will focus on this case.

Specifically, Rawls argues that his principles of justice are superior to the principle of average utility. Average utility represents a later and more plausible view than what Rawls calls "classical utilitarianism." According to the classical principle of utility, institutions should be "arranged to maximize the absolute weighted sum of the expectations of the relevant representative men"; or, more roughly but accurately enough, to maximize the *total amount* of satisfaction (happiness or utility) in society. By contrast, the principle of average utility enjoins maximizing the *average amount* of satisfaction. As Rawls notes, the two utilitarian principles are equivalent when the size of the population is held constant. But when population varies there are differences. For example, as population increases, the classical principle will require that we accept a continual lowering of the average utility as long as the total utility continues to increase. Rawls argues that the parties in the original position would prefer the average principle to the classical principle: "Since the parties aim to advance their own interests, they have no desire in any event to maximize the sum total of satisfaction" (163), particularly when this would probably lower their own individual levels of satisfaction.

Rawls' primary case for his two principles and against the principle of average utility is based on thinking of "the two principles as the maximin solution to the problem of social justice" (152). The maximin solution to a problem of decision under uncertainty tells us to act so as to maximize the value of the least valuable outcome: to make the best of the worst as opposed, for example, to a maximax solution (maximize the most valuable outcome). The general structure of Rawls' argument is this:

(1) The constraints defining the original position pose a decision problem.
(2) This problem requires a maximin solution.
(3) The two principles provide a maximin solution.
(4) The principle of average utility does not provide a maximin solution.
(5) Therefore, the two principles are superior to the principle of average utility (as a solution to the problem posed by the original position).

Premise (1) is unproblematic, since the original position is a clear case of decision under uncertainty. Premise (3) is readily established. Rawls' two principles of justice correspond to a maximin solution to the decision problem posed by the original position because they give those who are worst off in a society the best status that they could have in this position. The first principle guarantees that the worst off have the same basic rights as everyone else (giving them more rights would make them no longer the least advantaged), and the second guarantees that they benefit from any economic advantage that the better off have over them. There may be other forms of a maximin solution, but Rawls' principle undeniably provides one version. By contrast, choosing the principles of average utility does not follow the maximin strategy, since it maximizes the average satisfaction of members of society, even if this might require extreme hardship for some individuals. So premise (4) is also true.

Premise (2) is more difficult to establish, and the crux of the argument. Obviously, the conservative, risk-aversive maximin approach is not appropriate for every case. If, for example, a young person is investing discretionary funds, it may well make sense to accept the possibility of a significant loss for the chance of an even more significant gain. Only when it is of overriding importance to lose as little as possible is the maximin rule the best policy. If those in the original position knew that they would be among the least advantaged, then they would have good reason to prefer maximin. But, since they do not know what their position will be, why should they prefer the maximin strategy to one, like the principle of average utility, that tolerates higher risk for the sake of a better average outcome?

There are, Rawls maintains, three main features of a choice situation that tend to make the maximin rule preferable: (a) a need to pay little attention to the probabilities of possible outcomes (since the rule specifically ignores such probabilities); (b) a lack of interest in gaining anything beyond the minimum that can be guaranteed by the maximin rule; (c) the possibility that alternative choices, but not the preferred choice, may lead to intolerable results. Any one of these features gives some support for the maximin strategy, and all three together make a compelling case. He makes his case for premise (2) by arguing that all three conditions apply to the original position.

Condition (a) obviously applies because the veil of ignorance "excludes all but the vaguest knowledge of likelihoods" (155). The parties know hardly anything of what sort of society they will live in or what their place in it will be.

Condition (b) does not obviously apply to the original position. To show that it does, Rawls suggests (section 26), two complementary lines of thought in support of this condition, both developed in later parts of his book. The first is based on the project of Part II, which draws the consequences of the two principles for particular issues of social justice and argues that they "provide a workable theory of social justice, and . . . are compatible with reasonable demands of efficiency." Given a theory of justice that is satisfactory in practice, "there may be, on reflection, little reason for trying to do better," particularly if (as Rawls also tries to show) the utilitarian alternative risks producing unsatisfactory social results. The second line of thought derives from the priority of the principle of equal liberty over the difference principle that governs social and economic goods – again something Rawls will claim to establish later in the book. Adding this line of thought to the first is, Rawls says, "practically decisive" for establishing condition (b), since "this priority implies that . . . the minimum assured by the two principles . . . is not one that the parties wish to jeopardize for the sake of greater economic or social advantage" (156). In addition, two further "main arguments" for the principles (which we will discuss shortly) are also relevant to establishing condition (b).

Like condition (a), condition (c) unproblematically applies to the original position. There are obviously strong reasons to avoid principles of justice that may well have intolerable consequences for an individual who may well turn out to be me. Moreover, this condition would seem to favor Rawls' two principles over the utilitarian principles, since, whereas the maximin character of the two principles is a strong guard against intolerable outcomes, the principle of utility may well result in such outcomes. What, for example, is to prevent the utilitarian from accepting "if not slavery or serfdom, at any rate serious infractions of liberty for the sake of greater social benefits" (156)? A standard utilitarian response to this objection is that the possibility of utility's requiring moral outrages such as slavery is merely abstract. In any real society, there will almost certainly be no gain in utility from trading fundamental rights for social and economic benefits. Rawls cannot object in principle to this response because he himself makes a similar reply to a parallel objection to his second principle of justice. Critics note that the principle forbids decreasing the welfare of the least well off, even if a minuscule decrease would result in gigantic gains for everyone else. But why, for example, refuse to decrease the income of the least advantaged by \$1 a year if this would result in everyone else receiving \$1,000,000 more per year? Like the utilitarian, Rawls admits the absurdity, but insists that "the possibilities the objection envisages cannot arise in real cases; the feasible set [of social and economic arrangements] is so restricted that they are excluded" (158).

Nonetheless, Rawls points to what he regards as a decisive asymmetry between his theory and utilitarianism. Although both agree that "general facts as well as moral conditions are needed in the argument for the first principles of justice . . . it is characteristic of utilitarianism that it leaves so much to arguments from general facts." By contrast, his approach (like contract theories in general) "embeds the ideals of justice, as ordinarily understood, more directly into its first principles . . . [and] relies less on general facts in reaching a match with our judgments of justice" (160). This, he maintains, shows that the third condition relevant to choosing a maximin strategy holds in the original position choice between his principles and the principle of utility. Granted, the facts may turn out (however improbably) to require the counter-intuitive application of our principle of justice. But the two principles, unlike the utilitarian principle, minimize the disconcerting possibilities by minimizing their dependence on fallible factual assumptions. Accordingly, "it seems that the parties [to the original position] would prefer to secure their liberties straightaway rather than have them depend upon what may be uncertain and speculative actuarial calculations" (161) and so would judge the two principles superior to the principle of average utility as a way of meeting condition (c).

Having shown that conditions (a)–(c) apply to the original position, Rawls claims to have established premise (2) and so established his maximin argument for his two principles.

In section 29 of *A Theory of Justice*, Rawls formulates two further arguments that he describes as "some of the main grounds for the two principles of justice" (175). (But he also notes that they can also be regarded as reinforcements of the maximin argument, to which they are closely related.) The first is based on the formal constraint of finality for decisions made in the original position: "Since the original agreement is final and made in perpetuity, there is no second chance . . . A person is choosing once and for all the standards which are to govern his life prospects." Accordingly, "the parties must weigh with care whether they will be able to stick by their commitment in all circumstances" (176). Here, Rawls maintains, his two principles have a decided advantage over the principle of average utility, since, given their maximin motivation, they insure us "against the worst eventualities." By contrast, the principle of average utility may wind up requiring immense sacrifices from individuals for the sake of a greater average utility. We are far more likely to stand by the two principles than we are the principle of average utility.

The second argument employs the formal constraint of publicity: the requirement that the principles emerging from the original position be publicly known as such throughout the society. Because of this condition, members of a society will be able to know whether or not its basic structure in fact satisfies its principles. Such knowledge will have a stabilizing effect, assuming that it results in a firmer acceptance of the principles. Accordingly, "a conception of justice is stable when the public recognition of its realization by the social system tends to bring about the corresponding sense of justice" (177). Rawls argues that his conception of justice (the two principles) is stable in this sense. For, when the two principles are satisfied, "each person's liberties are secured and there is a sense defined by the difference principle in which everyone is benefited by social cooperation . . . Since everyone's good is affirmed, all acquire inclinations to uphold the scheme" (177). But when a society satisfies the principle of average utility, it does not follow that everyone has benefited from the regime; some may have had to accept major hardships for the sake of others. Accordingly, the stability of a society ruled by the utilitarian principle will require that those "who must make sacrifices strongly identify with interests broader than their own" (177–8). This is, as a matter of psychological fact, not a likely occurrence. Rawls does not deny that individuals frequently sacrifice themselves for others, but such actions are typically due to "affection and ties of sentiment" and "not demanded as a matter of justice by the basic structure of society" (178). Rawls also develops this point in a Kantian vein, arguing that his principles, as opposed to the utilitarian principle, fulfill the goal of treating everyone as an end and not just a means, thereby providing everyone with a sense of self-respect that is crucial for the psychological stability of the system.

Rawls thinks he has shown that the above arguments for his two principles are valid and that their premises are at least highly plausible. Nonetheless, he does not claim that they make an adequate case for his theory of justice. This is because the premises provided by the conditions are not self-evident or infallible and are open to revision. In particular, pressure for revision will arise if we find that the theory entailed by the conditions conflicts with our "considered convictions" about justice; that is, with judgments about the justice of certain practices or situations that "we now make intuitively and in which we have the greatest confidence" (17). (Rawls' examples include our judgments that religious tolerance is just and that racial discrimination is unjust.) If the theory of justice entailed by our characterization of the original conditions conflicts with our considered convictions about what is just, then we may want to revise our characterization of the conditions (and therefore our principles of justice). But, of course, our considered convictions about justice are in general no more self-evident and infallible than our intuitions about the original condition, so we may rather decide to revise our convictions to fit our conditions. (In fact, much of Rawls' discussion is of this latter sort.) There is, accordingly, a process of mutual adjustment between our formulation of the original conditions and our considered convictions about justice, a process which must continue until "eventually we . . . find a description that both expresses reasonable conditions and yields principles which match our considered judgments duly pruned and adjusted" (20). If and when this happens, we have reached what Rawls calls "reflective equilibrium." This reflective equilibrium may, of course, itself be upset by further reflection and discussion, but while it lasts it provides a justification for our theory of justice. Part II of *A Theory of Justice*, which is too extensive to consider here, develops this further stage in Rawls' justification of his two principles of justice.

But even the reflective equilibrium sought in Part II is not, Rawls thinks, sufficient to make his case. Even if the principles are superior to alternative conceptions of justice and even if they best match our considered judgments about particular cases, there are still two possibilities that would exclude them as the preferred choice from the original position. First, given truths of human psychology, the two principles might not be ones that most people will be able to accept in the long run; second, beyond questions of justice, they might not be consistent with our general view of what constitutes a good human life. We will focus on the second issue, which raises fundamental methodological questions and proved central to Rawls' own subsequent revision of his position.

In Part III, Rawls formulates a conception of the human good and argues for its consistency with the principles of justice. This formulation is subtle and complex, and its details need not concern us. The essential point is that it assumes what, in *Political Liberalism*,[3] Rawls calls a "comprehensive philosophical doctrine": roughly, that human nature, and hence the human good, is defined by a Kantian notion of rational autonomy. Given this, what we discussed earlier as a "Kantian

---

[3] John Rawls, *Political Liberalism*, New York: Columbia University Press, 1993. References will be given in the text.

interpretation" of the original position becomes not just an optional interpretation but also an essential premise in Rawls' case for the two principles of justice. In *Political Liberalism*, Rawls sees this as a "serious problem," since "a modern democratic society is characterized not simply by a pluralism of comprehensive religious, philosophical, and moral doctrines but by a pluralism of *incompatible yet reasonable* comprehensive doctrines" (xvi, emphasis added). Even if Rawls was not trying to argue from premises that would be accepted by any reasonable person, he was certainly trying to argue from premises that would be accepted by all reasonable fellow citizens of a modern democratic society. But Rawls now realizes that he is not prepared to judge a comprehensive moral view unreasonable simply because it is inconsistent with his own preferred position. Consequently, he concludes that his case for his two principles has not been adequately made.

CONCEPTIONS OF A PERSON AND THE REVISED CASE FOR THE PRINCIPLES

The remedy, developed at length in *Political Liberalism*, is to replace the Kantian comprehensive moral view – that persons have moral standing precisely because they are rationally autonomous – with a "political conception of the person" (29) as "free and equal" in the sense implicit in "the political culture of a constitutional democratic regime" (34). This political conception of the person will provide premises of the original position from which we can derive the two principles of justice, now presented not as philosophical conceptions that ought to be accepted by any reasonable person but as political conceptions that ought to be accepted by any reasonable citizen of a constitutional democratic regime.

The political conception of a person implicit in a constitutional democratic culture is, Rawls says, essentially that of a free citizen, where "free" is understood as having three aspects. First, "citizens are free in that they conceive of themselves and of one another as having the moral power to have a conception of the good" (30), a conception that they have the right, as citizens, to change for good reasons. Second, "citizens . . . regard themselves as being entitled to make claims on their institutions so as to advance their conceptions of the good." Such claims must "fall within the range permitted by the public conception of justice" but, given that limitation, they are "self-authenticating" in the sense of "having weight of their own apart from being derived from duties and obligations specified by a political conception of justice" (e.g., by what is "owed to society") (30). Third, "citizens ... are viewed as capable of taking responsibility for their ends"; in particular, they are "thought to be capable of adjusting their aims and aspirations in the light of what they can reasonable expect to provide for" and "they are viewed as capable of restricting their claims in matters of justice to the kinds of things the principles of justice allow" (33–4). Substituting this conception of a person for the controversial Kantian conception allows us, Rawls maintains, to derive the principles of justice from the conditions of the original position.

This alone, however, will not be enough to justify the principles of justice to those who, like most of us, hold comprehensive theories (religious or secular) that go well beyond anything implicit in the political conceptions derivable from our shared political culture. For it may be that views we would hold if our ultimate commitment were to democratic political culture are instead contradicted by our ultimate commitment to a comprehensive philosophical or religious theory. Such a contradiction may allow limited forms of participation in democratic culture, but at some point our comprehensive commitment will require withdrawal from the democratic commitment. So, for example, a fundamentalist Muslim might accept a role for a popularly elected legislature but insist that, on certain matters of ultimate religious principle, legislative decisions can be overridden by religious authorities.

Given this possibility, the existence of a democratic state requires that all (or at least a large majority) of the citizens see their comprehensive theories as at least consistent with a full commitment to the two principles of justice. There must be a *consensus* on these principles, even though the grounds for the commitment may be different (even mutually inconsistent) from citizen to citizen (which is what Rawls means by *overlapping* consensus). Those whose comprehensive theories do not allow such commitment are ipso facto outside the democratic community and must be judged "unreasonable" by those with an ultimate commitment to that community.

We are now in a position to see that Rawls' approach is fundamentally pragmatic in the sense that it grounds democratic consensus not in any shared theoretical knowledge but in the *practices* of a community. Implicit in these practices are assumptions necessary for them to make sense; for example, the egalitarian practices of a democracy are unintelligible without an assumption of the equality, in some specific sense, of all citizens. The ultimate premises that provide the public justification of the principles of justice (that is, the justification to which we are committed as citizens of our democracy) all derive from our practical commitment to life in a democratic culture. (This public justification is, of course, distinct from any further justification provided by our varying comprehensive theories.)

This pragmatic move allows Rawls to solve – at least in principle – the otherwise intractable problem of constructing a case for his principles of justice from premises shared by all citizens of a democratic society. At the same time, of course, the pragmatic move renounces, much more decisively than does *A Theory of Justice*, the traditional philosophical goal of a transcendent (that is, trans-historical and trans-cultural) theory, justified by arguments that should be accepted by any rational person. Some will see this renunciation as a sad abdication from the philosophical ideal, if not an implicit fall into skepticism.

Rawls, however, maintains that democratic liberty of thought will in all likelihood lead to an irreducible pluralism of reasonable, even though mutually incompatible, comprehensive theories: "Political liberalism assumes that, for political purposes, a plurality of reasonable yet incompatible comprehensive doctrines is the normal result of the exercise of human reason within the framework of the free institutions of a constitutional democratic regime" (xvi). It is not just that we will inevitably disagree on the fundamental philosophical issues but that proponents of conflicting views can all be rationally entitled to their convictions. It follows that our commitment to democracy entails an acceptance of irreconcilable philosophical disagreement due to mutually inconsistent pre-philosophical convictions.

CONCLUSION: REFLECTIVE EQUILIBRIUM AND CONVICTIONS IN PHILOSOPHICAL ARGUMENTATION

Rawls calls the method he uses to justify his two principles *reflective equilibrium*. This method is often characterized – by, for example, Norman Daniels – as a version of coherentist justification, a view that leaves Rawls open to the charge that he is engaged in the circular enterprise of using questionable assumptions to support one another.[4] But the language of coherence is appropriate only in the sense that Rawls rejects a classical (e.g., Cartesian) foundationalist approach in which we try to derive conclusions from premises that are entirely unproblematic

---

[4] Norman Daniels, "Wide Reflective Equilibrium and Theory Acceptance in Ethics," *Journal of Philosophy* 76 (1979), 256–82.

starting points. He denies that there are any such starting points, either in the sense of Cartesian self-evident truths or in the sense of an empiricist combination of obvious factual truths and incontestable analyses of the meanings of moral terms (577–8).

Nonetheless, as we saw, his case for his two principles centers on a core deductive argument based on the maximin solution. Reflective equilibrium develops as a method for critically evaluating the fallible premises of this argument. Although Rawls regards these premises as either obvious or justified by good arguments from obvious premises, he rightly sees a need to see if they are consistent with other claims that we find obvious (or justified by good arguments). This leads first to a reflection (in Part II) on our judgments about justice in particular cases and (in Part III) on various relevant aspects of our comprehensive worldviews.[5] In both cases, the point is to see if the premises and conclusions of Rawls' central argument are consistent with other claims to which we are committed. But Rawls is not claiming that the mere consistency of this set of beliefs justifies them as a whole. Rather, each belief has its own justificatory grounds (in either intuition or argument) and the point of reflective equilibrium is to make sure that we are not neglecting a possible challenge to our argument from other beliefs that we think we are justified in holding. Reflective equilibrium is not a matter of the weak supporting the weak; it is a way of showing how a core argument, from plausible but not indubitable premises, can be maintained (perhaps with revisions) in the light of possible challenges.

Accounts of reflective equilibrium often present it as involving the non-deductive mode of reasoning known as inference to the best explanation. Such reasoning is, of course, very common in science, and it is also tempting to think of Rawls and other philosophers as arguing for their principles on the grounds that they "explain" our intuitions about justice, freedom, consciousness, etc. In any case, this mode of inference has become very popular in many areas of philosophy.[6] Intuitions in a given domain are taken as "data" that need explanation; then general principles or definitions are presented as a "theory" from which the data can be logically deduced, further data are presented in search of further confirmation (or refutation) of the theory, alternatives theories are

---

[5] The first sort of reflection aims at what Rawls later calls "narrow reflective equilibrium" and the second sort aims at what he calls "wide reflective equilibrium."

[6] For an interesting discussion of best explanation in analytic metaphysics, see Chris Swoyer, "How Ontology Might Be Possible: Explanation and Inference in Metaphysics," *Midwest Studies in Philosophy* XXIII (1999), 100–31.

considered and found wanting, all leading to the conclusion that the theory should be accepted as (probably) true.

There is no doubt that inference to the best explanation is dramatically effective in some scientific cases (to cite one famous example, the inference to the existence of Neptune as the best explanation of anomalies in the orbit of Uranus). But these scientific cases are typically ones in which the inferred explanans entails phenomena that are in themselves improbable but are, surprisingly, observed to be the case. When there is no further surprising confirmation, the explanans remains at best a more or less plausible guess (as was the hypothesis of Vulcan, a planet between the sun and Mercury, posited to explain anomalies in the orbit of Mercury). In philosophical cases, where almost all our data are quite familiar intuitions, there is little room for a surprising new confirmation, and the inference to the best explanation by itself is seldom effective. At best, inference to the best explanation is just one element in a much more complex effort to persuasively elaborate a view.

In fact, reflective equilibrium (which involves far more than inference to the best explanation) is itself a particularly important means of persuasive elaboration. It is important, first, because it not only supports a view by showing how it can be fruitfully developed but also responds to objections that are potential defeaters of the view. Also, it is not, for most current analytic philosophers, an optional approach. Once we give up, as most of us have, the foundationalist ideal of arguing only from premises that are self-evident or otherwise entirely obvious, our views become open to challenges that can only be met by seeking reflective equilibrium. We have seen particularly clear examples of it in the dialectic of counterexamples in Kripke's critique of descriptivism and in Gettier epistemology. But Rawls goes much further than most other philosophers in raising the self-critical questions that require him to seek reflective equilibrium. In fact, *A Theory of Justice* provides within a single volume the sort of extended application of the method that typically results only from debates among the community of specialists in a given sub-area.

Our discussion of Rawls also provides an occasion to return to a perspective on intuitions and convictions that we have not yet sufficiently developed. Unlike many other philosophical appeals to direct intellectual insight, Rawls' intuitions are not in general the product of disengaged reflection on abstract propositions. Particularly in *Political Liberalism*, Rawls grounds democratic consensus in community practice. Correspondingly, the intuitive judgments he invokes typically derive from our engagement with practices that have an integral role in our concrete daily lives. They represent not isolated "inclinations to believe" but commitments flowing from our practical engagement in, for example, a moral or political form of life. As such, they express convictions rooted in lived experience and connected to our fundamental self-understanding. This gives them an epistemic status beyond that of ordinary beliefs or inclinations to believe – and far beyond isolated philosophical intuitions about whether barn-perceivings in Gettier circumstances are instances of knowledge or whether zombies are logically possible.

The fact that many of Rawls' intuitive judgments are so deeply rooted shows that his insistence that they are all subject to revision does not mean that they are necessarily lightly held or subject to easy rejection. The possibility of revision reflects merely a generic fallibilism, whereby any of our beliefs are subject to question if they turn out to conflict with more deeply held beliefs. Such fallibilism is consistent with a judgment's being entirely justified and confidently asserted as true. This retains the essential revisability of intuitions without necessarily reducing them to merely tentative intellectual seemings.

Basic convictions are intuitions and, in discussing religious belief and freedom, we have noted that such convictions are rooted in practices central to our way of life. Rawls' liberal democratic convictions about justice provide another example. More important, his development of these convictions through his core argument and use of reflective equilibrium provide an instructive model of how pre-philosophical convictions can function in philosophical argumentation.

To get a sense of the distinctive nature of this argumentation, it will be helpful to compare it to a more traditional approach, which I will call foundational argumentation, where convictions are allowed no role.[7] This approach corresponds to the following schematization:

Foundational argumentation
1. Begin with uncontroversial intuitions (based, for example, on conceptual analysis) about a given topic (e.g., justice).
2. Use the intuitions as premises in deductive arguments for a comprehensive philosophical doctrine (e.g., about the nature of justice).
3. Derive from this comprehensive doctrine a specific theory applicable to a domain of interest (e.g., principles of justice for ordering a society).
4. Use the specific theory to justify a particular set of practices (e.g., the practices of liberal democracy).

---

[7] Here, of course, the foundationalism in question is philosophical foundationalism.

5. Also use the theory to resolve disputed questions that arise regarding the practices (e.g., ethical and social issues).

By contrast, here is the schema for what I will call the convictional approach:

Convictional argumentation
1. Begin with a practice that we endorse as unquestionably appropriate (e.g., liberal democracy).
2. Reflect on this practice to formulate basic convictions relevant to the derivation of principles valid for a domain of interest (e.g., a just society).
3. Use various modes of deductive and non-deductive argumentation to arrive at a specific theory expressing the consequences of our basic convictions (e.g., Rawls' two principles of justice).
4. Test the principles against our considered judgments about particular cases and our comprehensive views, revising the principles, judgments, or views as appropriate (reflective equilibrium).
5. Apply the resulting theory to resolve disputed problems.

Note that whereas intuitions and comprehensive doctrines derived from them are the explicit starting points in the standard schema of foundational argumentation, they enter only indirectly into convictional argumentation, as premises (convictions) implicit in the practices from which we begin. Conversely, whereas acceptance of a relevant practice is the starting point of convictional argument, such acceptance is the outcome of foundational argumentation. The convictionalist will see the foundationalist as assuming the authority of special modes of philosophical knowing that have no purchase in the real world of intellectual debate, whereas the foundationalist will see the convictionalist presupposing the authority of practices that have no cognitive status unless justified by independent philosophical argumentation. Further, given their respective starting points, convictional and foundational arguments from them are radically different. Foundationalists require valid deductions of conclusions, whereas Rawls is content with an increasingly plausible case based on a variety of considerations.

These considerations include pointing out that a position explains most of the obvious truths in its domain, suggests new and fruitful ways of thinking, shows a high degree of logical coherence, can be revised in natural (non-ad hoc) ways to meet criticism, is supported by a variety of independent deductive arguments from plausible premises, and poses challenges to proponents of alternative views that they are not able to meet. There is no single knock-down argument for the position but the aggregated force of these diverse considerations makes an impressive case.

Despite the differences, much of foundational argumentation reappears in new ways in the convictional mode. For example, something akin to conceptual analysis (a primary source of foundational intuitions) may be used to "extract" considered judgments about principles and cases from our practices. The convictionalist will need to ask "what we would say" in various situations, not as a matter of exercising some abstract faculty of philosophical intuition or even of seeing what we mean or believe in some superficial sense, but in order to reveal what we are committed to by the fundamental frameworks in which we act. Further, once convictionalist "pragmatic analysis" extracts, from reflection on our practices, a set of judgments about principles and cases, these judgments can be used to construct arguments that mirror those put forward by foundationalists. For example, considered judgments about particular cases can function quite like Gettier counterexamples in modus tollens rejections of general principles; and it is at least ideally possible to use entirely deductive arguments in stage (3) of convictionalist argumentation. Conversely, the foundationalist model, purged of often unrealistic assumptions about, for example, the authority of isolated intellectual intuitions and demands for infallible premises and for purely deductive argumentation, converges towards the convictionalist model.

Although Rawls gives special prominence to convictions – and rejects the explicit use of conceptual and linguistic analysis – a major by-product of his work, like that of all good philosophers, is the discovery or development of important philosophical distinctions. Even those who have no sympathy with Rawls' liberal democratic convictions and no interest in his use of them to revive the Kantian picture of social ethics, will be at an intellectual disadvantage if they continue thinking about justice without taking account of Rawls' many perceptive and fruitful distinctions relevant to the topic.

In some cases, Rawls refines or transforms a distinction long employed in ethical and political thought. For example, his notion of the original position gives a novel way of reading the distinction between a historical social contract and a hypothetical contract, as well as a way of utilizing egoism as a methodological device rather than as a substantive ethical view. The related notion of a veil of ignorance gives a new way of deploying the distinction between autonomy and heteronomy and a new significance to the distinction of the general structure of a society and an individual's place in it. Rawls also introduces important new distinctions, especially in his effort to find agreement among people who have different substantive conceptions of the human good. Of particular significance are those between a comprehensive moral view of persons and a political conception of persons, and between a comprehensive consensus and an overlapping consensus. In yet other cases, he makes effective use of standard distinctions to develop or defend his positions. For example, the distinction between primary and ultimate goods points towards a way of getting agreement on principles of justice among people with different views of the ultimate good, the distinction between realistic and merely hypothetical cases provides a response to counterexamples to his difference principle, and the distinction between principles and cases underlies his method of reflective equilibrium. The way that perceptive and fruitful distinctions proliferate in Rawls' work, despite his eschewal of conceptual and linguistic analysis, illustrates that, even if not explicitly sought, they are an inevitable accompaniment of good philosophy.

PART III

Philosophical truth and knowledge

Rorty against the world: philosophy, truth, and objectivity

In this concluding case study, I turn to the work of Richard Rorty on the nature of philosophy. Rorty began as a practitioner of analytic philosophy and always gave it a central role in his thinking. Nonetheless, after the publication of *Philosophy and the Mirror of Nature* (1979), he became a *bête noire* for many analytic philosophers, who saw him as trying to undermine their enterprise by irresponsible defenses of outrageous claims. Others, myself included, find his work an engaging meld of erudition, penetration, and iconoclasm, which, even at its most problematic, always informs and stimulates. For our purposes, Rorty's work is of particular interest for its distinctive mode of philosophical argumentation, for the skeptical view of traditional philosophy defended by that argumentation, and for a perspective on the nature of the truth attained by philosophical knowledge.

RORTY'S PRAGMATIC METAPHILOSOPHY

Philosophy and the Mirror of Nature remains the only fully and systematically developed expression of Rorty's views on the nature of philosophy.[1] However, his position significantly changed over the last quarter-century, and he came to prefer explaining and defending his ideas not through unified treatises but in a mosaic of independent essays on intertwined topics. I begin by examining a set of four such essays, which Rorty grouped together, under the general heading "Philosophy's Place in Culture," in the collection he published shortly before his death in 2007.[2] Taken together,

---

[1] Richard Rorty, *Philosophy and the Mirror of Nature*, Princeton, NJ: Princeton University Press, 1979.
[2] Richard Rorty, *Philosophy as Cultural Politics* (*Philosophical Papers, Volume IV*), Cambridge: Cambridge University Press, 2007. The four papers are "Grandeur, Profundity, and Finitude," "Philosophy as a Transitional Genre," "Pragmatism and Romanticism," and "Analytic and Conversational Philosophy." References will be given in the text.

the essays delineate the intellectual significance of philosophy, particularly analytic philosophy, from four different perspectives, each representing a highly characteristic strain of Rorty's thought: the vicissitudes of Plato's founding philosophical project, a quasi-Hegelian (or, perhaps better, quasi-Comtean) progression of modern intellectual life, a critique of the correspondence theory of truth, and a reflection on the much derided but still hard-to-avoid distinction between analytic and continental philosophy.

The vicissitudes of Platonism

For Rorty, like Nietzsche, Plato is frequently the heavy in his *Geistesgeschichte* of Western thought. Plato, through his eulogization of Socrates, invented philosophy and, Rorty tells us, defended its prerogatives through three great battles: an internal fight between philosophical proponents of the gods (the immaterialism of the Forms) and the giants (the materialism of Democritean atoms) and two external quarrels, between philosophers and sophists and between philosophers and poets. Rorty traces the fall of Platonism through its ultimate loss, in modern and contemporary times, of all three of these battles.

The initial defeat of Platonic philosophy was by the giants in the form of Enlightenment materialism, a defeat that led to what Rorty sees as the modern marginalization of philosophy. On his view, philosophy is culturally important only when entrenched beliefs are threatened – e.g., when traditional Greek religion came under attack or the new science raised fundamental questions about Christian belief or democratic revolutions challenged convictions about the basis of society. Given such threats, philosophers are needed to "offer suggestions about what can be preserved and what must be discarded." There were no such threats in the twentieth century, since "the educated classes became complacently materialistic in their understanding of how things work . . . and complacently utilitarian and experimentalist in their evaluations of proposed social and political initiatives" (73). Further, "they share the same utopian vision: a global commonwealth in which human rights are respected, equality of opportunity is assured, and the chances of human happiness are thereby increased" (73–4). Thus the giants have won the struggle with the Platonic gods, and the resulting cultural complacency with materialism has marginalized philosophy, at least as Plato conceived it.

Nonetheless, within the limits of our materialistic/utilitarian consensus, the two other Platonic quarrels still have some resonance. Sophists and poets agree with one another in distrusting the philosophers' claim to reveal the deep truth of reality as such – to show us what is "really real" and thereby show us how, all things considered, we ought to live. Rorty calls this the philosophers' claim to "universalist grandeur" (76). He resists this claim by rejecting what Habermas calls "subject-centered reason" in favor of "communicative rationality"; that is, by thinking of "knowledge as the achievement of consensus" and denying that "human beings possess a faculty that enables them to circumvent conversation – to side-step opinion and head straight for knowledge" (77). (Rorty also puts this as the pragmatic substitution of "responsibility to other human beings for responsibility to a non-human standard" [77].) Rorty sees his resistance to a Platonist view of philosophy as putting him solidly in the camp of the sophists: "neo-sophists like myself" as opposed to "neo-Platonists such as Russell and Nagel" (77).

But the poets' challenge to philosophy raises a further issue. In rejecting Plato's universalist faculty of reason, should we also embrace what Habermas calls "an other of reason" (77) – e.g., emotion, imagination, mystical insight – as an alternative source of conviction? Romanticism – especially as understood by Isaiah Berlin – is the primary proponent of such an other. The romantic view is that there are no universally valid answers to questions about how we should live and that, therefore, individuals should make a passionate choice of a distinctive way of life, even though such choices will be rationally ungrounded and mutually incompatible. We should reject rationalist universalism in favor of personal depth of feeling (profundity), even when universalism is understood as merely the neo-sophist's agreement among human beings. For romantics, such agreement is "simply a way of procuring conformity to current beliefs and institutions" (84), a consensus that can and should be trumped by the depths of individual passion. Rorty thinks the romantics are right in emphasizing the human need for imaginative visions and passionate commitments that go beyond anything that could be arrived at by rational discussion. But what will satisfy this need varies among individuals. Imposing any one passionate commitment on humankind as a whole yields a fascist totalitarianism. Therefore, Rorty insists that such visions and commitments need to be constrained within the limits of one's private life. We must preserve a public domain of civic rights and duties that are required of everyone – precisely because this is the only way to ensure that the passion of one person or subgroup does not dominate the imaginative individuality of others.

Rorty presents his pragmatism as an alternative to both the rationalism of grandeur and the romanticism of profundity: "talk of universal validity is simply a way of dramatizing the need for intersubjective agreement, while romantic ardor and romantic depth are simply ways of dramatizing the need for novelty, the need to be imaginative" (85). Both needs are essential, so we will always require both intellectuals who are good at the kind of thinking that brings about intersubjective agreement and (usually other) intellectuals who are good at the kind of thinking that produces imaginative novelty. But neither of these enterprises can any more be plausibly taken as a penetration into the "intrinsic nature of reality"; neither reason nor imagination is attuned to any such thing. Once we've renounced both grandeur and profundity, what remains as the essential human project is to find ways of properly balancing "the need for consensus and the need for novelty" – the project Rorty calls "experimentalist tinkering" (86).

Once this project becomes our focus, we lose interest even in the philosophers' quarrels with the sophists and the poets because we agree with the sophists' claims against the philosophers and with the philosophers' claims against the poets. Neither philosophy nor poetry is the ground of any ultimate truth. The result, which Rorty sees as now becoming dominant in our culture, is a loss of interest in philosophy, which is no longer needed either as a critic of romantic pretensions to ultimate truth or as itself a source of such truth. We are now, he says, "in the habit of thinking horizontally rather than vertically – figuring out how we might arrange for a slightly better future rather than looking up to an outermost frame or down into ineffable depths." He concludes that philosophers like himself "who think all this is just as it should be can take a certain rueful satisfaction in their own steadily increasing irrelevance" (88).

Religion, philosophy, literature

Rorty's starting point here is his definition of *redemptive truth* as "a set of beliefs which would end, once and for all, the process of reflection on what to do with ourselves" (90). His historical narrative concerns the ways in which intellectuals (people who "read books to find out what purposes to have," 90) have sought redemptive truth. The narrative aims to support the thesis that "intellectuals of the West have, since the Renaissance, progressed through three stages: they have hoped for redemption first from God, then from philosophy, and now from literature" (91). Rorty's view is that this tri-part development, with its eventual superseding of philosophy by literature, has been a good thing.

Religion in its pure form, independent of philosophy, achieves redemption by direct relation to a divine person; it has no need for argument, merely the encounter with the divine. Literature too, apart from the influence of philosophy, has no need for argument, but, unlike religion, it finds redemption in "non-cognitive relations to other human beings," not in such relations to the non-human (93). It is only the philosophers who have insisted that redemption must take the form of *belief* in a body of redeeming truths. Those who "take philosophy as the guide to life" hold that "there is a single set of beliefs which can serve a redemptive role in the lives of all human beings, which can be rationally justified to all human beings under optimal communicative conditions, and which will thus form the natural terminus of inquiry" (93).

In its earlier stages (from Plato up through the early moderns), philosophy remained tied to the older religious viewpoint, trying to provide rational bases for a redemptive relation to a divine person. But in the nineteenth century, following the French Revolution, philosophy came into its own as an autonomous worldview and produced the "two great metaphysical systems": idealism and materialism. For all its greatness, idealistic metaphysics (paradigmatically, Hegel's) is a thing of the past, whereas materialist metaphysics remains as "pretty much the only version of redemptive truth presently on offer" (96). This is due to the fact that "by the middle of the nineteenth century, it had become clear that mathematics and empirical science were going to be the only areas of culture in which one might conceivably hope to get unanimous, rational agreement – the only disciplines able to provide beliefs unlikely to be overturned as history rolled along" (97). Since hardly anyone saw mathematical truths as redemptive, the conclusion, drawn by nineteenth-century positivists, was that empirical science had to be the source of redemptive truth.

But there was no basis for the authority of materialistic metaphysics beyond the sheer demand that something provide redeeming truth, coupled with the failure of all other alternatives. Once Western intellectuals got over their hope for redeeming truth, there was no plausible response to the literary intellectuals' challenge when confronted with the results of science: "That's nice, but is it really so important?" (100). The only remaining supporters of materialistic metaphysics are either philosophers who see natural science as the sole remaining bastion of objective truth or scientists convinced that their theories, beyond telling "us how things work and what they are made of," also say "something about how to live, about human nature, about what we really are" (98).

But the claims of neither group have any basis apart from their questionable assumption that the objective knowledge achieved by science is "a matter of more accurately aligning thought and language with the way things are" (99); that is, with the "intrinsic nature of things" (100). As we shall see, Rorty leaves no room for such a conception of scientific (or any other) truth.

Truth and romanticism

Rorty's third perspective centers on the correspondence theory of truth, which he understands as supporting the pretension of philosophy to a privileged access to the "really real" world behind the veil of appearances. In this discussion, he connects epistemological objections to the correspondence theory with the romantic claim that imagination has priority over reason.

Rorty's pragmatism rejects the correspondence theory's claim that "true beliefs are accurate representations of reality"; romanticism asserts "the priority of imagination over reason." In both cases, Rorty thinks, we have a reaction against "the idea that there is something non-human out there with which human beings need to get in touch" (105). Rorty proposes to trace the historical and conceptual ties between the pragmatic and the romantic reaction.

The correspondence theory rests on a distinction between what is merely apparent and what is real. A representation may seem to be correct but not really match the way things are. Rorty agrees that there is a common-sense distinction between appearance and reality: e.g., between real and fake Rolexes. But he rejects the "metaphysical" version of the distinction, which arises when we ask if things that common sense takes as real (as opposed to what it takes as merely apparent) are themselves merely apparent in comparison with some "higher" reality. The metaphysical distinction, then, arises when we ask if, for example, real Rolexes are *really* real, or, more generally, if the entire realm of common-sense reality is really real.

In opposition to this distinction, and hence to the correspondence theory, Rorty first appeals to Donald Davidson, "who has argued [that] most of our beliefs about such things as trees [generally, common-sense realities] have to be true." To establish this, Davidson notes that, if someone denies a large number of the claims we take as obviously true about trees, then the proper conclusion is not that she is deluded but that she is using the term "tree" in a different sense. From this it follows that "there have to be many commonly accepted truths about a thing before we can raise the question of whether any particular belief about it is erroneous." It further follows that "one can only dissent from common sense about a thing if one is willing to accept most of the rest of what common sense has to say about it" (106). Given this result, it is obvious that there is no sense to asking whether the entire realm of common-sense realities is itself unreal. We can "dissent from common sense" about this realm only to the extent that we "accept most . . . of what common sense has to say about it," which means not denying *en gros* the truths of common sense. Conversely, there is no way to argue for claims about the nature of the "really real" as opposed to common-sense reality. "Unlike the case of trees, there are no platitudes accepted by both the vulgar and the learned" about Reality; "when it comes to Reality . . . there is no such thing as common sense" (106) and so no solid starting points for arguments about what is Real and what isn't.

To the extent, then, that the correspondence theory goes beyond our common-sense distinction between how things appear and how they are and asks whether what common sense takes as real is really real (the question that motivates *ontology* as a philosophical discipline), the theory has no intellectual standing. Rorty suggests that the correspondence theory and ontology retain their grip only because we fear that, without them, there is no denying the romantic claim that "the imagination sets the bounds of thought" (106). But, Rorty maintains, this fear is in fact the sober truth, since "the imagination is the source of language, and thought is impossible without language" (106–7), so that thought derives from imagination. To avoid this conclusion, philosophers have claimed that thought (reason) has an access to reality unmediated by, and prior to, the use of language (107). To maintain the correct view of thought as impossible without language, Rorty says, "we need to think of reason as not a truth-tracking faculty but as a social practice"; specifically, "the practice of enforcing social norms on the use of marks and noises" (107).

Rorty thinks that the romantic point about the primary role of imagination can also be supported by arguments of various analytic philosophers, including Wittgenstein, Sellars, Davidson, and Brandom. These are arguments against empiricism, which regards the senses, as opposed to the imagination, as the primary source of knowledge because of their alleged "special relation to reality" (212). The force of the arguments is that the deliverances of the senses amount to nothing beyond physical modifications of our sense organs, which in turn initiate causal responses to the environment. Such responses, like the behavior of a thermostat, will usefully vary with the sensory causal input, but they are not based on knowledge, which requires *conceptual* awareness. As both Wittgenstein and Sellars have plausibly argued, we possess a concept only when we are able to use the corresponding *linguistic* expression. Accordingly, "before there were conversational exchanges . . . there were neither concepts, nor beliefs, nor knowledge" (113). At this point, the analytic argument converges with the romantic vision, since language is the result of a new set of social practices; that is, it is a work of the imagination. "It took imaginative genius to suggest that everybody make the same noises at the sight of blood, of certain maple leaves in autumn, and of the western sky at sunset" (114).

Rorty concludes that reason is a social practice, not a faculty for accurately representing the way the world really is. Given this conclusion, a number of other results follow directly. First, "what counts as rational in one society counts as irrational in another." This does not mean that Rorty is a relativist about rationality. He has no choice but to adhere to his own society's standards of rationality – that's what it means to say they are *his society's* standards.[3] But arguing in terms of those very standards leads him to the conclusion that there is no neutral way to ground the judgment that "some societies are more rational than others," since that would presuppose, contrary to what he has just claimed to prove, "that we have some access to a source of normativity other than the practices of the people around us" (107).

Second, imagination is not a faculty for forming mental images but "the ability to change social practices by proposing advantageous new uses of marks and noises" (107). As Rorty proposes to use the term, to be imaginative "one must both do something new and be lucky enough to have that novelty adopted by one's fellows"; otherwise, one is merely fantastical – foolish or even insane. Third, language is a social practice that originated "when it dawned on some genius that we could use noises, rather than physical compulsion – persuasion rather than force – to get other human beings to cooperate with us" (107). Although there is no need to deny that language from the beginning referred to people and things, its primary purpose was and remains not accurate representation but practical control. "On the pragmatic view I am putting forward, what

---

[3] Rorty sometimes weakens his own case by suggesting that accepting one's society's standards is a matter of a simple Sartrean choice, which could be readily revoked at the next instant. I've developed this criticism in my chapter on Rorty in *Pragmatic Liberalism and the Critique of Modernity*, Cambridge: Cambridge University Press, 1999.

we call 'increased knowledge' should not be thought of as increased access to the Real, but as increased ability to *do* things" (108).

Critics claim that his pragmatic view amounts to linguistic idealism, but Rorty demurs, noting that his position amounts to a "romantic" account of human progress and says nothing about the ultimate nature of reality (about which Rorty, like Nietzsche, thinks there is nothing to say). The criticism sometimes gains impetus because proponents of the view say that the world is "constituted" by language or that it is a "social construction" or that everything is "mind-dependent." Rorty, however, rejects all such language because it incoherently implies a causal influence of language on reality. Causal relations, he notes, obtain only between objects within the world. "We can investigate causal relations once we have identified such objects, but there is no point in asking where the world that contains such objects comes from" (116). The pragmatic point is simply that "there is no preconceptual cognitive access to objects." Like everything else, we humans are always causally involved with the world, but we have knowledge of it only after we have acquired language.

The priority of imagination entails that the Platonic and Cartesian idea that philosophy could be the foundation of all knowledge is misconceived. Philosophy is a deployment of reason, which is "a matter of making allowed moves within language games." But "imagination creates the games that reason proceeds to play . . . Reason cannot get outside the latest circle that imagination has drawn" (115). However, the achievements of many of the greatest among those we call philosophers can also be taken as achievements of the imagination. Rorty, for example, endorses Nietzsche's view that "Plato's success in putting the term 'really real' into circulation was a great imaginative achievement," and he further sees Nietzsche not as a thinker who refuted Plato but as one who saw that Plato's great metaphysical poem no longer suited human needs and was able to replace it with "a new better poem" (117). Indeed, it is generally possible to take philosophers' logical argumentation "as just one rhetorical technique among others" (118) and thereby read their books – from Hegel's *Phenomenology of Mind* to Kripke's *Naming and Necessity* – as stupendous feats of the imagination.

The cultural role of analytic philosophy

Rorty's final perspective on the cultural role of philosophy focuses on what he refers to as the "self-image" of analytic philosophers (122). Many analytic philosophers see themselves as complementing natural scientists'

206 Rorty against the world: philosophy, truth, and objectivity

discoveries of empirical, contingent truths with discoveries of necessary, non-empirical truth about the meanings (or natures) of things. They claim to do this by engaging in the activity of conceptual analysis. If there is something that remains invariable in the content of any assertion about, say, knowledge or justice – whether made by Plato almost twenty-five centuries ago or by you or me yesterday – then, as Rorty puts it, there "perhaps really are entities with intrinsic properties which philosophical analysis can hope to pin down." The idea of conceptual analysis, in other words, is to get right, once and for all, the invariant meanings of fundamental concepts. To the extent that philosophy can do this, it will achieve, in the manner of a science, an enduring body of knowledge. If philosophy cannot do this, if concepts are historically variable and do not admit a "final analysis," then "it is hard to see the history of philosophy as most analytic philosophers would prefer to see it – as a continuing examination of the same data as were examined by Plato and Aristotle, in the hope of finally getting knowledge, or morality, or mind, or justice, *right*" (123).

Against this goal of analytic philosophy, Rorty first notes that there are plausible accounts of concepts on which they are not invariant and so not a source of enduring knowledge. Rorty is particularly partial to Robert Brandom's inferentialism, according to which the content of our concepts derives entirely from our practices of inferring certain sentences from others. Since these practices vary as "individuals and communities go about revising their patterns of behavior, linguistic and non-linguistic," concepts are continually open to revision. Therefore, given Brandom's account, we must "give up the notion that concepts such as 'knowledge' or 'morality' or 'mind' or 'justice' have permanent, structural features that philosophers can discern, and that the vulgar may not have noticed" (123).

Beyond this question about the nature of concepts in general, Rorty notes that, as a matter of historical fact, philosophy (including its analytic version) has never been in a position to make credible claims that there is something that it "gets right." As he sees it, we can appropriately speak of a discipline "getting it right" only when "everybody interested in the topics draws pretty much the same inferences from the same assertions"; that is, "when a problem can be pinned down in such a way that everybody concerned is clear about what it would take to solve it" (124). We achieve such consensus on many topics treated on the level of common sense and also in a variety of "expert cultures." "Within such cultures there is agreement, for example, on when a gene has been located, a chemical compound analysed into its component elements, or a theorem proved. The members of such cultures all use the relevant referring expressions ('gene', 'element', 'proof') in pretty much the same way. They are also pretty much agreed about what exists" (124).

The problem with analytic philosophy is that it "as a whole is not, and has never been, an expert culture . . . What consensus has existed has been local and transitory" (125), with each generation of analytic philosophers looking on the problems discussed by the preceding generation as "merely quaint" (125) or even worthy of mockery (130). This unedifying "spectacle of the hungry analytic generations treading each other down . . . is the best reason to think that the slogan 'let's get it right' needs to be replaced by something like 'let's try something different'" (125). Rorty labels such a replacement as a move from analytic philosophy to "conversational philosophy," which abandons the quasi-scientific goal of truth for the imaginative goal of useful novelty. Further, Rorty says, "whenever philosophy has attempted to become [an expert culture] it has degenerated into scholasticism, into controversies which are of no interest to anyone outside the philosophical profession" (125). For these reasons, Rorty is "content to see philosophy professors as practicing cultural politics" by, for example, "suggesting changes in the use of words and by putting new words in circulation" (124), and, as we've seen, he typically reads major figures from Plato through Heidegger, as well as recent analytic philosophers such as Quine, Sellars, Davidson, and Brandom, in just this way.

RORTY'S ARGUMENTS

The idea of philosophy as conversation – in the sense of an open-ended generation of new and stimulating ideas – is the outcome of all four of Rorty's perspectives on the enterprise. There's no doubt that this imaginative role is an important aspect of philosophy, but Rorty claims that it exhausts the cultural significance of philosophy, that there is no significant body of disciplinary knowledge that philosophy has achieved or can be expected to achieve. Just how does he make a case for this conclusion? In particular, does Rorty – as some critics claim and as he himself suggests in some flamboyant passages – eschew standard modes of philosophical argumentation in favor of neo-sophistical rhetoric?

One of Rorty's central devices, particularly apparent in the articles analyzed above, is a distinctive sort of historical description that puts the philosophical enterprise in a broad cultural and chronological perspective. His history implicitly revolves around four forms of experience that seem to put us in direct contact with the world: the affective, the sensory, the intellectual, and the mystical. All four are undeniable aspects of human existence, and they are the only plausible sources of truth. On the common-sense level on which we all exist most of the time, the senses and intellect are undeniable sources of common-sense truths – the knowledge we need to get around in the natural world. But as far back as we know ourselves, humans have desired knowledge beyond that of common sense (the humdrum, the mundane), knowledge of transcendent truths that can guide us to a life beyond that of the natural world. The original claim to such knowledge came from the mystical experiences of religion. The claims of religion were very early called into question by science, which extended, eventually to extraordinary effect, the sensory and intellectual resources of everyday life to produce an impressive body of truth about the natural world. But science, although it could effectively criticize religion when it impinged on the natural domain, itself provided no account of any reality beyond the natural.

The founding idea of philosophy, invented by Plato, was that the intellect, deployed in essential independence of the senses, could grasp the transcendent truths humans desired. From Plato himself and Aristotle, through the great medievals and the early modern rationalists, to Kant and Hegel the main line of philosophical thought produced stunning intellectual constructions purporting to achieve Plato's goal. But there also developed uses of philosophical reason that launched subversive attacks on the possibility of transcendent philosophical truths: the ancient skeptics, Hume, Nietzsche, Rorty himself. In addition, from the late-eighteenth century on, the primacy of philosophy has faced the challenge of romantics who claim to find transcendent truth through the affectivity (emotion, imagination) of artistic experience. As Rorty reads this history, philosophers have been able to fend off the counter-claims to tran-scendent truth from religion and art, but they have failed to establish their own authority as the privileged source of such truth. Most intellectuals, he maintains, have become content to live their lives without tran-scendent truths that tell them how to do it. They find the common-sense and scientific truths of the natural world entirely sufficient. The only remaining resistance comes primarily from the analytic philosophers who dominate the philosophy departments of major anglophone universities but have little influence outside that rarefied domain.[4]

---

[4] Rorty also mentions a diverse group of "European and Asian philosophy teachers" (128) who have little use for analytic philosophy but endorse some version of continental philosophy (e.g., tran-scendental phenomenology or Heideggerian ontology) as the philosophy that gets ultimate reality right. Rorty himself reads most continental philosophy as the imaginative creation of new vocabularies, with no claim to transcendent truth.

The point of Rorty's story about the failures of philosophy is, of course, not simply to tell us that intellectuals in general do not accept the discipline's authority but to convince us that they have been right to do so. He invites us to review the successive efforts of philosophers to establish their authority (Plato's dialectic, Descartes' methodic doubt, Hegel's system, Husserl's phenomenology, Carnap's analysis, ...), recall the widely accepted reasons such efforts have been judged failures even among philosophers, and come to the judgment that philosophy as an intellectual discipline has never achieved an enduring body of knowledge. He further suggests the corresponding historical induction: that there is no reason to expect that philosophy will ever achieve such a body of knowledge.

Interwoven with Rorty's historical descriptions are what seem to be ahistorical philosophical arguments for propositions that support his rejection of philosophical authority. Here we may be tempted to object that he is inconsistently appealing to the established *results* of philosophical discussions, arguing, for example, that Davidson's (correct) thesis that almost all our beliefs about anything must be true provides a good argument against the correspondence theory of truth (and hence against the claim that there is a transcendent world for philosophy to be right about) or that Brandom's (correct) account of the nature of concepts undermines the claims of conceptual analysis. Rorty can hardly coherently argue that, because Davidson and Brandom are right about the nature of beliefs and concepts, getting things right is not an appropriate goal for philosophy. This, however, does not mean that he cannot dialectically deploy standard philosophical arguments to convince those who accept their premises. Rorty is in no position to maintain that these premises are self-evident or have some other special status that renders their denial impossible or essentially irrational. But, if the arguments are valid, they are compelling for anyone who accepts their premises, which in fact are accepted by many analytic philosophers. There is no basis to the suggestion that Rorty's rejection of traditional views on the cognitive authority of philosophy should prevent him from presenting arguments for philosophical conclusions.

Rorty himself suggests another way of taking his philosophical arguments. In deploying, for example, Brandom's arguments about concepts, he says that Brandom is not "trying to get reality or knowledge or meaning *right*" but is "expressing impatience with a certain familiar mind set, and [is] attempting to entrench a new vocabulary, one which uses old words in new ways" (125). It is not a matter of saying "everybody has been getting concepts wrong, and I am getting them right" but rather of saying "representationalist accounts of semantic content have become familiar, and the problems they raise increasingly tedious, so let us try an inferentialist account and see whether things go better" (126).

This is a plausible way of taking Rorty's use of these "arguments," although it is by no means clear that Brandom (or Sellars or Davidson) would endorse this characterization of what *they* were doing. Moreover, there need be no contradiction between this way of thinking about Rorty's use of the ideas of Brandom *et al.* and my above characterization of that use as argumentative in a more standard sense. Those who accept the premises Rorty takes from Brandom *et al.* will see them as compelling arguments in the usual sense. But even those who do not already accept the premises may be convinced by the way Rorty illustrates their power to illuminate puzzling questions and shows how to defend them against objections. Taken in this way, Rorty's "arguments" are examples of what I have previously called persuasive elaboration, and his use of the technique extends far beyond his appeals to arguments of his favorite analytic philosophers.

Rorty himself plausibly thinks of his persuasive elaboration as the deployment of a new vocabulary. Carrying out such a deployment is not a trivial matter. There is no a priori guarantee that Rorty will be able to find the resources (distinctions, arguments, concepts) needed to maintain the coherence of his new way of talking. Although the new vocabulary is designed to replace certain common-sense intuitions, there are still many common-sense claims it presupposes, and it is an open question whether the vocabulary can be developed consistently with these claims.

RORTY AND PHILOSOPHICAL KNOWLEDGE

We see, then, that Rorty makes his case against analytic philosophy via modes of persuasion that are quite typical of such philosophy. Although he himself rejects the goal of "getting things right," he does not – as many analytic philosophers claim – likewise reject the rational means that they themselves use in pursuing that goal. His case against analytic philosophy employs persuasive techniques that we have found in some of the most successful and influential analytic work. To this extent, Rorty's work poses no challenge to the conclusions I have drawn about philosophical argumentation from my previous case studies. To the contrary, Rorty is, like Rawls or like Plantinga, an excellent example of a philosopher who begins with a set of pre-philosophical convictions and defends and develops them by various techniques of persuasive elaboration.

In Rorty's case, the convictions are, first of all, those of the "educated classes" whose "complacency" he sees as the current cultural block to the transcendent claims of traditional philosophy. A good representative of his class, Rorty is, as we saw him describe it, "materialistic in [his] understanding of how things work," "utilitarian and experimentalist in [his] evaluation of proposed social and political initiatives," and committed to the "utopian vision" of "a global commonwealth in which human rights are respected, equality of opportunity is assured, and the chances of human happiness are thereby increased" (73–4). More distinctively, Rorty also holds the meta-conviction that his materialistic, utilitarian, and liberal utopian convictions do not require justification from philosophical argument. The brunt of his philosophical work from *Philosophy and the Mirror of Nature* on was to reply to objections derived from traditional philosophical standpoints; for example, that his position entails a self-refuting relativism, must deny obvious truths about the nature of truth and justification, etc. At the same time, he developed a variety of vocabularies, the success of which gave positive support to the coherence and plausibility of his position. Taking Rorty's work simply as a case study, it entirely supports the view of philosophy that has emerged from our other case studies. Rorty even makes important contributions to the first-order knowledge of philosophical distinctions. For example, he separates the unproblematic common-sense distinction between appearance and reality (the real and the fake Rolex) from the questionable metaphysical distinction between the real and the really real; and he offers helpful ways of taking the distinction between truth and justification. Rorty's challenge to my project comes not from the way in which he argues but from one major conclusion of this argument: that there is no body of disciplinary truth that philosophy has or could put forward.

I agree that Rorty's historical descriptions make a good case that philosophers have not answered the "big questions" of human life (God, freedom, immortality, etc.) and that there is no reason to think that they will do so in any foreseeable future. But this is entirely consistent with my claim that philosophers have, nonetheless, discovered some important truths in the course of vain efforts to answer the big questions. Against this, Rorty has maintained that there is not sufficient continuity of any problems over the history of philosophy to make sense of claims to have attained enduring results. Even in the limited sphere of twentieth-century philosophy, he says, the questions philosophers take as important change from generation to generation, so that even satisfactory answers to questions at one time later become irrelevant. But, as the work of Rorty's favorite philosopher of science, Thomas Kuhn, has shown, fundamental changes in the conceptual frameworks in which inquiry is conducted are consistent with enduring progress. Kepler's questions about the solar system were couched in (religious and astrological) terms that we find quite foreign, but nonetheless we incorporate his answers ("Kepler's laws") to those questions into our understanding of the solar system. Similarly, our current epistemological understanding of the difference between opinion and knowledge still retains results of Plato's original discussion in the *Theaetetus*, and Carnap's and Quine's results regarding the analytic-synthetic distinction are incorporated into the most recent rethinkings of the topic. In philosophy as in science, enduring achievements do not require a fixed framework of inquiry.

It is also worth noting that, contrary to what Rorty sometimes suggests, the failure of philosophers to answer the big questions does not mean that they should stop trying to answer these questions. Rorty can hardly claim that he has a philosophical proof that such questions cannot be answered, since that would amount to the sort of philosophical knowledge he thinks doesn't exist. As he himself insists, he is merely suggesting that it would be more useful for philosophers to start acting differently, by, in particular, proposing imaginative new ways of talking. But why think that changing the explicit focus from truth to imagination will be an improvement? It is, as Rorty points out, entirely possible to read the efforts of philosophers (from Plato to Kripke) wholly committed to objective truth as major achievements of the imagination. Would their thought be any less imaginative if they had renounced their drive for truth and simply tried to be creative?

Suppose, for example, that Hegel had done what Kierkegaard thought he should have done: "written at the end of his books that 'this was all just a thought experiment'" (96). What difference would this have made for the value of Hegel's thought to those, like Rorty, who appreciate it solely for its imaginative force? It is, in fact, not unreasonable to think that Hegel was all the more creative in developing his thought because he took himself to be elucidating the truth, not just making up another plausible story. It would seem that Rorty's worry should be that philosophers would finally agree on a set of "final truths," not that they are seeking such truths. But, then, since Rorty is quite certain that philosophers never will attain consensus about the big questions, there is no basis for his concern about their orientation towards truth. Finally, if, contrary to Rorty's expectations, philosophers do someday agree on the answers to the big questions, he surely has no basis for claiming that these answers might not be ones we should accept.

So far, then, we have seen how Rorty's arguments against philosophical knowledge are based on the questionable assumption that this knowledge must answer the traditional big questions or, at least, be developed within an unchanging framework of inquiry. But Rorty also sometimes argues that, in any case, there is no reason for thinking that any knowledge philosophers might realistically attain could add anything significant to what non-philosophers already know.

Rorty makes this claim, at least for the case of ethics, in a critique of some comments by Peter Singer.[5] He notes his "embarrassment" when he long ago read an article by Singer[6] in *The New York Times Magazine*, where Singer maintained that moral philosophers have something to tell the general public because they have "'soundly based theories' that are grounded on something quite different from the moral intuitions of the public." Although he agreed that the work of moral philosophers, such as Rawls and Singer himself, is more accessible to non-philosophers and would seem to be relevant to their concerns, he found it hard to see how philosophers can "claim an ability to see more deeply into matters of right and wrong than most people" (184). Specifically, he questioned the claim that moral philosophers have a "superior grasp of what Singer calls 'the nature of moral concepts [and] of the logic of moral argument'." This alleged superiority of philosophers is, according to Rorty, entirely bogus. As to the nature of moral concepts, he thinks that "concepts like 'right', 'ought', and 'responsible' are not technical concepts, and it is not clear what special training could enable you to grasp the uses of these words better than do the laity" (185). As to the logic of moral argument, he thinks it very unlikely that "judges and social workers, for example, are less familiar with this logic than are trained moral philosophers" or "that philosophical training would help such people do their jobs better" (186).

Rorty rejects a special role for philosophy in moral decisions because he sees such decisions as closely tied to questions of a person's "practical identity" and thinks that such questions are best answered by imagining alternative identities, not by proving from first principles that one identity is better than another. Accordingly, he sees moral decisions as a matter of imagination rather than reason: "The advantage that well-read, reflective, leisured people have when it comes to deciding the right thing to do is that they are more imaginative, not that they are more rational" (201).

[5] Richard Rorty, "Kant vs. Dewey: The Current Situation in Moral Philosophy," in *Philosophy as Cultural Politics (Philosophical Papers, Volume IV)*, Cambridge: Cambridge University Press, 2007, 184–202. All references will be given in the text.
[6] Peter Singer, "Philosophers Are Back on the Job," *The New York Times Magazine*, July 7, 1974, 6–7; 17–20.

214 *Rorty against the world: philosophy, truth, and objectivity*

I have no quarrel with Rorty's rejection of reason in morality to the extent that it is simply a rejection of philosophical foundationalism, the idea that philosophers have special access to some basic truths that are the premises of arguments needed to justify our moral convictions. Morality cannot and should not wait on philosophical theorizing.

We start from our moral convictions (our sense of "practical identity"), rooted in our moral practices, and go on to raise questions about how to apply or revise these convictions. But Rorty can ignore the distinctive role of philosophers in this process only because he works with too facile a distinction between reason and imagination. Moral imagination requires not only vivid and rich portraits from literature, history, and experience but also precise conceptual discriminations provided by philosophical reflection. To properly "imagine" alternatives, it is not enough to have concrete examples of them. We must also be able to understand just how the examples differ. Moral reflection requires not only, to use an example of Rorty's, Dostoyevsky's portrayal of Alyosha and Ivan but also the ability to see whether these vividly contrasting portraits really correspond to essentially different moral orientations and, if so, just how they do. We can be as much misled by the moral irrelevancies of concrete literary portrayals as by those of abstract philosophical analyses. Does the attractive optimism of Alyosha's belief in resurrection require his intellectual naiveté? Is Ivan's rejection of the utilitarian sacrifice of a shivering child based on sentimentality? To answer such questions, we need to understand and apply philosophical distinctions that track the complex paths between faith and reason and between reason and emotion.

So far, I have responded to three versions of Rorty's case against philosophical knowledge: that based on the fact that there are no answers to the "big questions," that based on the alleged lack of continuity of philosophical problems, and that based on the priority of imagination over reason in moral reflection. Rorty has, however, a deeper reason for rejecting any claim to a distinctive body of philosophical knowledge. This is his belief that any such claim is based on a peculiar and indefensible conception of objective truth. If, as Rorty maintains, the traditional enterprise of philosophy depends on a peculiar conception of truth and objectivity that should be abandoned, then there is no point to speaking about philosophical truth, either as a present achievement or as a future goal. The arguments from Davidson and Brandom discussed above give a preliminary sense of Rorty's case here, but I now turn to the fuller treatment in, first, Rorty's article, "Objectivity or Solidarity" and then in his debate with John McDowell over issues raised in that article.

RORTY ON TRUTH AND OBJECTIVITY: THE PRIORITY
OF SOLIDARITY

Rorty crystallizes his challenge to epistemology-based philosophy in the question: "objectivity or solidarity?"[7] The terms of this dichotomy correspond, he says, to two opposing ways of approaching philosophy's *ur*-question of how to make sense of our lives. One, the mainline of the philosophical tradition, running "from the Greek philosophers through the Enlightenment," requires describing ourselves "as standing in immediate relation to a nonhuman reality" – e.g., God or some secular surrogate such as human nature or scientific truth. For this tradition the meaning of our lives must be grounded in objective truths about the way the world really is, quite apart from any human preferences or commitments. Proponents of this view Rorty calls "realists." The opposing camp, including himself, are "pragmatists," who see the meaning of our lives as grounded merely in our allegiance to a particular community. For the pragmatist, we establish the meaning of our lives simply by "telling the story of [our] contribution to a community" (21), not by discovering objective truths about God, human nature, or any other reality beyond our individual, contingent lives. The meaning of our lives is rooted not in *objectivity* but in *solidarity*. Accordingly, Rorty rejects most traditional philosophy from Plato on – and in particular current analytic philosophy – because it is opposed to his pragmatic account of truth in terms of solidarity rather than objectivity.

Rorty's own communal allegiance is to the liberal practices and institutions of the Western democracies created by "the hopes of the Enlightenment." His goal is to show that these practices and institutions do not require a grounding in realist objective truths that are independent of pragmatic commitments to these practices and institutions. As he puts it elsewhere, he is asserting "the priority of democracy to philosophy."[8]

On Rorty's view, the realists' insistence on objectivity requires them to "construe truth as correspondence to reality." Metaphysically, such a theory requires "a special relation between beliefs and objects which will differentiate true from false beliefs." Epistemologically, it requires "a kind of justification which is not merely social but natural, springing from

---

[7] Richard Rorty, "Objectivity or Solidarity," in his collection, *Objectivity, Relativism, and Truth*, Cambridge: Cambridge University Press, 1990, 21–34. References will be given in the text.
[8] Richard Rorty, "The Priority of Democracy to Philosophy," in *Objectivity, Relativism, and Truth*, 175–96.

human nature itself," rather than from "the various procedures which are thought of as providing rational justification by one or another culture." Pragmatists, since they reject truth as correspondence, need no metaphysical account of what it means for beliefs and objects to "correspond" and no epistemological account of how we can bring our beliefs into this state of correspondence. Rather, they understand justification entirely in terms of the standards by which a given society judges that something is good to believe and regard the gap between justification and truth as due to the fact that "there is always room for improved belief, since [to use the terms of our view of justification] new evidence or new hypotheses, or a whole new vocabulary may come along" (23). Similarly, whereas for realists objectivity is a matter of escaping "the limits of one's community" to reach a standpoint free of any particular society's viewpoint, pragmatists see objectivity as merely a matter of intersubjective agreement.

Realists, Rorty notes, standardly criticize pragmatism as a form of relativism, taken as the self-refuting view that "every belief is as good as every other." But this, he says, is a misrepresentation, since, for example, the pragmatist "thinks his views are better than the realists'," even though he does not, of course, "think that his views correspond to the nature of things." Properly understood, Rorty's pragmatism is ethnocentric – quite the opposite of relativism.

But the realists' accusations of relativism are indicative of their way of thinking. They cannot, Rorty says, "believe that anybody would seriously deny that truth has an intrinsic nature." Accordingly, when pragmatists say that truth is merely what is good to believe according to the standards of a given society, the realist takes this as a claim about the intrinsic nature of truth: that it is, by definition, "simply the contemporary opinion of a chosen individual or group" (24). But what the pragmatist actually means is that there is no point to trying to formulate a substantive general theory of what truth in itself is, since there is just a contingent set of practices that we characterize as "seeking the truth." Similarly: we have contingent practices that correspond to what we call "playing sports" or "being married"; but there is no point asking whether these practices properly express the objective, intrinsic nature of sports or marriage. These, like the rational pursuit of truth, are merely practices that have an important role in particular societies, not more or less "correct" expressions of ideals that exist independent of all societies.

Realists, of course, will maintain that such views of truth, knowledge, and objectivity misrepresent their intrinsic natures, but this response, Rorty notes, begs the question against the pragmatist, who is precisely claiming that there are no such natures. Conversely (although Rorty does not here explicitly make the point), pragmatists will beg the question if they argue that the realist view does not fit well with "a sociohistorical account of how various people have tried to reach agreement on what to believe" (24). The issue between realists and pragmatists cannot be fairly drawn either in the former's metaphysical or epistemological terms or in the latter's sociological or anthropological terms. It can, however, Rorty suggests, be fairly drawn in ethical terms. Realists and pragmatists both agree on the central value of "certain habits of intellectual, social, and political life" that have been traditionally described as directed towards the rational pursuit of truth. Realists, however, think that these habits have no ethical standing unless they can be justified, in the traditional manner, by appealing to "Reason, conceived as a transcultural human ability to correspond to reality," whereas pragmatists think the habits can be justified by "a conception of rationality as criterionless muddling through, and by a pragmatic conception of truth," expressing nothing more than the contingent practices of a particular historical community (28).

To this point, Rorty has not made any positive case for his view of truth and objectivity. He has formulated it as an alternative to realism and, specifically, done so in ethnocentric terms that avoid the charge of relativism. He has also pointed out that each side of the debate between realism and pragmatism has a characteristic mode of argument (normative analysis of concepts and description of social practices, respectively) that does not resolve the debate because it begs the question against its opponent. But, finally, he has suggested an ethical approach to settling the dispute. Since both sides are trying to justify certain communal values, we can ask which does a better job of justifying those values. The question of which account of justification is better turns on which account provides a more effective way of convincing people to accept the values.

The pragmatist position rejects the project of constructing an argument for the preferability of Enlightenment values from premises that any rational person would have to accept. But the pragmatist can present people with a comparison of societies that exemplify these values with those that don't, "leading up to the suggestion that nobody who has experienced both would prefer the latter" (29). Such an approach will not convince everyone; indeed, there are no doubt people who have experienced both Enlightened and non-Enlightened societies and do prefer the latter. But there is also no doubt that it will convince many people who do not live in liberal democratic societies and that it does reinforce the commitment of most people who do live in such societies. Realists seek the sorts of arguments pragmatists eschew, but they do not find any that are convincing. As Rorty puts it, "the traditional Western metaphysico-epistemological way of firming up our [democratic] habits simply isn't working anymore." There are no convincing philosophical arguments for the preferability of democratic values, and the philosophies that generate such arguments are open to Nietzschean and Foucaultian critiques revealing their roots in the power structures of the society they support. According to Rorty, this is "the best argument we partisans of solidarity have against the realistic partisans of objectivity" (33).

I agree with Rorty that there is no way and no need of justifying our commitment to Enlightenment values by showing that they correspond to some reality transcending the contingencies of our historical human existence, such as the Form of the Good, the will of God, or ahistorical human nature. But I nonetheless wonder why Rorty thinks that making this claim requires rejecting the very idea of objective truth, independent of human concerns and projects. There are at least two other plausible possibilities. First, basic value-beliefs, even if fully justified, may not be the sorts of things that correspond to objective reality, although there may still be other sorts of beliefs – say of science – that do. Second, even if basic value-beliefs cannot be justified by deriving them from other objective truths, it may still be that believing that they are true, no matter how justified, requires believing that they correspond to the way things objectively are. Perhaps, for example, the way we use "truth" requires such correspondence. This is not to say that Rorty can make no case for his across-the-board rejection of objective truth. My point is just that this case must go beyond his case for solidarity over objectivity as the basis for our commitment to Enlightenment values.

RORTY ON TRUTH AND OBJECTIVITY: THE DEBATE WITH MCDOWELL

This further case is the focus of John McDowell's analysis and critique of Rorty. By following in some detail McDowell's discussion and Rorty's response, we will be able to see that there need be no essential tension between pragmatic solidarity and realist objectivity.

McDowell[9] begins by noting the deeply ethical roots of Rorty's rejection of objectivity: his conviction that objectivity is a remnant of the

[9] John McDowell, "Towards Rehabilitating Objectivity," in Robert B. Brandom (ed.), *Rorty and His Critics*, Oxford: Blackwell, 2000, 109–23. References will be given in the text.

religious abasement of the human before the non-human that the Enlightenment tried to extirpate. As Rorty sees it, the idea of an objective world, a domain of things-in-themselves, which serves as the standard we must meet for our beliefs to be knowledge, is just a secular surrogate for the divine. Realism, particularly the scientific realism that makes scientists the new priests who mediate between us and the non-human truths of nature, has replaced theism. "Full human maturity" requires getting beyond both these hedges on our commitment to the human community. Just as working together is our only hope of salvation, so too is striving to reach intellectual agreement with one another our only hope of knowledge. This is the ultimate motive for "Rorty's call . . . to abandon the discourse, the vocabulary, of objectivity, and work instead towards expanding human solidarity" (110).

But just as a thoroughly secularist view of reality collapses if there in fact is a God who judges our lives, so Rorty's rejection of objectivity collapses if there is a real world that sets the standards for our knowledge. Rorty's radicalization of atheism will give him reason to rejoice at the overthrow of realism, but it does not provide the intellectual resources to effect this overthrow. That requires a critique of the epistemological tradition that, according to Rorty, has sustained the myth of objectivity. Rorty developed this critique in a variety of modes: historical reflection on the classical epistemological tradition from Plato on (with special emphasis on the classical modern period from Locke through Kant); deployment of twentieth-century critiques of empiricism (especially logical positivism) by Wittgenstein, Quine, Sellars, and Davidson; his reading of the pragmatist tradition of James and Dewey; and his engagement with continental figures, especially Heidegger and Derrida.

McDowell is very sympathetic with this critique but thinks that Rorty mistakes the scope of its effectiveness. It is entirely successful against a particular formulation of realism, associated with Descartes and the British empiricists, but it has, he maintains, no force against more plausible versions of realism. Specifically, McDowell argues that we need to distinguish the mere contention that "inquiry is answerable to the world," which is eminently plausible, from the classical modern idea that this world is withdrawn from our experience to the point at which we must worry that it is inaccessible. It is, McDowell contends, only this latter conception of the "real world" that leads to the incoherent notion of the "thing-in-itself" as a standard for our knowledge claims and the pointless epistemological project of trying to bridge the gap separating us from this world.

To establish the minimal claim that inquiry is answerable to the world and not just to the judgment of our epistemic peers, McDowell appeals, as we would expect, to our use of the term "true," which seems inevitably to imply correspondence to reality. Rorty tries to avoid this implication by showing that we require only three uses of "true," none of which requires a notion of correspondence.[10] These uses are: (1) an endorsing use, whereby we simply assert a belief; (2) a cautionary use, whereby we note that any belief, no matter how well justified, may eventually lose its justification; (3) a disquotational use, whereby we allow inferences between object-language sentences ("Snow is white") and meta-linguistic sentences about their truth ("'Snow is white' is true"). McDowell, however, maintains that the disquotational use in fact involves a notion of correspondence that sets a norm of answerability to the way the world is:

This idea of disquotability is not separate, as Rorty suggests, from anything normative. For a given sentence to be true – to be disquotable – is for it to be correctly usable to make a claim just because _____, where in the gap we insert, not quoted but used, . . . the sentence itself . . . (116)[11]

So, for example, for "Snow is white" to be true (i.e., for "'Snow is white' is true" to be inferable from "Snow is white" and vice versa) is for "Snow is white" to be correctly usable to make a claim just because snow is white. "Correctly usable" expresses a norm that is specified by snow's being white, the aspect of the world to which our assertion "Snow is white" is answerable.

McDowell goes on to point out that Rorty's cautionary use of truth can itself be understood in terms of disquotability, and so shares in the latter's normative answerability to the world. For example, the cautionary "Although supported by all current evidence, 'All life forms are carbon-based' might not be true" can just as well be put as "There may (after all) be life forms that are not carbon-based," which is to say that "All life forms are carbon-based" may not be disquotable.[12] Rorty, he concludes, simply

[10] See "Pragmatism, Davidson, and Truth," in *Objectivity, Relativism, and Truth*, 127–8. Here Rorty makes his point by saying that none of our uses of "true" is explanatory; that is, it does not explain the success of a belief by referring to its correspondence to reality.

[11] Here, for simplicity, I am restricting the principle of disquotation to cases in which the object-language and the meta-language are the same (e.g., both English, as in "'Snow is white' iff snow is white"). Expansion to cases in which the two languages are different (as in "'Schnee ist weiss' iff snow is white") is straightforward.

[12] McDowell also claims that truth understood as "that which is preserved by valid inference" also amounts to truth as disquotability, pace Rorty's suggestion that this use of "true" has nothing in common with the cautionary use.

has a "blind-spot" that makes him unable to see the unproblematically normative sense of truth in virtue of which truth-claims are answerable to the world (117).

The same blind-spot, McDowell maintains, affects Rorty's account of justification. On this account, justification is always relative to an audience, never to the evidence (facts about the world). In other words, for Rorty, when someone claims that p is justified, we must always ask "to whom?" but never "in light of what?" So, for example, if I claim that "Cold fusion has not been achieved" is justified, it makes sense to explain my claim by saying that this is the judgment of all reputable physicists, but, according to Rorty, it makes no sense to say that this is because cold fusion has not been achieved. But "Cold fusion has not been achieved" is an entirely different claim from "All reputable physicists agree that cold fusion has not been achieved," and, corresponding to each claim, there is a different sense of justification. In particular: "There is a norm for making claims with the words 'Cold fusion has not occurred' that is constituted by whether or not cold fusion has occurred, and whether or not cold fusion has occurred is not the same as whether or not saying it has occurred will pass muster in the current practice" of physics (118).

Finally, McDowell insists that appealing to the way the world is as a norm for truth and justification does not amount to the impossible project of trying to, in Thomas Nagel's phrase, "climb outside of our own minds" and judge our claims from an absolute standpoint (a "view from nowhere"). Rather, the distinction between *how we think things are* and *how they are in fact* is one essential to our own epistemic perspective. "To insist on this distinction is not to try to think and speak from outside our practices; it is simply to take it seriously that we can really mean what we think and say from within them" (118). Here there is no incoherent appeal to norms external to our epistemic practices. The norms requiring our claims to be answerable to the world and not just to our judgments about the world are norms "internal to our world view . . . It is just that the world view to which they are internal has the world in view otherwise than as constituted by what linguistics performances will pass muster in our present practices" (119). Rather, our worldview has the world in view as constituted by the way things are, independent of our judgments about how things are.

Rorty's reply to McDowell[13] is, as he himself notes, characteristically pragmatic. He does not deny that there is a difference between the questions

---

[13] Richard Rorty, "Response to John McDowell," in Brandom (ed.), *Rorty and His Critics*, 123–8. References will be given in the text.

"Did X happen?" and "Can saying X happened pass muster in the current [epistemic] practice?" But he maintains that this difference "makes no difference" in the sense that "anything that helps you decide to answer either question in the affirmative will, assuming you are a participant in the current practice, let you answer the other question the same way" (125). Rorty also notes that it is possible to question the authority of current epistemic practices – "to murmur things like '*Eppur se muove*'"; but, he maintains, this is simply to appeal to "some possible better alternative" to current practices, that is, to the judgment of some other epistemic community. The point, then, is that our only access to truth is through our practices of justification, the practices that, if successful, lead to agreement (consensus) about what to believe. Given this, there is no practical role to be played by norms other than those that govern our practices of justification.

McDowell says that there is also a norm, tied not to our practices but to the world itself, that requires that our beliefs correspond to the world. But how could such a norm be actually applied? Suppose McDowell is right that, when I say that "Snow is white" is true, I am implicitly saying that you should believe the claim "Snow is white" because in fact snow is white. We know what you should do to see whether my claim is justified: look at examples of snow, study the optics relevant to how snow reflects light, etc. But what else should you do to make sure that "Snow is white" is not only justified but also true? McDowell states the relevant norm like this: "What makes it correct among speakers of English to make a claim with the words 'S' is that S" (116). So to apply the norm, you need to determine whether S obtains. But the only procedures for doing this are those for justifying S. As Rorty puts it, you "can reasonably say that the only way to find out whether S is to follow the same old norm [you have] been following all the time – getting on with our current attempts to justify belief that S" (126).

At this point, we see that the dispute between McDowell and Rorty reduces to a fruitless quarrel about how we should use the term "norm." McDowell's defense of the correspondence theory of truth turns on his assertion that, since "S" is true if and only if S, the sheer fact of the world's being such that S is a norm for our acceptance of S. Certainly, S's being the case is a necessary condition for "S" to be true. If a norm of truth is nothing more than a condition that must be met for a claim to be true, then S's being the case is a norm for the truth of "S"; and, in that sense, truth is correspondence: corresponding to the world is a standard a claim must meet in order to be true. But Rorty maintains that a norm must be more than a necessary condition; there must also be some distinctive procedures specified for determining whether the condition is met. In this case there are no such procedures, since any procedure for determining the truth of "S" is also a procedure for justifying "S." In this sense, corresponding to the world is not a norm for the truth of "S." But surely nothing substantive turns on whether we define "norm" in Rorty's way or in McDowell's. In either case, McDowell and Rorty agree on all the essential points. Regarding truth, they agree that there is a world, that we are in direct causal contact with this world, and that our true statements are about that world; regarding justification, they agree that our procedures of justification are our only access to the truth of a statement and that even a statement fully justified by those procedures might turn out not to be true. Given this agreement, what does it matter whether we say that truth is a norm governing our assertions and, in that sense, agree that truth is correspondence? If Rorty suffers from a blind-spot here, it is not in failing to see that answerability to the world is an essential epistemic norm; it is in failing – just as McDowell does – to see that it makes no difference whether we say such answerability is a norm or not. One last turn of the pragmatic screw eliminates Rorty's disagreement with McDowell – and his need to reject any notion of objective truth.

My conclusion is that Rorty has no basis for insisting on solidarity to the exclusion of objectivity. There are construals of objectivity – in particular, the veil-of-ideas realism of some early modern philosophers – that do fall to his critique; but there is no point to his absolute insistence that there is no viable sense in which true statements must correspond to the way the world is. Given the right sorts of formulations, Rorty's insistence that there is no justificatory appeal beyond community consensus is consistent with McDowell's insistence that true beliefs must correspond to the way the world is. The differences between McDowell and Rorty do not make a difference. It follows that the philosophical ideal of objective truth need not be taken as contrary to Rorty's pragmatism. As a result, Rorty's critique of objectivity provides no basis for rejecting the enterprise of analytic philosophy, nor for denying that this enterprise has achieved a substantial body of disciplinary knowledge.

CHAPTER 10

Philosophical knowledge: conclusions and an application

The question I've posed in this book is why people outside the discipline of philosophy should pay attention to what philosophers say, and my answer is that philosophers know things about topics that are important to non-philosophers. In this conclusion I first summarize the view of philosophical knowledge that has emerged from my case studies and then offer the example of religious belief as one illustration of the essential role philosophical knowledge should play in non-philososphical thinking.

A PICTURE OF PHILOSOPHICAL KNOWLEDGE

On any account, philosophy is concerned with our convictions – beliefs about fundamental human issues that are deep-rooted in our experiences and practices. According to the view that I've called philosophical foundationalism, the project of philosophy is to provide compelling arguments for or against our convictions, so that our beliefs and lives can be put on a solid rational basis. But, I have maintained, one of the most important achievements of recent philosophy has been to discredit this foundationalism. Philosophers themselves have given good reason to believe that our convictions do not require (and are unlikely, in any case, to receive) compelling philosophical justification. This, of course, is hardly news to most analytic philosophers. Nonetheless, our commitment to rigorous argument as the principal engine of philosophical inquiry often implicitly brings us back to the foundational model, even though we know we have little hope of finding the sort of premises that will make this model effective. Lacking an alternative that would preserve the analytic ideal of argument, we fall back on the foundational model in spite of ourselves.

To avoid this impasse we need to give up the analytic ideal of argument and forthrightly admit that philosophy must begin from pre-philosophical convictions that have no need for justification by philosophical argument; that, in other words, convictions – and, more broadly, the practices that embed them – do not require *philosophical foundations*. But, although convictions do not require philosophical justification, they do require *philosophical maintenance*. We are intellectual creatures and cannot avoid thinking about our convictions – about what they mean, how we can defend them against challenges, etc. To adapt Lévi-Strauss' well-known terminology: we need practices (and so convictions) that are *good-for-living*. But as intelligent humans, what we find good-for-living must also be *good-for-thinking*, and the continual probing and refining of our convictions through philosophical reflection is the way we ensure that they remain good for thinking.

Philosophical thinking, then, is an inevitable aspect of developed human life, a necessary reflection on our basic convictions, even though not a source of their justification. Such reflection will always emerge, both on the public level of, say, the self-justifications of a regime and the manifestoes of revolutionaries trying to overthrow it, and on the private level of, say, late-night dorm conversations and mid-life brooding about what it all means. It does not follow that such thinking must be done in the context of a specific discipline – philosophy – dedicated to the pursuit of fundamental questions. But, at least in the Western world, there has long been such a discipline, and it has been a powerful source of materials for thinking about such questions. Our case studies have shown, more-over, that recent analytic philosophy has achieved (or is heir to) a sig-nificant body of knowledge relevant to such thinking – knowledge both about the epistemological status of convictions and about conceptual distinctions needed to think fruitfully about them.

Prior to philosophical reflection, our convictions are not very well articulated and can be profitably regarded as expressing general *pictures*; that is, general schemes for thinking about some major aspect of the world. One of the main projects of philosophical thinking is the development of the precise and detailed formulations of important pictures that I have called *theories*.[1] Once philosophers have an apparently plausible, suffi-ciently detailed theoretical formulation of a picture, the next task is to see

---

[1] The distinction between pictures and theories is flexible and relative, since pictures and theories differ merely in degree of specificity. What functions as a theory in one context (e.g., Plato's "theory of Forms" in the *Phaedo*) may function as a picture in another (e.g., discussions of universals among contemporary analytic metaphysicians). The value of the distinction – like that of any distinction – lies not in its universal correctness but in the light it is able to shed on particular cases to which it can be applied.

if they can refute it. There are various techniques of refutation: showing that the theory is self-contradictory, showing that it is inconsistent with obvious truths, showing that it has no intelligible content (e.g., is based on a distinction that makes no sense). Once a theory is refuted, a philosopher can either try to formulate a better theory expressing the picture or develop a new picture. Formulating a new theory is a matter of revising the old one in the light of its refutation. This means not only dropping the claims that have been shown false but also replacing them with claims that both avoid the refutations and seem plausible in their own right. Here it is common to move through several successive theories, particularly though the dialectic of counterexamples. Our case studies have shown numerous examples of this approach: Kitcher's formulation of a theory of reference for scientific terms to support his convictions about the rationality of science; Plantinga's development of a theory of warrant in support of his religious convictions; Rawls' efforts to reach a theory of justice through reflective equilibrium.

So far I have been speaking as if philosophical theorizing always works with pictures derived from convictions. But, like other disciplines, philosophy, particularly as it becomes more specialized and technical, takes on a life of its own and raises questions for their own sake, not for the sake of coming to terms with convictions. Initial responses to such questions are strictly philosophical pictures, corresponding not to convictions, with their roots in central practices, but merely to intuitions – in the sense of either strongly held beliefs or even just intellectual seemings. Quine's radical empiricism, Kripke's essentialism, and Goldman's reliabilism are good examples. Since such pictures are not, like those tied to convictions, rooted in long-established practices central in people's lives, they especially need to be given an initial plausibility through the processes of persuasive elaboration that we've seen in our case studies. Of course, sometimes a picture corresponding to an apparently moribund conviction will be revivified through a surprising persuasive elaboration. Also, it is always possible that the development of a purely philosophical picture may turn out to lend support to a picture based on pre-philosophical conviction. For example, Kripke's picture of metaphysical necessity led, in Plantinga's development, to a new version of the ontological argument for God's existence.

Once a picture has shown a capacity for inspiring viable theories, the development and continuing viability of these theories becomes the central locus of the persuasive elaboration of the picture. Ideally, philosophers would be able to arrive at a theory that survived all criticism and could, moreover, be shown superior to all rival theories. Such a theory would stand as a prime example of philosophical knowledge, and would no doubt be justified by either a deductive or non-deductive foundational argument. But as we know, philosophers almost never achieve this sort of theoretical success. Theories either require successive modification in the light of ever new difficulties or, at least, cannot be shown to be decisively superior to rival theories. But successful theoretical development does show that a given picture is capable of generating progressively better theoretical formulations. This may demonstrate, for example, an ability to meet counterexamples and other objections or an ability to extend the picture to new domains. Philosophers can and do agree about the present status of the theoretical development of a given picture (even though they may themselves hold different views about the ultimate acceptability of the picture). For example, it is uncontroversial that, after Kripke, the picture of metaphysical necessity as an objective fact is far more viable than it was before and that, similarly, the theistic picture and the dualist picture are in much better shape after the work of Plantinga and Chalmers, and that the utilitarian picture was significantly challenged by Rawls.

Judgments of this sort are obviously important for those holding the relevant convictions or beliefs, but they can also be significant for those who do not. If the picture associated with the convictions is shown to be internally consistent, to cohere with well-established bodies of knowledge, and to suggest interesting and fruitful responses to questions important even to those not sharing the convictions, then even non-believers will need to take these convictions seriously. So, for example, an atheist reading Plantinga or a utilitarian reading Rawls may, even though still unconvinced, become much less dismissive of these convictions.

Efforts at theoretical development of a picture can also lead to refutations of convictions or, conversely, defenses of convictions against purported refutations. The latter is well exemplified by Plantinga's free-will defense against the deductive argument from evil, which makes a compelling case for the logical compatibility of an all-powerful, all-good God and the existence of evil. This was not merely a matter of showing the viability of the theistic picture but of proving, from premises acceptable even to atheists, that there is no contradiction between "An all-good, all-powerful God exists" and "There is evil." Convictions can also be decisively refuted by, for example, showing them to be logically contradictory or inconsistent with established facts. The fundamentalist who insists that the Earth is no more than a few thousand years old or that the great dinosaurs were contemporary with early humans can be shown to be wrong. But convictions are typically formulated in terms of pictures and can take on a variety of specific theoretical formulations, so that refuting one such formulation will not decisively discredit the picture or the conviction. On the other hand, pictures and associated convictions that persistently fail to generate defensible theories will be rightly judged non-viable.

The above discussion summarizes the various ways in which philosophy yields highly significant knowledge about our convictions. But our case studies have also shown that the processes of theoretical development yield some important *first-order knowledge* about fundamental questions. This comes about because developing and criticizing philosophical theories requires the making of *distinctions*. A distinction is a claim that where we have implicitly supposed there was just one relevant concept, there are in fact two or more. Distinguishing among these concepts allows us to separate theoretical claims that would otherwise be conflated. This separation of claims typically allows us to show that one is true (or plausible) and the other false (or problematic). This, in turn, allows us to attack or defend a theory by showing that its claims are true on one interpretation but false on another, the distinction working for or against the theory depending on whether or not the correct interpretation fits with key features of the picture the theory is trying to articulate.

Philosophical knowledge of distinctions typically begins with an intuitively obvious or plausible difference between two notions (fact/value, knowledge/opinion), based on clear examples of the difference. We then *use* the distinction to make various points; for example, criticize a certain claim, argue for a positive conclusion, understand a certain concept. This use may extend the distinction to new areas and raise questions about whether it holds there and, if so, in what sense. It may also call into question views we find plausible or support views we find suspect. This may lead us to reexamine the distinction, leading either to a revised version or to restrictions on its domain of validity. The entire process is in some ways more like the invention of a new tool than the discovery of a new fact. Because of this, it might be tempting to treat our knowledge of philosophical distinctions as *knowing how*, not *knowing that*. On the other hand, this is also a case in which the knowing how depends on knowing that. I know how to think about freedom and causality because I know that there is a distinction between causality and compulsion and, indeed, have considerable information about just what this distinction amounts to.

While claiming that there is a substantial body of philosophical knowledge, I have said little about the question of the nature of this knowledge and the methods by which it is attained. This has been for two reasons. First, to a great extent, philosophical knowledge is developed in the same ways as most other cognitive enterprises: there are deductive and inductive arguments from obvious truths, persuasive elaborations of pictures (e.g., via theoretical specification), showing their explanatory power and fruitfulness, challenge arguments strongly suggesting that what has not been shown cannot be shown, all leading to shared judgments among a community of inquirers (à la Kuhn) regarding the overall import of a body of evidence. Second, even if there are special faculties involved in philosophy, identifying and justifying them is not essential to showing that there is a body of philosophical knowledge. (Similarly, there is no need to have identified and justified a special "scientific method" to show that there is significant scientific knowledge.) I have noted various senses in which intuitions operate in philosophy and it may be that some of them – perhaps modal intuitions – depend on distinctive abilities not deployed in, say, the natural sciences. (Correspondingly, the natural sciences obviously use methods such as the prediction of surprising new results that have little or no role in philosophy.) But questions about the nature of such intuitions are not prerequisites to accepting the reality of philosophical knowledge.

From the standpoint of philosophical foundationalism, knowledge about distinctions – e.g., between an act's being compelled and its being caused, between true opinion and knowledge, between a functional concept and a phenomenal concept – is a means of answering fundamental questions about whether we are free, how to define knowledge, or the reducibility of consciousness to matter. Once we find that the relevant distinctions do not yield answers to these questions, they seem to be of no real significance.

But rejecting foundationalism and recognizing the irreducible role of pre-philosophical convictions reveals the true importance of philosophical distinctions. As thinking beings, we need to reflect on our convictions – deriving their implications, giving them more precise expression, defending them against objections, even revising or eventually rejecting them. Philosophy is our model for such reflection and it is based on the distinctions that drive the process of theoretically developing pictures that express our convictions. Without knowledge of these distinctions, we have few resources for dealing responsibly with our convictions.

Nonetheless, it is easy – even after rejecting foundationalism – to fail to appreciate the importance of distinctively philosophical knowledge of distinctions. For example, it might be argued, most distinctions are rooted in common-sense judgments (things can appear other than they are, something isn't so just because it ought to be so, etc.) and to that extent they do not originate in specifically *philosophical* thinking. Further, although philosophers have introduced more subtle and more interesting extensions or refinements of common-sense distinctions, these specifically philosophical distinctions give rise to the disagreements typical of philosophers. There is still, for example, significant controversy about the nature and extent of distinctions between value/fact, appearance/reality, form/matter.

But, although there are legitimate disputes about some formulations and applications of the more refined distinctions, there is also a body of accumulated knowledge about how to understand and make use of these distinctions. We saw, for example, how discussions following Quine's critique clarified the analytic-synthetic distinction, how Kripke gave new depth to the distinctions between naming and description, how Gettier epistemology opened up new dimensions of the difference between knowledge and true opinion, how philosophers of mind have illuminated the differences between the phenomenal and the physical, and how Rawls reformulated the autonomy-heteronomy distinction. The main obstacle to recognizing such cognitive achievements is the assumption (another form of the Philosopher's Fallacy) that, short of a "perfect" definition that catches every intuition we have about a distinction, there is no substantial knowledge of that distinction. On the contrary, in many cases (knowledge and freedom are good examples) there is reason to think there is no perfect definition but nonetheless a detailed knowledge of the scope and limits of a variety of complementary definitions. As in science, philosophical knowledge is often not a matter of discovering the (perhaps illusory) ultimate nature of the object being investigated but of appreciating the value of various approaches to that object.

The value of their knowledge of distinctions becomes particularly apparent when philosophers discuss topics such as freedom or necessity with those who do not have an adequate grasp of the relevant distinctions. Our students often think that they cannot win arguments with us because we are just too smart or too dialectically adept (and we ourselves often succumb to this flattering conclusion). But our ultimate advantage is not our superior intelligence but our access to a body of knowledge that our discipline has developed over the centuries. Even the brightest and most motivated students will continually fall into basic confusions until we teach them the crucial distinctions, honed over the centuries by our predecessors. The same is true of our discussions with colleagues in other disciplines. Even an experimental psychologist developing empirical measures of freedom or a mathematician concerned with the sense in which theorems are necessarily true will be at a severe disadvantage without a thorough acquaintance with the relevant philosophical distinctions.

Philosophers do themselves a signal disservice when they disregard the significance of the distinctions they employ even in unsuccessful efforts to resolve fundamental problems. We need a reorientation towards our own work – one that makes room for reflective assessments not only of how we continue to disagree about fundamental problems but also of what we have learned from our continuing refinement of basic distinctions.

APPLYING PHILOSOPHICAL KNOWLEDGE: RELIGIOUS BELIEF

We have looked at the discipline of philosophy and found that, contrary to the views of many philosophers themselves, it has produced an important body of knowledge. It would take at least another book to demonstrate in detail the illumination that knowledge provides for questions important to those who are not philosophers. But before I conclude, I want to give at least one example of the power of philosophical knowledge to shed decisive light on issues that many non-philosophers encounter in their lives. The example concerns religious belief, where, contrary to common opinion, I maintain that philosophical knowledge is essential for many struggling with questions of faith.

Some people have definitely made up their minds about religion and live as either contented believers or contented non-believers, but many genuinely ask (with a combination of hope and fear) whether religious accounts are true. It is easy to conclude that philosophers have nothing to teach such people because they themselves have reached no agreement about the claims of religion. This, however, is a serious mistake. One of the first things someone inquiring about the truth of religious claims will want to know is whether there is any decisive intellectual case for or against these claims. Is there any compelling argument from the nature of the world or our understanding of the divine essence for the existence of the God of traditional Christianity? Is there any compelling case from the fact and amount of evil in the world against the existence of such a being? Here it's important to remember that many believers and non-believers rely on such arguments to support their positions. There are many atheists for whom the argument from evil is an extremely important support for their position, and many theists who are seriously motivated by popular versions of the design argument or the cosmological argument. So whether or not such arguments are cogent is a question of major importance to many concerned about religious belief. Further, philosophy has a decisive answer to this question: no standard popular version of a theistic or atheistic argument makes an adequate case for its conclusion. The point is not that philosophers disagree about whether such arguments are sound. For any standard version of such an argument – the versions repeatedly invoked by ordinary people in their reflections and debates about religious belief – there are solid philosophical reasons that show just why the argument fails.

Consider a standard atheistic argument from evil: An all-good being would have wanted to prevent the Holocaust, and an all-powerful being would have been able to do so; therefore, since the Holocaust did occur, there is no being that is both all-good and all-powerful – hence no God in the traditional sense. No one familiar with Plantinga's free will defense can think that there is a compelling case for the initial premise of this argument. It is logically possible that an all-good being would permit the Holocaust for the sake of avoiding even greater evils and that even an all-powerful being could not have prevented the Holocaust and avoided greater evils. The argument as formulated is demonstrably inadequate, and anyone who rejects the existence of God on the basis of this argument has been misled. A similar point holds for those who accept the existence of an all-good and all-powerful God because there is no other way to explain the very existence of the universe as a whole. Any standard version of such an argument fails because it provides no compelling reason to think that the existence of the universe requires an explanation or that, if such an explanation is need, it must be given by positing a being of maximal power and goodness. Both the atheistic and the theistic arguments are inadequate in the light of well-established philosophical distinctions such as that between being all-good and permitting nothing but the good and between explaining things that are parts of the universe and explaining the universe itself.

Of course, there are more sophisticated versions of such arguments that are invoked by religious inquirers, but these typically also involve just somewhat more sophisticated inadequacies. At the highest level – beyond the intellectual competence of almost all religious inquirers – there are the intricately wrought arguments of professional philosophers such as Plantinga's ontological argument or William Rowe's probabilistic argument from evil. But even the proponents of such arguments admit that they require at least one premise that is not itself an established philosophical result and can be rightly rejected by anyone who does not see it as rationally compelling. The situation, then, is this: the arguments to which the vast majority of religious inquirers have intellectual access are demonstrably inadequate, and there are no arguments to which they do not have intellectual access that they can accept as endorsed by a consensus of expert opinion. There is, therefore, for the vast majority of religious inquirers, no generally compelling argumentative basis for accepting or rejecting the existence of God.[2]

This, of course, is a conclusion widely accepted, particularly by religious believers who see their commitment as a matter of faith rather than reason. But what is not widely recognized is that this conclusion is itself a significant instance of philosophical knowledge. It is not simply obvious that theistic and atheistic arguments will be inconclusive. Rather, the point has been solidly established by a long and rigorous process of philosophical analysis and discussion and represents a major cognitive achievement of philosophy as a discipline. The irony is that so many, including many philosophers themselves, see the failure to decide the issue of theistic belief as nothing more than a failure of philosophical reason. There is no denying that philosophers have not achieved the very enticing goal of proving either that God does exist or that God does not exist. But what philosophers have achieved is a clear understanding of precisely why successive versions of theistic and atheistic proofs are not adequate, an understanding based on truths discovered by philosophical reflection. It is only the Philosopher's Fallacy that leads us to conclude that a failure to answer an ultimate question implies that we have not achieved a substantial body of knowledge in the course of trying to answer the question. Moreover, in the present case, this body of knowledge is of major importance for non-philosophers inquiring about religious matters. It is precisely because of the results of philosophical discussion that religious inquirers are entitled to judge theistic proofs and disproofs unconvincing.

Lacking decisive proofs, many conclude that religious commitment is, as they often put it, simply a "matter of faith rather than reason." But, once again, philosophical results provide essential guidance to any

---

[2] This does not exclude the possibility that some individuals may be in epistemic situations that entitle them to the premises of valid arguments for or against religious beliefs. If, after careful reflection, it just seems overwhelmingly obvious to me that, say, the universe must have an intelligent cause or that certain sorts or amounts of evil are just incompatible with an all-good, all-powerful creator, then I have an intellectual right to accept the conclusions that follow from these premises. But I still have no basis for claiming that others, who see things differently, are not epistemically entitled to their views.

reflective inquirer. There is, for example, the question of just what might be meant by faith as opposed to reason. The history of philosophy offers crucial distinctions between various senses of faith: a Kierkegaardian embrace of the absurd, a Marcelian fidelity to mystery, a Thomistic trust in another's cognitive authority, a Plantingian basic belief, a Pascalian calculation, a Jamesian pragmatic choice, a Wittgensteinian commitment to a religious form of life. Each of these philosophical understandings of faith catches at least some of the tone of the religious belief of many people, and each understanding has been philosophically explored with meticulous attention to the religious authenticity and epistemic integrity of each mode of belief. Intellectually mature believers, even if they are free of doubts, need to know more about the precise nature of their commitment. Philosophical accounts of the faith–reason distinction are a major source of such knowledge.[3]

Further, the fact that religious convictions, like any others, do not, in principle, need prior authentification from philosophy does not mean that a particular conviction in the mind of a particular believer is epistemically unassailable. As we saw in our discussion of Plantinga, convictions that are properly basic for a paradigmatic believer may well require argumentative support for those whose belief is not so strong. I might, for example, realize that *my* belief in God is not properly basic but sustained only by my acceptance of reports of miracles (e.g., in the Bible considered as a historical document or from the testimony of those cured at Lourdes). In such a case, philosophical discussions about the reasonableness of believing testimony about miracles or about whether the occurrence of a miracle is good evidence for the existence of the God of traditional Christianity become highly relevant. Similarly, if (like many, it seems) my adherence to a religion is due to Pascalian cost–benefit calculations, then philosophical discussions of the famous wager (e.g., William James' suggestion that such calculators might be the very people God would surely exclude from heaven) become of great interest. More generally, we need to remember that those with religious convictions (or an interest in them) may also have equally deep convictions about responsible belief, which will lead them directly to philosophical discussions about the consistency of or the evidence for religious beliefs.

---

[3] The variety of such accounts is a good example of how there can be different "analyses of a concept" that are valid in different domains. There are likely to be different types of religious belief, corresponding to a Kierkegaardian or a Jamesian leap, a Wittgensteinian participation in a form of life, a Thomistic reasoned acceptance of a religious authority, etc.

Finally, the mere fact that I am entitled to my convictions – as basic beliefs or as derived conclusions – does not mean that my self-understanding of these convictions is unquestionably adequate. If, for example, my conviction is an expression of a legitimate emotional need or a morally appropriate deference to parental or other social authority, it does not follow that it can be properly taken as a literal expression of truths about the world. Another, more common, example: Many believers evade objections to religious claims by altering the content of what they assert; for example, defining God not as an all-good, all-powerful person involved in the history of the world but as an ideal of perfection to which we strive or a reality beyond all meaningful thought. Such redefinitions may result in a belief to which I am entitled: I may have reason to believe there is an ideal of perfection towards which I am striving even though I am not entitled to believe that there is an all-good, all-powerful being guiding the world. But there is an unfortunate tendency for believers to move to a deflated formulation of their belief ("God is the object of mankind's ultimate concern," "The Resurrection is our affirmation of hope in the face of evil") for the sake of meeting legitimate epistemic challenges, only to revert to the original problematic beliefs ("God exercises providential care over the world," "Christ's Resurrection guarantees our eternal life") once the challenge is met. Philosophical distinctions about just what can be meant by "God" and what sort of evidence or argument is relevant to claims about the existence of God in various senses of the term are essential for avoiding a faith based on bad faith.

A main reason that philosophical considerations seem irrelevant to the convictions of actual religious believers is that philosophers have typically tried to formulate universal master-arguments that would, for example, compel any rational person to agree that theism is inconsistent with the reality of evil or that undeniable principles of causality entail the existence of a first cause. Such arguments assume the foundationalist conception of philosophy that we have found wanting. The sorts of universally accepted premises such arguments require are just not available. Once we abandon the foundationalist conception, the door opens to much more focused "regional" or "individually tailored" philosophical considerations that will be highly relevant to those in particular epistemic situations; that is, to those who accept certain convictions as properly basic but are inquiring as to the truth of others. Philosophy cannot supply universal solutions to the great questions of religion, but it does offer resources of great value, although in quite different ways, to a wavering atheist with a strong commitment to objective moral values, to a traditional Catholic who has come to have doubts about Thomistic philosophy, to a fundamentalist Muslim worried about the fact that thinkers he has come to respect disagree with his deepest convictions, or to a humanist agnostic surprised by some vivid religious experiences. For such religious inquirers, philosophy provides a treasure trove of essential knowledge.

Religious beliefs concern not only God but also the nature of human beings. Although there is not a necessary correlation, atheism has often associated itself with materialism and theism with some form of dualism. This is particularly true because materialism seems to tell against the likelihood of life after death, whereas dualism seems to at least keep the door to eternity open. It is, accordingly, plausible to think that philosophical debates in the philosophy of mind are relevant to questions of religious belief. To see how this might be, let us reflect a bit on how even non-philosophers are likely to come to questions about mind and body.

We all begin with a common-sense distinction between the mental and the physical. No one denies that there are important prima facie differences – at root the differences Nagel formulates via the distinction between a first-person, subjective perspective and a third-person, objective perspective. Accordingly, the suggestion that there are really nothing but physical states seems, initially, at odds with common sense. On the other hand, we are all very impressed with the ability of natural science to describe and explain the world, and we realize that the basic entities of science do not include any mental states, although science has been very successful in finding physical explanations for mental states. There is, in fact, no reason in principle to think that science will not someday have discovered a causally sufficient physical antecedent for every mental state. This is where the philosophical mind–body problem begins – from two unquestionable pre-philosophical certainties: the reality of mental states and the possibility of a completely physical causal explanation of all mental states. Given these certainties, the question becomes: Is there ultimately any need to view mental states as an independent kind of reality, or can we place them entirely in the realm of the physical? And, if the mental is reduced to the physical, what prospects remain for our hopes of human distinctiveness and survival of death?

The two great rival pictures, materialism and dualism, provide opposing answers to the first question, materialists claiming that the mental can be reduced to the material, dualists that the mental is irreducibly immaterial. Until recently, the materialist picture dominated analytic philosophy of mind, generating a series of increasingly sophisticated theories: behaviorism, contingent identity theory, anomalous monism, various forms of functionalism. Dualism, by contrast, seemed unable to move beyond the classic problems of how immaterial entities could interact with material entities. There was little or no sense of how to give the dualist picture plausible and fruitful theoretical expressions, nor any rigorous argumentative formulation of the widespread anti-materialist intuition that thoughts and feelings just can't be merely material. Materialism, for all its intuitive implausibility, was sustaining a progressive philosophical research project.

As we have seen, however, there has been a recent revival of the dualist picture, effected by a detailed and progressively improving case for the logical irreducibility of at least some mental states and events to matter. The case is not decisive, but there has been no decisive refutation of the zombie and other anti-materialist arguments and little current prospect for a materialist counter-demonstration that the purely qualitative aspects of consciousness logically supervene on matter. As Jaegwon Kim, one of the most meticulous and cogent materialists, has put it, "Qualia . . . are the 'mental residue' that cannot be accommodated within the physicalist [materialist] domain."[4] It is, then, fair to conclude that the dualist picture is once more a viable contender.

This fact, however, provides less support than it might seem to religious beliefs that we survive death. If the anti-materialist arguments are sound, then the mental does not supervene on the physical; that is, the mere existence of an appropriate physical state or event is not logically sufficient for the existence of the corresponding mental state or event. But to what extent does this support the hopes traditionally sustained by the dualist picture? Central to these hopes is personal survival of the body's death. Such survival requires far more than the failure of supervenience; it requires that there be something mental for which the body is neither a logically nor a causally necessary condition, and this something must be identifiable as the person that I am. None of the current anti-materialist arguments supports such a conclusion. On the contrary, even dualist philosophers of mind generally accept a nomologically necessary dependence of the mental on the physical that would require miraculous intervention to bring about our survival of death. If we distinguish between a *strong dualism* that at least makes plausible personal survival of death from a *weak dualism* that does not, then contemporary philosophy of mind at best supports weak dualism.

---

[4] Jaegwon Kim, "The Mind–Body Problem at Century's Turn," in Brian Leiter (ed.), *The Future for Philosophy*, Oxford: Oxford University Press, 2004, 343.

Strong dualism corresponds to a supernaturalist picture of the human person, for which personal existence continues after death; weak dualism and materialism correspond to a naturalist picture that has no place for such continued existence. Despite the new life of dualism, the present state of philosophy of mind still supports the naturalist over the supernaturalist picture. Almost all the main contributors to the discussion are naturalists (that is, materialists or weak dualists). The rise of weak dualism has served the cause of naturalism, not supernaturalism, which has found few defenders and failed to produce a progressive series of theoretical formulations.

But what is the cognitive significance of this situation? We can hardly claim that philosophy of mind has refuted supernaturalism and established the truth of naturalism. Nor does it show that accepting supernaturalism is necessarily intellectually irresponsible. As we have seen, if a conviction remains firm after full and honest reflection on the case against it, there is no epistemic fault in retaining it as a basic belief. It need not depend on the availability of philosophical arguments in its favor; it can simply remain as a properly basic belief. Nonetheless, supernaturalists whose convictions fall short of those of Plantinga's paradigmatic believer do not have an epistemic right to maintain the sort of commitment that would be proper for such a believer. To the extent that they are aware of the current status of the philosophical discussion, they ought to retreat from full commitment to personal survival of death. Depending on the details of their assessment of the situation, this will mean at least a significant decrease in the strength of their belief if not a move to withholding judgment on the question. Even in the latter case, however, the belief might be retained in the form of hope rather than conviction and, for those with appropriate philosophical skills, this hope could well inspire an effort to revive the supernaturalist picture, perhaps by developing strong dualistic theories (as Richard Swinburne has done in recent years). Short of this, supernaturalists can at least try to legitimate their hope by showing that, even given the truth of materialism, personal survival is possible (logically and even perhaps nomologically) via resurrection of the body.[5]

At the same time, the revival of dualism poses a significant obstacle to the atheism of scientists such as Richard Dawkins and philosophers such as Daniel Dennett based on the claim that science provides a complete

---

[5] See, for example, Dean Zimmerman, "Materialism and Survival," in E. Stump and M. Murray (eds.), *Philosophy of Religion: The Big Questions*, Oxford: Blackwell, 1999, 379–86.

explanation of everything that needs explaining. They argue, in particular, that we have decisive evidence that evolutionary biology provides (or will provide in the future) a complete account of the origins of human beings. This is true for the human body and even for the mind insofar as it can be treated in a functional manner. But, given the results of current philosophy of mind, it is simply false for the qualitative aspects of consciousness. It remains an open question whether there will be satisfactory evolutionary (or other scientific) explanations of qualia, either by somehow reducing them to matter or by viewing them as irreducible but nonetheless somehow included in our scientific accounts (the approach Chalmers and others are trying to implement). Of course, even if qualia lie beyond scientific explanation, it by no means follows that they require a supernaturalist explanation. But given the results of recent philosophy of mind, the assertion that science has provided (or will provide) an explanation of all aspects of the human mind, including qualia, is a matter of materialist conviction, not scientific knowledge. Religious believers who reject the entire process of evolution or even those who deny that the process applies to human beings are in clear conflict with the scientific facts. But those who question whether there are good evolutionary explanations of *all* aspects of human consciousness are not contradicting established science and have at least some support for their view from recent philosophy of mind.

The above applications of philosophical knowledge to debates about religion do not, of course, answer the big questions about God's existence or life after death. If we restrict ourselves to inferences from established philosophical results, our conclusion about religion will be agnosticism. On the other hand, the anti-foundationalist results of recent philosophy show the legitimacy, in appropriate epistemic situations, of both religious and anti-religious convictions. Given our convictions as a starting point, philosophy serves as an essential guide to developing, revising, or even (if they conflict with other convictions) rejecting these convictions.

Someone may object that this is fine as far as it goes, but the real question is whether our pre-philosophical convictions are true, and philosophy, as I'm presenting it, has nothing to say to this. It might even be said that, if our convictions (which will, in general, be substantive assumptions, not shared by other competent inquirers) are not themselves justified but are just taken as arbitrary starting points, then we fall into a relativism in which different groups or even individuals have the right to say that they "know" (or have justification for believing) contradictory claims, simply because they happen to start from (equally dubious) convictions.

This objection slips back into philosophical foundationalism, and does so because it ignores the proper meaning and role of convictions in our thinking and knowing. A conviction is not an arbitrary starting point – a whimsically chosen position, a self-deceptive prejudice, or an idiosyncratic opinion. My conviction is what I truly and deeply believe, what, in my most honest self-assessment, I can scarcely think of giving up because it is rooted in practices of thought and action central to my conception of myself. Much of what falls into this category are beliefs that everyone sees as obvious and unquestionable.

But there are also convictions that others may not share, including fundamental views not just on religion but also on morals, politics, and art. Here there is room for deception, including self-deception, and others may have good reasons for thinking that I simply can't have a conviction that, say, every statement of the Bible is literally true, that human lives have no value, or that Andy Warhol was a great artist. I may need considerable hermeneutic resources to untangle just what I am fundamentally committed to, and these commitments themselves may only gradually emerge from shadows of doubt, particularly when others I respect disagree with an emerging conviction. (I may, for example, realize, on reflection, that I was not actually committed to the literal truth of the Bible but to the value of taking what it says seriously.) In the end, each of us is responsible for an honest formulation of convictions, an individual *Here I stand, I can do no otherwise*. It is when they have questions arising from these sorts of "thick" convictions (as opposed to the "thin," trivially obvious convictions) that non-philosophers will most profit from applying philosophical knowledge. On the other hand, non-philosophers will often be understandably uninterested in philosophical discussions that don't deal with their convictions or that are arguing for or against a conviction with which they are entirely content.

ENVOI: DOUBT, FAITH, KNOWLEDGE, AND WISDOM

A panoramic view of philosophy reveals three different roles in which the philosopher can lay claim to knowledge: as skeptic, as apologist, and as expert. Although the role of skeptic is important, I have paid little attention to it, primarily because the associated knowledge is entirely negative. Skeptical philosophers at most show the falsity of various positions but can arrive at no firm cognitive ground of their own. Trying to parlay philosophical skepticism into a body of positive knowledge leads to the Cartesian project of trying to prove what everyone else takes as obvious truths, by extending skepticism to the point of self-refutation and building up from there. One of the most important results of recent epistemological discussions has been the realization that this is an impossible and inappropriate project; the philosopher, like everyone else, must simply start with a set of properly basic truths (truths we're entitled to hold without justification). But once we avoid the Cartesian trap, philosophy is a highly useful technique for clarifying what we actually know by subjecting our obvious truths to critical scrutiny – not to show that they're false or doubtful, but to make clearer the meaning they must have as obvious truths. For example: colors exist; we are free; lying is wrong. There are senses in which these are utterly undeniable, but they can also be taken in senses that are legitimately questionable, and philosophy can discover these senses (the limits of the obvious).

Our last few chapters have put considerable emphasis on the philosophical defense of pre-philosophical convictions. The idea of philosophers as apologists is immediately distasteful, but less so when we realize that we all come to the philosophical table with some convictions. I have no patience with the facile claim, usually by those whose questionable views have come under heavy fire, that critics are just as much "persons of faith" as believers. It's important to distinguish kinds and degrees of beliefs, and there is a huge distance between a traditionally orthodox Christian, say, and an agnostic committed to basic canons of rationality and open to a wide range of views on ethical and religious truths. But there is also a great distance between such an agnostic and a dogmatic atheist who refuses to consider the possibility of any significant religious truth. Nonetheless, once all this is acknowledged, the fact remains that convictions of one sort or another are woven into the fabric of our thinking, and there is no realistic hope that philosophy can replace all convictions with rigorously argued conclusions from obvious premises. Accordingly, we should expect that philosophers will think out of one or another set of convictions. We will find this less distasteful the closer the convictions assumed are to our own, and we should develop a habit of giving even quite alien convictions a respectful hearing, although never forgetting that there will always be some convictions that we find entirely gratuitous or even repugnant.

The main thesis of this book – and one I did not expect to arrive at when I began writing it – is that philosophers have expert knowledge about a large and important domain of conceptual (or linguistic) distinctions. I have given numerous examples of such knowledge and also tried to give some sense of the intellectual processes that generate it. At the same time, I have insisted that there is no mysterious source of philosophical knowledge, which is just the application of widespread modes of thinking to a distinctive subject-matter. Correspondingly, there is no need for any special defense or justification of the intuitions and inferences from which this knowledge flows.

In arguing for a body of first-order philosophical knowledge, I have come to feel like a foil of the little boy in the Hans Christian Andersen tale, insisting that the Emperor everyone thinks is naked is actually clothed. The distorting expectations of philosophical foundationalism, I have argued, make us unable to see the achievement that is right before our eyes. Admittedly, we philosophers are not garbed in the royal raiment our forebears claimed as their right, but we are still entitled to a distinctive place at the intellectual table. We have knowledge but not the wisdom to which our name and tradition aspire. Even so, applying philosophical knowledge to improve and revise our convictions will bring us as close as possible to this wisdom.

References

Audi, Robert, *The Good and the Right: A Theory of Intuition and Intrinsic Value*, Princeton, NJ: Princeton University Press, 2004.

Bealer, George, "Intuitions and the Autonomy of Philosophy," in DePaul and Ramsey (eds.), 201–39.

Burge, Tyler, "Logic and Analyticity," *Grazer Philosophische Studien* 66 (2003), 199–249.

Burgess, John, "Quine, Analyticity and Philosophy of Mathematics," *Philosophical Quarterly* 54 (2004), 38–55.

Chalmers, David, *The Conscious Mind*, Oxford: Oxford University Press, 1996.
"Phenomenal Concepts and the Knowledge Argument," in P. Ludlow, Y. Nagasawa, and D. Stoljar (eds.), *There's Something about Mary*, Cambridge, MA: MIT Press, 2004, 269–98.
"The Two-Dimensional Argument Against Materialism," in his *The Character of Consciousness*, Oxford: Oxford University Press, forthcoming (a draft is available on Chalmers' website at http://consc.net/papers/2dargument.html)

Chomsky, Noam, Review of *Verbal Behavior*, *Language* 35 (1959), 26–58.

Clark, Michael, "Knowledge and Grounds: A Comment on Mr. Gettier's Paper," *Analysis* 24(2) (1963), 46–8.

Creath, Richard (ed.), *Dear Carnap, Dear Van: The Quine–Carnap Correspondence and Related Work*, Berkeley: University of California Press, 1990.

Cummins, Robert, "Reflections on Reflective Equilibrium," in DePaul and Ramsey (eds), 113–27.

Daniels, Norman, "Wide Reflective Equilibrium and Theory Acceptance in Ethics," *Journal of Philosophy* 76 (1979), 256–82.

Davidson, Donals, "Quine's Externalism," *Grazer Philosophische Studien*, 66 (2003), 281–97.

Dennett, Daniel, "The Zombic Hunch: Extinction of an Intuition?," in A. O'Hear (ed.), *Philosophy at the New Millennium*, Cambridge: Cambridge University Press, 2001, 27–43.

DePaul, Michael R., "Reflective Equilibrium and Foundationalism," *American Philosophical Quarterly* 23 (1986), 59–69.
"Why Bother with Reflective Equilibrium?," in DePaul and Ramsey (eds.), 293–309.

DePaul, M. R. and W. Ramsey (eds.), *Rethinking Intuition: The Psychology of Intuition and Its Role in Philosophical Inquiry*, Lanham, MD: Rowman & Littlefield, 1998.

DeRose, Keith, "Plantinga, Presumption, Possibility and the Problem of Evil," *Canadian Journal of Philosophy* 21 (1990), 497–512.

Evans, Gareth, "The Causal Theory of Names," *Collected Papers*, Oxford: Oxford University Press, 1985.

Fitch, G. W., *Saul Kripke*, Montreal: McGill Queen's University Press, 2004.

Flew, Anthony and Alasdair MacIntyre (eds.), *New Essays in Philosophical Theology*, London: Macmillan, 1955.

Fodor, Jerry, "Water's Water Everywhere," *London Review of Books*, October 21, 2004.

Frankfurt, Harry, "Alternate Possibilities and Moral Responsibility," *Journal of Philosophy* 66 (1969), 829–39.

Friedman, Michael, "Kuhn and Logical Empiricism," in Thomas Nickles (ed.), *Thomas Kuhn*, Cambridge: Cambridge University Press, 2003, 19–44.

Gettier, Edmund, "Is Justified True Belief Knowledge?," *Analysis* 23 (1963), 121–3.

Gibson, Roger F., Jr. (ed.), *The Cambridge Companion to Quine*, Cambridge: Cambridge University Press, 2004.

Giere, Ronald, "Kuhn's Legacy for North American Philosophy of Science," *Social Studies of Science* 27 (1997), 496–8.

Glock, H.-J., K. Glürt, and G. Keil (eds.), *Fifty Years of Quine's "Two Dogmas"* (*Grazer Philosophische Studien* 66 [2003]), 1. Also published as a book by Rodopi, 2003.

Goldman, Alvin, "A Causal Theory of Knowing," *Journal of Philosophy* 64 (1967), 335–72.

"What is Justified Belief?," in George Pappas (ed.), *Justification and Knowledge*, Dordrecht: Reidel, 1979, 1–23.

Grice, H. P. and P. F. Strawson, "In Defense of a Dogma," *Philosophical Review* 55 (1956), 141–58.

Gutting, Gary, *Pragmatic Liberalism and the Critique of Modernity*, Cambridge: Cambridge University Press, 1999.

Hardcastle, Valerie Gray, "The Why of Consciousness: A Non-Issue for Materialists," in Jonathan Shear (ed.), *Explaining Consciousness – The "Hard Problem,"* Cambridge, MA: MIT Press, 1997, 61–8.

Hoyningen-Huene, Paul and Howard Sankey (eds.), *Incommensurability and Related Matters*, Boston: Kluwer, 2001.

Hughes, Christopher, *Kripke: Names, Necessity, and Identity*, Oxford: Oxford University Press, 2004.

Jackson, Frank, *From Metaphysics to Ethics: A Defense of Conceptual Analysis*, Oxford: Oxford University Press, 1998.

"Reference and Description Revisited," in J. Tomberlin (ed.), *Philosophical Perspectives 12: Language, Mind, and Ontology*, Oxford: Blackwell, 1998, 201–18.

Katz, Jerrold, "Names without Bearers," *The Philosophical Review* 103 (1994), 1–39.

Kim, Jaegwon, "The Mind–Body Problem at Century's Turn," in Brian Leiter (ed.), *The Future for Philosophy*, Oxford: Oxford University Press, 2004, 129–52.

Kirk, Robert, "Zombies v. Materialists," *Proceedings of the Aristotelian Society*, Supplementary Vol. 48 (1974), 135–52.

Kitcher, Philip, "Theories, Theorists and Theoretical Change," *The Philosophical Review* 87 (1978), 519–47.

Klein, Peter, "A Proposed Definition of Propositional Knowledge," *Journal of Philosophy* 68 (1971), 471–82.

Kripke, Saul, *Naming and Necessity*, Cambridge, MA: Harvard University Press, 1980.

Kuhn, Thomas, *The Structure of Scientific Revolutions*, second edition, Chicago: University of Chicago Press, 1970 [first published 1962].

Lakatos, I. and A. Musgrave (eds.), *Criticism and the Growth of Knowledge*, Cambridge: Cambridge University Press, 1970.

Laudan, Laurens, *Progress and Its Problems: Toward a Theory of Scientific Growth*, Berkeley: University of California Press, 1978.

Lewis, David, "Are We Free to Break the Laws?," in his *Philosophical Papers, Volume II*, Oxford: Oxford University Press, 1986, 291–8.

"Elusive Knowledge," *Australasian Journal of Philosophy* 74 (1996), 549–67.

Loar, Brian, "Phenomenal States (Revised)," in P. Ludlow, Y. Nagasawa, and D. Stoljar (eds.), *There's Something about Mary*, Cambridge, MA: MIT Press, 2004, 219–39.

Lycan, William, "Definition in a Quinean World," in J. Fetzer, D. Shatz, and G. Schlesinger (eds.), *Definitions and Definability: Philosophical Perspectives*, Dordrecht: Kluwer, 1991, 111–31.

"On the Gettier Problem Problem," in Stephen Hetherington (ed.), *Epistemology Futures*, Oxford: Oxford University Press, 2006, 148–68.

Machery, E., R. Mallon, S. Nichols, and S. Stich, "Semantics Cross-Cultural Style," *Cognition* 92 (2004), B1–B12.

Mackie, J. L., *The Miracle of Theism*, Oxford: Oxford University Press, 1982.

Martin, Michael, *Atheism: A Philosophical Justification*, Philadelphia: Temple University Press, 1990.

McDowell, John, "Towards Rehabilitating Objectivity," in Robert B. Brandom (ed.), *Rorty and His Critics*, Oxford: Blackwell, 2000, 109–23.

McGinn, Colin, "Can We Solve the Mind–Body Problem?," *Mind*, New Series, 98 (1989), 349–66.

Nagel, Thomas, "Conceiving the Impossible and the Mind–Body Problem," *Philosophy* 73 (1998), 337–52.

"What Is It Like to Be a Bat?," *The Philosophical Review* 83 (1974), 435–50.

Pickering, Andrew, *Constructing Quarks: A Sociological History of Particle Physics*, Edinburgh: Edinburgh University Press, 1984.

Plantinga, Alvin, *God and Other Minds*, Ithaca, NY: Cornell University Press, 1967.

The Nature of Necessity, Oxford: Oxford University Press, 1974.

Warranted Christian Belief, Oxford: Oxford University Press, 2000.

Putnam, Hilary, "The Analytic and the Synthetic," in his *Mind, Language, and Reality, Philosophical Papers*, Volume II, Cambridge: Cambridge University Press, 1975. [First published 1962.]

"The Greatest Logical Positivist," in his *Realism with a Human Face*, ed. James Conant, Cambridge, MA: Harvard University Press, 1990.

Reason, Truth, and History, Cambridge: Cambridge University Press, 1981.

Quine, W. V. O., "Two Dogmas of Empiricism," in his *From a Logical Point of View*, Cambridge, MA: Harvard University Press, 1953.

"Two Dogmas in Retrospect," *Canadian Journal of Philosophy* 21 (1991), 265–74.

Word and Object, Cambridge, MA: MIT Press, 1960,

Rawls, John, *Political Liberalism*, New York: Columbia University Press, 1993.

A Theory of Justice, Cambridge, MA: Harvard University Press, 1971.

Rorty, Richard, "Response to John McDowell," in R. Brandom (ed.), *Rorty and His Critics*, Oxford: Blackwell, 2000, 123–8.

"An Imaginative Philosopher: The Legacy of W. V. Quine" [obituary notice], *Chronicle of Higher Education*, February 2, 2001.

Objectivity, Relativism, and Truth, Cambridge: Cambridge University Press, 1990.

Philosophy as Cultural Politics (Philosophical Papers, Volume IV), Cambridge: Cambridge University Press, 2007.

Philosophy and the Mirror of Nature, Princeton, NJ: Princeton University Press, 1979.

Salmon, Nathan, *Reference and Essence*, Oxford: Basil Blackwell, 1982, 23–31.

Scheffler, Israel, *Science and Subjectivity*, Indianapolis: Bobbs-Merrill, 1967.

Scheffler, Samuel, "Rawls and Utilitarianism," in Samuel Freeman (ed.), *The Cambridge Companion to Rawls*, Cambridge: Cambridge University Press, 2003.

Searle, John, *Intentionality: An Essay in the Philosophy of Mind*, Cambridge: Cambridge University Press, 1983.

Shapere, Dudley, "The Structure of Scientific Revolutions," *The Philosophical Review* 73 (1964), 383–94.

Shope, Robert K., *The Analysis of Knowledge*, Princeton, NJ: Princeton University Press, 1983.

"Conditions and Analyses of Knowing," in Paul Moser (ed.), *The Oxford Handbook of Epistemology*, Oxford: Oxford University Press, 2002, 25–70

Singer, Peter, "Philosophers Are Back on the Job," *The New York Times Magazine*, July 7, 1974, 6–7; 17–20.

Soames, Scott, *Philosophical Analysis in the Twentieth Century, Volume I: The Dawn of Analysis*, Princeton, NJ: Princeton University Press, 2003.

Philosophical Analysis in the Twentieth Century, Volume II: The Age of Meaning, Princeton, NJ: Princeton University Press, 2003.

Sosa, E. and J. Kim (eds.), *Epistemology: An Anthology*, Malden, MA: Blackwell, 2000, 340–53.

Stoljar, Daniel, "Physicalism," *Stanford Encyclopedia of Philosophy* (online), http://plato.stanford.edu/entries/physicalism/

Swoyer, Chris, "How Ontology Might Be Possible: Explanation and Inference in Metaphysics," *Midwest Studies in Philosophy* XXIII (1999), 100–31.

Van Inwagen, Peter, *An Essay on Free Will*, Oxford: Oxford University Press, 1983.

"Freedom to Break the Laws," *Midwest Studies in Philosophy* XXVIII (2004), 334–50

"Free Will Remains a Mystery," in Robert Kane (ed.), *The Oxford Handbook of Free Will*, Oxford: Oxford University Press, 2002, 158–77.

"The Incompatibility of Free Will and Determinism," *Philosophical Studies* 27 (1975), 185–99.

Weatherson, Brian, "What Good Are Counterexamples?," *Philosophical Studies* 115 (2003), 1–31.

Weinberg, J., S. Nichols, and S. Stich, "Normativity and Epistemic Intuitions," *Philosophical Topics* 29 (2001), 429–60.

Whitehead, Alfred North, *Adventures of Ideas*, New York: Free Press, 1967 [first published 1933].

Williams, Bernard, *Ethics and the Limits of Philosophy*, Cambridge, MA: Harvard University Press, 1985.

Williamson, Timothy, *The Philosophy of Philosophy*, Oxford: Blackwell, 2007.

Zammito, John H., *A Nice Derangement of Epistemes: Post-Positivism in the Study of Science from Quine to Latour*, Chicago: University of Chicago Press, 2004.

Zimmerman, Dean, "Materialism and Survival," in E. Stump and M. Murray (eds.), *Philosophy of Religion: The Big Questions*, Oxford: Blackwell, 1999, 379–86.

Index

a posteriori 31, 35, 44–7
a priori 22, 31, 45
ability (to do otherwise, to render false) 139,
    140–1, 143
agreement 19, 194, 199–200, 219, 222
  in philosophy 1–2, 90, 95–6, 230, 231
  in science 201, 206
Albritton, Roger 78
Alston, William 106
analytic philosophy 3, 197
  Rorty on 198, 205–7, 208, 215
analytic-synthetic distinction 5, 11, 12–30, 90,
    212, 230
  defenses of 11–24, 75–6, 83
  Kripke on 32
  Quine's critique 3–4, 12–30, 73, 74–6,
    82–3
Aquinas, Thomas 48, 234
argument 1–2, 5, 6, 32, 43–4, 47–50, 207–10
  challenge 73, 82–3, 229
  consequence 139–47
  from evil 227, 231–2
  zombie 5, 123, 125–38
argumentation 6, 13, 38, 191–4
  convictional 192–3
  foundational 191–3
Aristotle 47, 48, 78, 149, 208
Audi, Robert 91, 106
authority 95, 98, 99, 100–1, 129, 193, 201, 222,
    234, 235
  philosophical 168, 192, 208–9
  scientific 151, 156–7, 167, 168, 170, 171
Ayer, A. J. 51

Bealer, George 76, 91, 93
behaviorism 236
  Quine and 21–2, 24, 75
belief
  Christian 111–20, 231–40
  properly basic 171, 234, 238
Berlin, Isaiah 199
Bradley, F. H. 29

Brandom, Robert 203, 206, 207, 209–10, 214
Broad, C. D. C. 139
Burge, Tyler 13, 24, 25, 28
Burgess, John 21

Carnap, Rudolf 12, 15, 16, 18, 20, 21, 23, 26, 27,
    29, 156, 209, 212
causal theory of reference 41–2, 78, 84–5,
    164–5
causality
  mind–body 131–3
Chalmers, David 4, 125, 132, 227, 239
  on conceivability (vs. metaphysical
    possibility) 134–7
  on epiphenomenalism 131
  on functional states 127
  on phenomenal concept 230
  on two-dimensional semantics 136–7
  zombie argument 5, 123, 125–38
Chastain, Charles 78
Chisholm, Roderick 51
Chomsky, Noam 21
cluster theory 36–41
coherentism 112, 188
compatibilism 122–3, 145, 148
conceivability 132–3, 134–7
concepts
  nature of 206, 209
  phenomenal 230
consciousness 123–38
consequence argument 123, 139–47
contextualism 65–72, 88
convictions 5–6, 31, 77–82, 120–1, 147–8, 173,
    184–5, 190, 224, 242
  pre-philosophical 130, 133–4, 137–8, 152, 170–1,
    188, 210–11, 241
  religious 101, 171, 234–6, 237, 239–40
counterexample(s) 51–7, 61–3, 84, 190
  barn 51, 54, 99, 191
  Frankfurt 138
  Gettier 3, 51, 52–7, 65, 86–9, 95, 99,
    190, 193

counterfactuals 34, 35
Creath, Richard 30
Cummins, Robert 91–2, 93

Daniels, Norman 188
Darwin, Charles 2
Davidson, Donald 24, 79, 202–3, 207, 209, 210, 214, 219
Dawkins, Richard 238
death, survival of, 237
defeasibility analysis (of Gettier problem) 54–5
definite descriptions 33, 35–44
definition 16–17, 18, 20, 21, 22, 87–9, 230
Dennett, Daniel 130–1, 132, 133, 238
DePaul, Michael 91, 101
Derrida, Jacques 219
DeRose, Keith 111
Descartes, René 4, 209, 219
descriptivism 44, 49, 83–6, 230
determinism 138–9, 139–42, 145, 148–50
Devitt, Michael 162
Dewey, John 219
disagreement *see* agreement
distinctions 4–5, 6, 40, 45–7, 77, 225, 235, 241
    role in philosophy 193–4, 211, 228–31
Donnellan, Keith 78, 162
Dostoyevsky, Fyodor 214
Dretske, Fred 71
dualism 122, 236–9
    strong vs. weak 237, 238
Duhem, Pierre 27–8
Duhem's thesis 27–8, 166

elaboration, persuasive 77–82, 88, 89–90, 92, 94, 100, 190, 210, 229
empiricism 16, 74, 78, 219, 226
    dogmas of 13–14, 25–6
Enlightenment 198, 215, 217, 218, 219
epiphenomenalism 131
essence; *see also* essentialism 14–15
essentialism 27, 31, 32–5, 44, 45, 48, 50, 76, 78–9, 226
Evans, Gareth, 42, 85
evidence 27, 33, 46–7, 54, 56, 59, 62, 65–7, 83, 91, 93, 114, 119, 146, 165, 221, 229
evil 231–2
    moral 107, 109–10
    natural 110
    problem of 233
experimental philosophy 95–9, 100
explanation 1, 66, 69, 70, 88, 89, 124, 130–1, 232, 238–9
    inference to best 189–90

Feyerabend, Paul 152, 156, 158, 160
Findlay, J. N. 105

Flew, Anthony 105–6
Fodor, Jerry 76
foundationalism 5–6, 112–17, 120, 190
    classical 112, 147, 188
    epistemic 112
    philosophical 7, 171, 191, 214, 224, 229–30, 235, 240, 242
Frankfurt, Harry 138, 149
free will 122–3, 138–50
    defense 106, 107–11, 227, 232
Frege, Gottlob 15, 31, 36, 160
Friedman, Michael 156
fruitfulness 4, 73–6, 77, 79, 81, 167, 225, 229
function, proper 113–14

Galileo Galilei 2
Gettier, Edmund 3, 5, 51, 52–7, 73, 86–9, 230
Gettier problem 55, 90, 113
Giere, Ronald 158
Ginet, Carl 139
God 1, 2, 234, 235
    and evil 227
    arguments against 227, 232
    arguments for 226, 231–3
    power of 107–10
    see also Plantinga, Alvin
Goldman, Alvin
    on justified belief 57
    on self-evidence 58–9
    reliabilism of 4, 81, 88, 226
    use of counterexamples 51
good, conception of 179, 185–6, 194
Goodman, Nelson 12
Grice, H. P. 19, 20, 21, 23, 25

Habermas, Jürgen 199
Hanson, Norwood Russell 152, 156, 158
hard problem (of consciousness) 127
Hardcastle, Valerie Gray 133
Harman, Gilbert 25
Hegel, G. W. F. 78, 201, 205, 208, 209, 212
Heidegger, Martin 207, 219
Hesperus/Phosphorus 36, 45–7
holism (Quine) 23, 24, 25–6, 27–30, 74–6, 83
Hoyningen-Huene, Paul 165
Hughes, Christopher 31, 43, 48, 49–50
Hume, David 147, 149, 208
Husserl, Edmund 209

identity 33, 35, 36, 44–7
    practical 213
imagination 73–6, 86
    Rorty on 74, 199–200, 202, 203–5, 207, 208, 212, 213–14

incommensurability 156, 170
  epistemological 165–70
  semantic 159–70
indexicals 161
infallibilism 64–72
intension 136–7
  primary 136
  secondary 136
intuition(s) 5, 32, 43, 47–50, 76–7, 89–101,
  146–7, 189, 190–4, 226
  phenomenality 137–8
  zombie 129–38
Isaacson, Daniel 23, 25–6

Jackson, Frank 76, 85, 96, 126
James, William 219, 234
judgment 56, 96–8, 184, 190, 230
  in philosophy 23, 49, 193
  in science 6, 90, 158, 165–70, 171–2
justice 171
  as fairness 177
  Rawls' two principles of 173–9, 186–8
  utilitarian account of 173, 180–4, 227
justification 52, 53, 59–61, 65, 70, 95,
  113, 115, 187, 211, 216, 221,
  223, 225

Kant, Immanuel 12, 14, 174, 178–94, 208, 219
Katz, Jerrold 85
Kepler, Johannes 212
Kierkegaard, Søren 176, 212, 234
Kim, Jaegwon 124, 237
Kirk, Robert 125
Kitcher, Philip 159, 160, 161, 162, 226
Klein, Peter 54
knowledge 1, 74, 191, 206, 230
  a posteriori 11
  a priori 11
  as justified true belief 3, 5, 51–7, 86–9
  philosophical 2, 3–7, 11, 40, 73, 82–9,
  89–101, 148, 171, 173, 197,
  210–14, 224–31, 231–40, 241–2
Koyré, Alexandre 157
Kripke, Saul 3, 31–50, 51, 73, 76–80, 162,
  164, 212
  and essentialism 31, 32–5, 44, 48, 76,
  78–9, 226
  and intuitions 32, 35, 43, 47–50, 74,
  76–7, 100
  and necessity 3–4, 31, 32, 76, 78, 134–7,
  226, 227
  and Quine 31, 32–3, 44, 76
  and Searle 37, 41, 84–5
  critique of descriptivism 35–44, 49, 190, 230
  modal argument 43

Naming and Necessity 78, 79, 205
  on identity 33, 35, 44–7, 77
  on mind–body problem 135
  on naming 33, 34, 35–44, 44–7, 76–7, 83–6,
  90, 92, 230
  on necessary a posteriori 17, 22, 31, 35,
  44–7, 73
  on pictures–theory distinction
  4, 40–4, 78–80
  on possibility (epistemic vs. metaphysical) 31
  on possible worlds 32–5
  on rigid designators 31–5, 35–44, 49,
  76–7, 85–6, 90, 92
  use of counterexamples 37, 95, 190
Kuhn, Thomas 6, 90, 101, 151–72, 211, 229
  and logical positivism 153, 156–9, 170
  and the rationality of science 151, 152–3,
  155–9, 159–72
  Kitcher's response to 159
  Laudan's response to 165–6, 168
  on incommensurability 156, 159–70
  on paradigms 153–6, 159, 165
  on scientific revolutions 151, 153–4, 159, 165
  Scheffler's critique of 152, 153–4
  Shapere's review of 155–6, 157

Lakatos, Imre 152, 154, 165, 168
Lamb, Charles 139
Laudan, Larry 165–6, 168
Lavoisier, Antoine 161, 163
Leibniz, G. W. F. 14
Lévi-Strauss, Claude 225
Lewis, David 51, 80–2, 148
  and closure 81
  and compatibilism 142–7
  and contextualism 65–72, 81, 88
  critique of consequence argument 141, 142–7
  on freedom 142–7
  on Gettier counterexamples 65, 67–8
  on infallibility 64–72, 80
  on knowledge 88
  on lottery paradox 67–8
  on modal epistemology 66–72
  on philosophical arguments 146
  on skepticism 64–72, 171
  on "was able to render false" 139,
  140–1, 142–7
  rules for ignoring possibilities 66–72,
  80–1, 88
liberalism, political 6, 188
libertarianism 123
Loar, Brian 137
Locke, John 112, 174, 219
logic
  modal 34, 49

logical positivism 31, 219
  on science 6, 153, 156–9, 170
  Quine and 23, 74–6
lottery paradox 67–8
Lycan, William 13, 56–7, 99

Machery, Edouard 96, 97
MacIntyre, Alasdair 105–6, 176
Mackie, J. L. 107, 110
Marcel, Gabriel 234
Martin, Michael 115–16
materialism 122–38, 201, 236–9
maximin strategy 180–4, 189
McDowell, John 6, 214, 218–23
McGinn, Colin 133
meaning 14–22, 25–6, 36, 37, 160–5
metaphilosophy 2–3, 6
Mill, John Stuart 36, 43
mind–body problem 133, 236–9
Moore, G. E. 70

Nagel, Thomas 123–5, 130, 132–3, 199, 221, 236
names 33, 35–44, 76–7, 78
  proper 31, 44–7, 83–6
naming 14, 34, 44, 90, 92, 230
naturalism 29–30, 76, 86, 91–101, 117, 168–9, 238
necessary a posteriori 17, 22, 31, 35, 44–7, 76
necessity 3, 11, 17–18, 22, 31, 32, 73, 83, 134–7
  metaphysical 74, 78, 226, 227
Newton, Isaac 2
Nietzsche, Friedrich 198, 205, 208
Nozick, Robert 71

objectivity 6, 215–18, 218–23
ontology
  Quine on 15–16, 29–30
  Rorty on 203
original position 173–9, 185, 186, 193
  constraints on 181–4
oxygen theory 161–2

pain 61, 135, 136–7
paradigm 151, 153–6, 159, 165, 171
Pascal, Blaise 234
Perry, John 130, 131, 132
person 194
  political conception of 186–8
Philosopher's Fallacy 89, 149, 230, 233
philosophy
  analytic 197, 198, 205–7, 208
  cognitive authority of 168, 192, 208–9
  experimental 95–9, 100
  of science 6, 151–2, 165–70, 170–1
phlogiston theory 161–4
physicalism: *see* materialism

Pickering, Andrew 166–7, 169
pictures; *see also* theories 4, 6, 78–80, 225, 225–31
Planck, Max 158
Plantinga, Alvin 5, 28, 50, 79, 105–21
  and Kripke 226
  free will defense 106, 107–11, 227, 232
  God and Other Minds, 106
  Nature of Necessity 79
  on foundationalism 112–17
  on problem of evil, 106–11, 227
  on (properly) basic beliefs 112–17, 234
  on religious belief 101, 106, 111–20, 171, 226, 227, 238
  on warrant 113–14, 115–17, 226
  ontological argument 232
Plato 4, 11, 51, 198, 205, 207, 208, 209, 212, 219
Platonism 14, 198
Polanyi, Michael 151, 158
possibility 31
  epistemic 134–7
  metaphysical 134–7
possible worlds 13, 32–5, 44
practice 2, 78, 156–7, 168, 170–1, 187, 190, 191–2, 203, 204–5, 215, 221–2, 225
pragmatism 199–200, 202, 204–5, 215–18, 218–23
Priestly, Joseph 161–3
psychology
  folk 49
Putnam, Hilary 23, 25, 75–6, 78, 83, 154, 162, 165

qualia 237, 239
Quine, W. V. O. 3, 31, 50, 51, 73, 76, 77, 79–80, 207, 219, 226
  and behaviorism 21–2, 24, 75
  and Carnap 20, 23, 27
  and Duhem's thesis 27–8, 166
  and Kripke 17, 33
  and naturalism 29–30, 76, 86
  holism of 23, 24, 25–6, 27–30, 74–6, 83
  imagination in 73–6, 77, 86
  on analytic-synthetic distinction 3–4, 5, 12–30, 73, 74–6, 82–3, 90, 212, 230
  on essences 14–15
  on meaning(s) 14–22, 25–6, 79
  on necessity 17–18, 19, 32–3, 44
  on ontology 15–16, 29–30, 79
  on synonymy 16–18, 21, 73
  on verification 25–6
  "Two Dogmas" 13–30, 32, 73–6
  Word and Object 15, 24, 79

rationalism 78, 91–101, 208
rationality 151, 178–9, 204

Rawls, John 3, 6, 101, 171, 173–94, 213, 230
  and Kant 186, 187
  on conceptions of the good 179, 185–6, 194
  on conceptions of the person 186–8, 194
  on maximin principle 180–4, 189
  on the original position 173–9, 181–4, 185, 186, 193
  on reflective equilibrium 185, 188–94, 226
  on utilitarianism 180–4, 227
  on veil of ignorance, 177–8, 184, 193
  political liberalism 6, 188
  the two principles of justice 173–9
    arguments for, 179–86, 186–8
realism 215–18, 218–23
reductionism 13, 14, 25–30, 74
reference 1, 14–15, 36–42, 43, 49, 79, 160–5, 169
reference potential 163–4
reflective equilibrium 185, 188–94
relativism 204, 211, 216, 239
reliabilism 4, 81, 88, 226
religion 224, 231–40
  philosophy of 5, 105–21
  Plantinga on 15, 101, 227
  Rorty on 200–2, 208
revolutions, scientific 151, 153–4, 156, 159, 165
rigid designators 31–5, 35–44, 45, 49, 76–7, 85–6, 90, 92
Romanticism 199–200, 202–5, 208
Rorty, Richard 2, 6, 12, 13, 197–223
  and relativism 204, 211, 216
  argument in 207–10, 210–11
  critique of Singer 213–14
  debate with McDowell 6, 218–23
  on analytic philosophy 198, 205–7, 208, 215
  on imagination 74, 199–200, 202, 203–5, 207, 208, 212, 213–14
  on the nature of concepts 206, 209
  on objectivity 215–18, 218–23
  on philosophical knowledge 197, 210–14
  on Platonism 198
  on realism 215–18, 218–23
  on religion 200–2, 208
  on Romanticism 199–200, 202–5, 208
  on truth 101, 198–200, 200–2, 202–5, 207, 208–9, 211, 215–18, 218–23
  pragmatism of 199–200, 202, 204–5, 215–18, 218–23
Rousseau, Jean-Jacques 174
Rowe, William 232
rules
  Lewis' 66–72, 80–1, 88
  semantical 18, 20
Russell, Bertrand 15, 36, 199

Sankey, Howard 165
Sartre, Jean-Paul 176

Scheffler, Israel 152, 153–4, 160
Scheffler, Samuel 173
science 74, 122–3, 125, 127, 130–1, 201–2, 205, 238–9
  cognitive authority of 151, 156–7, 167, 168, 170
  normal 153
  rationality of 152–3, 154, 155–9, 159–72
Searle, John 37, 41, 49, 84–5, 99
self-evidence 58–9
Sellars, Wilfrid 158, 203, 204, 207, 210, 219
semantics, two-dimensional 136–7
sense; *see also* reference 160, 163, 164
Shapere, Dudley 155–6, 157
Shope, Robert 55
Singer, Peter 213–14
skepticism 64–72, 116, 169, 171, 240–1
Skinner, B. F. 21
Slote, Michael 78
Soames, Scott 19, 22–3, 31, 43–4, 45, 47
Society of Christian Philosophers 106
Socrates 89, 198
solidarity, Rorty on 215, 218–23
sophists 198–9
Sosa, Ernest 76, 91, 93, 94
states, psychological vs. phenomenal 127
Stevens, Wallace 3
Stoljar, Daniel 134
Strawson, P. F. 19, 20, 21, 23, 25, 39, 41, 42
Stump, Eleonore 106
supervenience 126–9, 237
  logical 131, 237
  nomological 131, 237
Swinburne, Richard 238
Swoyer, Chris 189
synonymy 16–18, 21, 25, 73, 83
system, systematic 76–80

theories; *see also* pictures 4, 25–6, 42, 146, 166–7, 225–31
  philosophical 40, 78–80
Toulmin, Stephen 165
transworld depravity 110
truth 82, 200–2, 202–5, 207, 208–9, 211, 215–18, 218–23
  and disquotation 220–1
  correspondence theory of 198–200, 202–3, 215, 220
  philosophical 101

underdetermination 166–7
utility, principle of 182, 183
  average utility 180
  classical 180

Van Inwagen, Peter 139, 148, 123, 139–47
   consequence argument 5
   debate with Lewis 142–7
   on philosophical arguments 146
   on "was able to render false" 140, 142–7
veil of ignorance 177–8, 181, 193
verification 25–6, 74

warrant 113–14, 115–17
Weatherson, Brian 56–7, 76

White, Morton 12
Whitehead, Alfred North 29
Williams, Bernard 68, 176
Williamson, Timothy 91, 93
Wittgenstein, Ludwig 158–65, 203, 204,
   219, 234

Zammito, John 151, 158
zombie argument 5, 123, 125–38,
   191, 237